The Wisdom and t

The Wisdom and the Folly

An Exposition of the Book
of First Kings

Dale Ralph Davis

Christian Focus

Christian Focus Publications publishes biblically-accurate books for adults and children. The books in the adult range are published in three imprints.

Christian Heritage contains classic writings from the past.

Christian Focus contains popular works including biographies, commentaries, doctrine, and Christian living.

Mentor focuses on books written at a level suitable for Bible College and seminary students, pastors, and others; the imprint includes commentaries, doctrinal studies, examination of current issues, and church history.

For a free catalogue of all our titles, please write to
Christian Focus Publications,
Geanies House, Fearn,
Ross-shire, IV20 1TW, Great Britain

For details of our titles visit us on our web site
http://www.christianfocus.com

ISBN 1 85792 703 6

Published in 2002, reprinted in 2003
by Christian Focus Publications
Geanies House, Fearn, Ross-shire
IV20 1TW, Scotland

www.christianfocus.com

Cover design by Alister MacInnes

Printed and bound by
Mackays of Chattham

Contents

Preface

First Kings covers such a swath of history, in royal time from the death of David to the death of Ahab, or in prophetic time from Nathan to Micaiah, blending together royal records, detailed descriptions, repetitive formulas, and tense narratives in the whole effort. I try to avoid both being aridly historical and sentimentally devotional. As with my previous commentaries, I seek to grasp the theological nerve of the text and cast it in an expository form, without being allergic to application.

One always owes thanks. I pushed one of my Hebrew exegesis classes through some of the least interesting material in 1 Kings just to see if we could preach it. They did grandly and proved an immense help to me. The powers that be at Reformed Seminary have accelerated the pace of writing by granting an eight-month sabbatical. Ken Elliott and John McCarty have been more than gracious with research space in 'their' library. And Ruth Bennett's sharp eye nailed numerous glitches and follies before the manuscript was in the mail.

The appearance of this volume coincides with a milestone. Knox Chamblin, my colleague in New Testament, will soon retire from full-time teaching duties at Reformed Theological Seminary, Jackson, Mississippi. He is both Jesus' disciple and Paul's admirer, as one should be. This book goes forth as a small tribute to Dr. Chamblin, for we have found and enjoyed him as a rigorous scholar, moving preacher, mischievous colleague, and gracious friend.

Reformation Day 2000

Abbreviations

ABD	*Anchor Bible Dictionary*
ANET	*Ancient Near Eastern Texts*, 3rd ed.
BDB	Brown, Driver, and Briggs, *Hebrew and English Lexicon*
DCH	*Dictionary of Classical Hebrew* (ed. D. J. A. Clines)
IDB	*Interpreter's Dictionary of the Bible*
IDBS	*Interpreter's Dictionary of the Bible/Supplementary Volume*
ISBE	*International Standard Bible Encyclopedia*
JB	Jerusalem Bible
JSOT	Journal for the Study of the Old Testament
KJV	King James Version
LXX	The Septuagint
NASB	New American Standard Bible
NBD	*New Bible Dictionary*
NIDOTTE	*New International Dictionary of Old Testament Theology & Exegesis*
NIV	New International Version
NJB	New Jerusalem Bible
NJPS	Tanakh: A New Translation of the Holy Scriptures according to the Traditional Hebrew Text (1985)
NKJV	New King James Version
NLT	New Living Translation
NRSV	New Revised Standard Version
REB	Revised English Bible
RSV	Revised Standard Version
TDOT	*Theological Dictionary of the Old Testament*
TEV	Today's English Version
TWOT	*Theological Wordbook of the Old Testament*
ZPEB	*Zondervan Pictorial Encyclopedia of the Bible*

Introduction

Sorry about the title. It would be nice to call this volume *The Power and the Glory,* but 1 Kings' story of the sadness and stupidity of sin forbids it. The power and the glory is not yet. There is, to be sure, a flash of glory (Solomon) but it fades.

Bible readers who have braved their way through 1 and 2 Kings are sometimes dazed by the apparent maze of detail, especially when the writer takes us through the various kings of Israel and Judah, switching back and forth along the way. We can handle two Jeroboams in one kingdom and a Rehoboam in the other contemporary with one of the Jeroboams, but when there is a Jehoram (or Joram) in each kingdom at about the same time, not to mention double Ahaziahs, we go into historical overload. Like warm jello it all seems to melt into hopeless confusion. 'Too much history!,' we sigh.

Not really. Actually, the writer has been very kind to us, deliberately trying to prevent cranial fatigue. No one has said it better than Charles Martin:

> 1 and 2 Kings ... give a continuous narrative of the Hebrew monarchy from the time when David handed on a rich and extensive kingdom to the time of its final destruction. Four hundred years in little more than 50,000 words means a drastic reduction of detail.[1]

In other words, the writer of Kings left out most of what he could have said! Four hundred years in little more than 50,000 words. The history of my own country (USA) extends a little over half that long but its history is written in thick tomes not brief booklets (like 1–2 Kings). This means, as Martin says, a 'drastic reduction of detail.' The writer of (1–2) Kings must be very *selective*, which implies that what he *does* include must be of vital importance. It also means the writer has no intention of providing us with an exhaustive history but maybe with a prophecy – a God-authorized

---

[1] '1 and 2 Kings,' *The New Layman's Bible Commentary* (Grand Rapids: Zondervan, 1979), 425.

version of how we should view that history.

I have imposed a policy of planned neglect on this treatment of 1–2 Kings. Temptation lurks in the text at every turn; one can easily get sucked into all the chronological, historical, and critical matters that beg attention and solution. But one must be rather ruthless about excluding these unless they directly affect the expositional task. In any case, such matters have been covered elsewhere.[2]

I should, however, explain a bit of terminology. The Books of Kings are part of what scholarly jargon calls the Deuteronomistic History, said to encompass the books of Deuteronomy-2 Kings (excluding Ruth). One influential view holds that this 'history' came out in two editions, one in King Josiah's time (ca. 622 BC), which may have been more hopeful, and one in the exilic period (ca. 550) in which the theme of condemnation was prominent. Most do not think of a single Deuteronomist living at one address. Scholars often posit a Deuteronomistic 'school' – these Deuteronomistic editors being at work from the late seventh century on into the exilic period. Now the 'Deuteronomistic History' is only a hypothesis and this is not the place to evaluate it. I myself have problems with its assumptions and its application. Usually (note the qualifier), those who follow this theory assume that the Book of Deuteronomy itself is a product of the seventh century BC rather than coming substantially (according to its own claim) from Moses. However, I primarily object to the way the theory's practitioners mangle the biblical text when using the theory allegedly to explain the text. One then realizes that one is dealing with a pool of deuteronomists, a 'prophetic' deuteronomist adding this snip, a legalistic one responsible for this verse or half-verse, and so on. The text becomes a collage, a product of multiple contributors grinding their specialized deuteronomistic axes. Such detailed theorizing is largely guesswork. Even that might be stomached if, at the end of it all, such writers looked at the text as a whole and told us how it addresses us as the word of God. This they rarely do.

---

[2] See, to begin, David M. Howard, Jr., *An Introduction to the Old Testament Historical Books* (Chicago: Moody, 1993), 169-229.

Readers will run into other terminology, which I hope will be clear in the context. Occasionally, one will bump into terms like 'hermeneutics' or 'hermeneutical,' which I use in a non-technical sense, the former referring to the process of interpretation, the latter as synonymous with 'interpretive.'

First and Second Kings were originally one book. We don't know who the author was (some prefer to speak of authors). He used earlier materials for his work, but the whole work cannot date earlier than 560 BC since the final composition must post-date Babylon's smashing of Judah and Jerusalem in 2 Kings 24–25. The material of 1–2 Kings falls into three major chunks:

I. The Golden Age, 1 Kings 1-11
II. The Torn Kingdom, 1 Kings 12-2 Kings 17
III. The Last Days, 2 Kings 18-25

Let us hurry to the text.

Part 1
The Golden Age
1 Kings 1–11

Chapter 1

Kingdom, Kingdom, Who's Got the Kingdom?

1 Kings 1

Some days he would simply sit, moody and depressed, for long periods of time, and matters of state were allowed to slide. It was 1724, in Russia, Peter the Great within a year of his death. Unless Peter's motor would drive affairs, very little was done. Unfortunately, now his motor seemed to idle in neutral. A diplomat wrote back to his home government, reporting that currently in Russia nothing was considered important until it came to the edge of a precipice.[1]

We meet a similar scene about 970 BC, recorded in the first four verses of our passage. Here is an old, cold king who seems not to be long for this world. We cannot even be sure if the heat therapy administered by the stunning Abishag was effective.[2] Not a promising beginning.

Before jumping into an exposition of the chapter let us review a literary map of the narrative and add a few footnotes about the manner of the story.

---

[1] Robert K. Massie, *Peter the Great: His Life and World* (New York: Ballantine Books, 1980), 865.

[2] I am aware that a number of scholars look on vv. 1-4 as a virility test that David failed, i.e., if super-model Abishag could not get David excited, then his loss of sexual prowess was a sign of his inability to rule. But this more sensational view has to be divined into the text. David's problem in the text is body heat not dysfunctional sexuality; and v. 4c ('But the king did not know her [sexually]') reads more like a simple qualification than a failure to succeed.

Proposed Structure of 1 Kings 1
> Setting, vv. 1-4
> Adonijah's royal party, vv. 5-10
> > Informing the ignorant king, vv. 11-27
> > > Plan, 11-14
> > > Bathsheba's speech, 15-21
> > > Nathan's speech, 22-27

> > The king's decision, vv. 28-37
> > > Announcement to Bathsheba, 28-30
> > > (response by Bathsheba, 31)

> > > Announcement to Zadok & Co., 32-35
> > > (response by Benaiah, 36-37)

> > Execution of the king's decision, vv. 38-40

> > Informing the ignorant pretender, vv. 41-48

> > The party's over, vv. 49-53

Some (additional) observations: (1) The prevalence of *speeches* (Bathsheba, vv. 15-21; Nathan, vv. 11-14, 22-27; David, vv. 28-31, 32-35; Jonathan, vv. 41-48); the writer tells much of his story through the mouths of lead characters; (2) how the writer engages in *repetition*, e.g., via David's speech (vv. 33-35), his own report (vv. 38-40), and Jonathan's speech (vv. 43-48); and (3) the dominant idea of 'sitting on the throne and ruling' mentioned nine times (vv. 13, 17, 20, 24, 27, 30, 35, 46, 48). Other repeated vocabulary occurs, but this last is the central theme: Who's got the kingdom? And the central contention of the text is: *Yahweh maintains his kingdom in all its precarious moments*. Now for some expository reflections.

The Peril that Threatens the Kingdom (vv. 1-10)
Not all kings are decrepit like David in verses 1-4. Note the contrast between verses 1 and 5. Adonijah is everything David is not. Here

is a vigorous would-be king! He has ambition (v. 5a), style (5b), image (6b), position (6c, apparently next in line by order of birth), and support (7, 9 – both military and religious, among others).

At one level the writer simply describes Adonijah and his activity. It seems a very objective, here-are-the-facts description. I hold, however, that he takes a negative view of Adonijah – especially if he means us to view him in light of preceding texts or traditions. The writer's description of Adonijah's fine looks recalls the glossy word picture of Absalom in 2 Samuel 14:25-27, as well as the depictions of Saul (1 Sam. 9:2; 10:23-24) and Eliab (1 Sam. 16:6-7). All these royal or potentially royal persons were physically impressive and either disastrous or rejected. Adonijah, our writer implies, belongs to that class. Moreover, Adonijah's freedom from discipline (v. 6a) reflects both on David and himself and places him in the category of Amnon (2 Sam. 13:21), who was high in glands but low on brains and restraint.[3]

Several applications arise from the text. The first is an observation: the kingdom of God frequently passes through precarious moments in this world. It may be the passing of Joseph and the rise of bondage (Gen. 50 – Ex. 1), the death of Moses and the transition to Joshua (Deut. 34 – Josh. 1), the burial of Joshua and the apostasy to Baal worship (Josh. 24 – Judg. 2) – others are not lacking. The situation in our text is one of them. Here in David's nearing death is a transition point in the kingdom of God, one of those critical situations where a wrong move, a false step, a stupid turn, could spell disaster. It seems that the contemporary church might benefit from this text. How frequently we are deluged with the various crises the church faces, with the perils she must meet in days of unprecedented moral decadence, ethical relativism, global upheaval, or whatever. I do not wish to downplay the crisis element in 1 Kings 1 or at any time among the people of God, but the church has repeatedly passed through such times when she has had to walk on the edge of disaster. Apparently, there is a hand that steadies her.

---

[3] This comparison with Amnon is more explicit if one follows LXX at 2 Samuel 13:21, as does REB: 'but he [David] would not hurt Amnon because he was his eldest son and he loved him.'

The text also suggests that the kingdom of God can suffer from unqualified leadership. When Peter the Great (allow me to re-resurrect him) wanted to launch a Russian navy at Archangel on the White Sea, he promoted three of his comrades to high office, appointing them as admiral, vice admiral, and rear admiral, respectively. The first two had never been on a boat, but the last, Patrick Gordon, a Scotsman in Peter's service, had had nautical experience. He had been a passenger on ships crossing the English Channel![4]

Our writer (for reasons given previously) sees Adonijah as unqualified for kingdom leadership. There is far more to it than saying, '*I* will be king' (v. 5). Lust for power and position are not the marks for leadership among God's people.

I think there is an applicational spillover here for the church. In 1 Timothy 3, Paul lays down qualifications for church leaders, elders, deacons, and deaconesses (or deacons' wives). Isn't it telling that those qualifications almost totally stress godliness rather than giftedness, character rather than skills? Nor should we delude ourselves by thinking Adonijah is dead in the church. He lives under a different name perhaps. Do we not find him in 3 John 9-10 in Diotrephes, 'who loves to be first' (NIV), using his royal tyranny to domineer and boss the congregation? Adonijah still struts in the church. He may be the elder who can't distinguish between authority and authoritarianism; he may be corporate – the one 'family' that runs the church; or he may be the dominant dame, the woman who either visibly or cryptically calls the shots.

The Servants who Love the Kingdom (vv. 11-27)
Adonijah's party is in full swing at En-rogel (v. 9), a spring several hundred yards south of the City of David. Not everyone, however, is at Adonijah's party or on his bandwagon.

Nathan the prophet decides something must be done to alert the uninformed king about the state of affairs. So he goes to Bathsheba and briefs her on his plan. The narrative falls into three chunks: (1) Nathan to Bathsheba, vv 11-14; (2) Bathsheba to David, vv. 15-21; and (3) Nathan to David, vv. 22-27. Bathsheba

---

[4] Massie, *Peter the Great*, 134.

is to inform the king of Adonijah's coup-in-progress, and Nathan will come in and, in line with the at-least-two-witnesses requirement (Num. 35:30; Deut. 17:6; 19:15), confirm her story (v. 14).

Apparently, David had gone on oath to Bathsheba, assuring her that Solomon would succeed him as king (v. 17). But David had taken no public action in this regard, and, while David shivered and vegetated, Adonijah decided to make a move and present Israel with a *fait accompli*. Adonijah also surely knew that Solomon was privately the favored successor; otherwise, one cannot explain his excluding Solomon from his invitation list (vv. 10, 19, 26). Nathan and Bathsheba were probably right to infer from this fact that once Adonijah reigned Solomon would be eliminated (vv. 12, 21).[5] So now (at the end of v. 27) the king knows what he didn't know and knows the danger in which his own faithful servants, and especially Bathsheba and Solomon, stand.[6]

How crucial Nathan's role (vv. 11ff.) is in this story! He even had to inform Bathsheba. Looking back on the whole affair, everything rests on Nathan. He not only intervened but had a plan by which to stir David to action. Nathan was the man who stood in the gap – his vigilance goaded David off his couch and protected

---

[5] 'The pointed exclusion of Nathan, Benaiah and his officers ... and Solomon from the meal at En Rogel indicates that Adonijah was not prepared for "peaceful coexistence", to which, by ancient Semitic convention, he would have been committed by such a meal. He obviously trusted in the strength of his party to liquidate the opposition (cf. v. 12)....' (John Gray, *I & II Kings*, Old Testament Library, 2nd ed. [Philadelphia: Westminster, 1970], 84).

[6] I am aware of the hermeneutics-of-suspicion approach to Nathan's intervention. Such expositors view Nathan as a ruthless conspirator who is 'pulling a deception on the senile king' (Nelson). The vow David is said to have sworn (vv. 13, 17) is something Nathan and/or Bathsheba have made up out of whole cloth to deceive and exploit the infirm king. See Walter Brueggemann, *1 Kings*, Knox Preaching Guides (Atlanta: John Knox, 1982), 4-6; Richard D. Nelson, *First and Second Kings,* Interpretation (Louisville: John Knox, 1987), 19-20; and Tomoo Ishida, 'Solomon's Succession to the Throne of David – A Political Analysis,' in *Studies in the Period of David and Solomon and Other Essays*, ed. Tomoo Ishida (Winona Lake, IN: Eisenbrauns, 1982), 178-79.

Bathsheba and Solomon from almost certain death. One non-royal servant makes the difference and preserves the kingdom.

Trouble was brewing in Richmond. It was 1863 and some of the women in the Confederate capital were incensed over the rise in food prices. They decided to protest. Minerva Meredith, a butcher's assistant, six feet tall and brandishing a navy revolver and a Bowie knife, led the rampage. Some three hundred women plus children screaming, 'Bread! Bread!,' rioted, smashing plate-glass windows and carting off – not surprisingly – far more than food from the shops. They ignored the mayor's warning, as well as a company of militia that threatened to fire on them. Then a few of them noticed a tall thin man in gray walk up and climb on to a loaded cart and begin to address the mob in no uncertain terms. They quieted when they saw him empty his pockets and throw money in their direction. 'You say you are hungry and have no money. Here is all I have. It is not much, but take it.' Then, with open watch in hand and an eye on the company of militia, he assured the furious females that he wanted no one injured. Nevertheless the lawlessness must stop. He held his watch. They had five minutes to disperse – then they would be fired on. The women knew he was not given to idle threats and within five minutes all targets had vanished. So Jeff Davis, president of the Confederacy, dispersed a mob. The difference one man made.[7]

That is the situation in 1 Kings 1: Everything, humanly speaking, hinges on Nathan. I do not think we should use this text as a piece of Christian cheer-leading or religious rah-rah. I don't think the text is grabbing me by the lapels telling me to 'become a Nathan.' But surely it implies that one's service in Christ's kingdom has a real dignity about it and that one can never tell how crucial one servant's labor may prove to be. Surely a Lord who remembers cups of water handed to his people (Mark 9:41) does not think lightly of our faithfulness, major or minor.

---

[7] Shelby Foote, *The Civil War: A Narrative*, vol. 2: *Fredericksburg to Meridian* (New York: Vintage Books, 1986), 163-64.

The Zeal that Preserves the Kingdom (vv. 28-40)

What a change comes over David! When Bathsheba had first come in (v. 16), David, as though out of gas (petrol), gets out two Hebrew syllables, literally translated, 'What to you?' But at verse 28 he is full of gusto: calling for Bathsheba (v. 28), reaffirming his previous oath to her (vv. 29-30); calling for Zadok, Nathan, and Benaiah (v. 32); giving detailed orders for anointing and installing Solomon as king (vv. 33-35) – all of which were executed with vigor and dispatch (vv. 38-40). David was not doddering but decisive: '*he* will reign in my place, and I have ordered *him* to be leader over Israel and over Judah' (v. 35, emphasis in Hebrew). That takes care of the major issue (see discussion of literary features/themes at beginning of this chapter). God was the one who would establish David's dynasty (2 Sam. 7:12-16), and yet that assurance seems to call for a component of human responsibility. God had promised David a kingdom and dynasty, and David dare not be apathetic toward what happened to it.

This section suggests two matters for reflection. First, it was the fate (I speak loosely) of the kingdom that stirred David to action. What stirs us, as kingdom servants, to life? What catches our zeal? Our portfolio? The auto shop that still hasn't correctly diagnosed and repaired my ailing vehicle? Inability to find just the right drapes? Your high school football team blew its chance to make the district playoffs? Do the *first* three petitions of the Lord's Prayer move, grip, and stir us? What stirs us reveals us. And must we not confess that frequently only our comfort zone has the ability to ignite any real zeal in us?

Secondly, notice how much of the narrative – not only in this section but in the whole story so far – describes nothing but human activity. Adonijah's quest for the throne is met by Nathan's vigilance and countered by the orders of a resurrected David. But there is little if any reference to divine intervention. As Ronald Wallace has put it:

> Yet God had made no spectacularly miraculous intervention in human affairs. He had not struck Adonijah down with any sudden illness nor had he sent a bolt of lightning from heaven to spoil his celebration. At the right time, and in the right situation he had simply inspired

minds with thoughts that moved them on, and given the exact words that were required to turn events in the right direction.[8]

Why is God's hand so invisible, his ways so hidden? Why does he seem to allow things to take their course rather than put things right? Why does he seemingly commit to fragile human hands such critical matters? Why do we constantly long for one of the days of the Son of Man and never see it (cf. Luke 17:22)?

The Submission that Marks the Kingdom (vv. 41-53)
Adonijah and his cronies all hear the racket up in the city but haven't a clue about its meaning until Jonathan, Abiathar's son, arrives. Jonathan must have been on site for most of Solomon's coronation; he even has intelligence about conversations and statements. But his first words contain the long and the short of it: 'Our lord King David has made Solomon king' (v. 43). End of party (v. 49). Everyone scurries or slinks home to begin looking like ideal citizens in Solomon's kingdom. Adonijah himself submits and is allowed to live in spite of his attempt to seize the kingdom for himself (vv. 50-53).[9]

Now not everything is peaches and cream at this point, but to date Adonijah has made the proper response. That is all that is required. So long as he continues this submission he is safe (v. 52). Yet we know there can be such a thing as an outward, external submission that stands miles apart from a glad, internal one, a formal submission given because of conditions or circumstances – something like the sixty-seven standing ovations Ceausescu of Romania once received during a five-hour speech.[10] In the latter

---

[8] *Readings in 1 Kings* (Grand Rapids: Eerdmans, 1996), 7. Johannes Fichtner nicely points out the hints of sovereign work amid the barrage of human activity (*Das erste Buch von den Königen*, Die Botschaft des Alten Testaments, 2nd ed. [Stuttgart: Calwer, 1979], 46).

[9] One can understand the picture we have here as a foreshadowing of what is to come, when every knee will bow, whether voluntarily or necessarily, before the final Davidic king, Jesus (Isa. 45:23; Phil. 2:9-11).

[10] Paul Johnson, *Modern Times*, rev. ed. (New York: Harper Perennial, 1991), 761.

case no one would imagine such tedium could call forth totally genuine enthusiasm.

Do not believing parents face this concern with their children? From birth we teach them the Scriptures, the doctrines and precepts of the faith, including the kingship of Jesus, and they usually assent to all this. Even into their teen years there is this general acceptance of what has been taught. And that is not disappointing! It's not like we want them to go become Baal worshipers to prove how authentic they are. But there is a subtle concern: Will what has been taught not merely be acknowledged but embraced? Will the catechetical become the experiential? Will there be more than outward assent? Will they sit in willing bonds at Jesus' feet?

Chapter 2

How Can a Kingdom Be Safe?

1 Kings 2

The Washington Times recently carried a story about the abduction of a police officer. Officer Reinhold, as he was called, sat in his patrol car at various locations in the Maryland village where he served as a deterrent to speeding motorists. Officer Reinhold was, however, a mere mannequin, dressed as a police patrolman and plunked behind the wheel of a departmental cruiser. After he had been sitting in the same location for two days (he was usually moved every twelve hours), someone smashed his car window and pilfered him. Ultimately police work cannot be done passively (i.e., with dummies); it takes, as people say today, a pro-active approach.

The kingdom of God is like that. It will not be secure with merely passive attention. If Yahweh's kingdom, which in 1 Kings 2 is also Solomon's kingdom, is to be made secure, active and vigilant measures will have to be taken. No Officer Reinhold technique will do. Before we tackle the text via exposition let us quickly observe some of its literary features.

Literary Features

I draw your attention to the following items. First, as in chapter 1 when David swears an oath at mid-chapter in response to Bathsheba (1:29-30), so here (2:23) Solomon swears an oath in response to Bathsheba. Second, in chapter 1 Nathan approaches the king through Bathsheba (1:11ff.); here Adonijah does the same (2:13ff.). Third, the root *kûn* (to be/make firm, be established) is used four times (vv. 12, 24, 45, 46). This repeated vocabulary provides the theme for the chapter. In chapter 1 the concern was for the succession in the kingdom; in chapter 2 the focus is on the security of the kingdom. Fourth, the last half of the narrative reports a series of deaths, executions actually. Hence in verses 24ff. one meets repeated use of *mût* (to die; or once the noun *māwet*; see vv. 24, 25, 26, 30, 34, 37, 42, 46). One suspects these deaths may have a relation to the kingdom being established.

More could be said but these items will suffice. The chapter breaks down into three major chunks, verses 1-12, 13-35, 36-46, or, more broadly yet more properly, into two divisions, verses 1-12 and verses 13-46. Note that the thematic verb *kûn* (be established) occurs at the end of each of these sections (vv. 12, 46).[1] Since most of David's advice in verses 5-9 is carried out in verses 13-46, our exposition will deal primarily with verses 1-4 and then with verses 13-46.

Expository Discussion

The premier question this chapter asks is: How is the kingdom to be made secure, to be established? And the narrative answers: Chiefly by two means ...

By Obeying the Covenant Law (vv. 1-4)

David is nearing death and knows it and so charges Solomon with what matters most.[2] Solomon is to show manhood and strength (v. 2b), 'walking in [Yahweh's] ways' (v. 3), which are *clear* (they are spelled out in his laws, commandments, rules, and admonitions

---

[1] Some puzzle over how the writer could say Solomon's 'kingship/ kingdom was securely established' in verse 12 when, in fact, it is not established until verse 46 after all the perceived threats against it have been eliminated. But this is the way of Hebrew narrative. In Joshua 10, after a relatively succinct story, the writer has Joshua and Israel returning to their boot camp at Gilgal (v. 15); he then immediately describes an extended military campaign in southern Canaan (vv. 16-42), which he closes by noting that Joshua and Israel returned to Gilgal (v. 43). The writer doesn't mean the Israelites were trying to chalk up frequent flier miles. They only returned to Gilgal once. But the writer inserts the Gilgal note at verse 15 as both an anticipation of verse 43 and in order to close off the earlier and briefer part of his story. See my *Joshua: No Falling Words* (Ross-shire: Christian Focus, 2000), 86-87, for discussion.

[2] Note the exhortations of others who are near their earthly end: Joseph (Gen. 50:24-25), Moses (Deut. 31:1-8), and Joshua (Josh. 24:1-28).

[NJPS] – all these terms used to suggest totality, i.e., *all* Yahweh's word is to be kept), *available* ('according to what is written in the torah of Moses'), and *beneficial* ('in order that you may have success in whatever you do and wherever you turn'). Indeed, should Solomon and other Davidic kings give whole-hearted obedience to Yahweh's word, Yahweh will see that his promise to David (namely, 'there shall never cease to be a man of yours on the throne of Israel,' NJPS mg.) remains in effect (v. 4). The point is plain: law-obedience is the condition for promise-enjoyment.

Here we have, side-by-side, the promise to David and the law of Moses. And there is no conflict between them; indeed they are perfectly compatible. I believe that on the basis of 2 Samuel 7:14-15 one can say that the unfaithfulness or disobedience of Solomon (or of any Davidic king) would not negate the promise to David; but that text assumes there will be no *enjoyment* of the blessedness of that promise unless a king remains faithful. David says it all in verse 4: obedience is the internal means of kingdom security.

This catches us by surprise, doesn't it? We don't normally think this way. Why, a kingdom will be secure if it concludes advantageous trade agreements or cements a suave set of alliances with other states or maintains a sizable and state-of-the-art military. Obedience to the torah of Moses? No self-respecting political scientist thinks that has much to do with state security.

We find the same sort of teaching in the New Testament. The man who hears Jesus' words and *does* them is like a wise man who builds his house on a rock. The storms and floods and winds of life may beat upon him/it, but he will not fall (Matt. 7:24-25). Others will seem to believe that their ministry dossiers are a substitute for obedience to Jesus' words. They rehash the healing services they've held for Jesus, the Bible conferences they've preached, the evangelism programs they've administered – and none of it holds water at the last day (Matt. 7:21-23).

That is the point of 1 Kings 2:1-4. Whether it is the Davidic king or the disciple of Jesus, true stability only comes through obedience to the Lord's commands. What is true on the personal level holds also for the people of God as a corporate body. Kingdom stability is not anchored in our experiences or profession, nor in our education or pedigree, nor in our ministerial achievements, but only in obedience to the clear word we have long possessed.

By Eliminating the Kingdom's Enemies (vv. 13-46)
Here we see the external means of securing the kingdom. Here Solomon basically carries out the advice of David in verses 5-9. Here we meet with execution upon execution (in one case commuted to banishment and/or village arrest, vv. 26-27). The key characters in the order of their elimination are:

Adonijah, vv. 13-25
Abiathar, vv. 26-27
Joab, vv. 28-35
Shimei, vv. 36-46

Adonijah is executed because he seems to be making another play for the throne (more on him below). Abiathar is banished from office (vv. 26-27) and Joab executed (v. 34) because they were assumed to be still in cahoots with Adonijah (1:7). David also wanted Joab put to death for the murders he had committed (vv. 5-6, 31-33).[3] Shimei made David's dispensable list for his tirade against the king when he fled from Absalom (2 Sam. 16:5-13); David had nevertheless granted him a reprieve (2 Sam. 19:18b-23). However, Shimei's mouth had made him a marked man, and Solomon had confined him to Jerusalem with appropriate threats (vv. 36-37).

Adonijah approached Bathsheba (v. 13), doubtless reasoning that Solomon would more likely consent to his request if it were mediated through the king's mother.[4] He wanted Abishag (1:1-4)

---

[3] Why David hadn't dealt with Joab for the latter's bloodying of Abner (2 Sam. 3:27) and Amasa (2 Sam. 20:10) remains a puzzle. Some suggest David felt he was too weak at the time to do without Joab's support.

[4] Some interpreters view Bathsheba as a passive, naïve player in this whole affair, as though the possible significance of Adonijah's request did not faze her. But she may have been suave rather than naïve. She may well have realized exactly what Adonijah was doing and have determined to play along with him, knowing he was sealing his own doom. See Paul R.

for his wife. What did this mean? It *could* mean that Adonijah was beginning another play for the throne, for though Abishag had not been sexually intimate with David (1:4), she would have been considered one of his wives or concubines. Obtaining a previous king's wife was tantamount to claiming that king's position (see 2 Sam. 3:7; 12:8; 16:21). Hence Adonijah's request could be construed as another (devious) move for the throne. And maybe it was. At any rate, there was nothing implausible in Solomon's choosing to interpret it that way (v. 22).

David and Solomon commonly receive hermeneutical beatings for their words and actions in this story. The narrative recounts, we are told, Solomon's 'callous, systematic elimination of all threats',[5] and Solomon is 'a man of ruthless action, pursuing power by all means at his disposal'; hence this is a 'fairly sordid story of power-politics thinly disguised as a morality tale'.[6]

I cannot follow this anti-Solomon view. I readily admit David should have addressed these matters (e.g., Joab's murders) earlier; and I think we can assume that Solomon was no political nincompoop. But tagging him callous and ruthless likely goes beyond the text. After all, Adonijah's request for Abishag *may have been* subversive; Solomon may only have assessed it accurately. The text provides as much or more evidence for this view as it does for a 'poor, vulnerable Adonijah' theory. However, even if Adonijah's request was not sinister, it *was* stupid. Assuming Adonijah had a modicum of sense he would surely understand that Solomon could reasonably interpret his request as subversive, should he choose to do so. If Adonijah wanted to live, he had only to sit still (1:52-53). The same goes for Shimei (vv. 36-46). Solomon ordered him to live confined in Jerusalem and to go nowhere else (v. 36), including his old home at Bahurim a little

---

House, *1,2 Kings*, New American Commentary (n.p.: Broadman & Holman, 1995), 100.

[5] Walter Brueggemann, *1 Kings*, Knox Preaching Guides (Atlanta: John Knox, 1982), 5. Brueggemann also speaks of Solomon's 'shrewd and ruthless advisors' (Nathan, Benaiah, and Zadok) and refers to 'the cunning Bathsheba, the bloodthirsty Benaiah, the vulnerable Adonijah' (pp. 4, 7).

[6] Iain W. Provan, *1 and 2 Kings*, New International Biblical Commentary (Peabody, MA: Hendrickson, 1995), 40.

east of Jerusalem (v. 37; cf. 2 Sam. 16:5).[7] Did Solomon keep Shimei under surveillance? I should think so. And if Shimei wanted to live, all he had to do was stay put and not go traipsing off to Philistia to catch up with his runaway slaves (vv. 39-40). Can we really castigate Solomon if Adonijah was stupid and Shimei careless?

Immediately before Adonijah's demise Solomon had claimed that Yahweh had 'established' him on David's throne (v. 24), and after the executions of Adonijah, Joab, and Shimei and the banishment of Abiathar, the narrator concludes, 'Now the kingdom was established in the hand of Solomon' (v. 46). These statements reflect the theological drive of the narrative: if the kingdom is to be secure, the threats against it must be neutralized. That is what 'establishing' the kingdom demands.[8]

We may wince at the severity this may require, yet there is no getting around it. In my last pastorate I was spending what had been a quiet morning working in my study at the church building. Suddenly I noticed a bat swooping and swerving beneath the cool glow of the fluorescent lighting. Nothing like this had ever disturbed my study. I had no idea how it had gotten in there. The room was only about twelve by twenty feet, so there was no hiding from the intruder. I hastily exited in order to arm myself. In my haste I obtained a dust mop from the church kitchen. That was a mistake, for one swing at the circling bat only filled the study air with nasty particles gleaned from dirty floors. I returned again, this time, as I recall, with a broom, with which I at last succeeded in knocking the bat out of the interior sky. He/she fell stunned on the carpet, where I proceeded with all pastoral authority to beat it to death until bat blood stained the ancient gold carpet. Readers who are bat lovers will be upset with me. Other readers will simply wonder if I did not, after all, over-react. Why not ignore it with a live-and-let-live policy? But such folks have never had a bat in

---

[7] Jerusalem at that time would have been quite restricted, a site of about eleven acres and a population in the city itself of perhaps 2,000-2,500. Cf. Tomoo Ishida, *The Royal Dynasties in Ancient Israel* (Berlin: Walter de Gruyter, 1977), 130-35.

[8] I found Ronald Wallace takes a similar view; see his *Readings in 1 Kings* (Grand Rapids: Eerdmans, 1996), 16-17.

their studies. And peace came when the bat died. Sometimes it is like that and must be like that.

Here in 1 Kings 2 it is like that. The security of the kingdom requires the elimination of its enemies. The kingdom must be preserved from those trying to destroy and undermine it. This text then has a 'last day' dimension to it, for ...

> so it will be at the end of the age. The Son of Man will send out his angels, and they will weed out of his kingdom everything that causes sin and all who do evil. They will throw them into the fiery furnace, where there will be weeping and gnashing of teeth. Then the righteous will shine like the sun in the kingdom of their Father (Matt. 13:40b-43a, NIV; see also 2 Thess. 1:9-10).

First Kings 2 shares the same kingdom theology with the rest of Scripture. That's why 1 Kings 2 is such a searching text. The final Davidic king will follow the same principle in finally establishing his kingdom. My only safety then is in submitting to the monarchy of Jesus.

Chapter 3

To Have a Hearing Heart

1 Kings 3

Scholars argue over verse 1 and about whether it paints Solomon in primarily positive colors or in suspiciously sinister tones. Is Solomon's marriage to Pharaoh's daughter a sign that Israel now holds a place of honor among the nations, or is it the beginning of infidelity (marrying a foreign wife)?[1] Or maybe both? Are the qualifications (the 'only'-clauses) in verses 2 and 3 the bungling efforts of those ubiquitous Deuteronomic editors to excuse the use of the normally detestable high places,[2] or are they simply a straight-forward 'allusion to a state of incompleteness that did

---

[1] See S. G. De Graaf, *Promise and Deliverance*, 4 vols. (St. Catharines, Ont.: Paideia, 1978), 2:197-98, for the former, and Iain W. Provan, *1 and 2 Kings*, New International Biblical Commentary (Peabody, MA: Hendrickson, 1995), 44-45, for the latter. Yahweh's prohibitions on intermarriage in Exod. 34:11-16 and Deut. 7:1-5 focus on pagan groups in the land and do not explicitly mention Egyptians. Provan sees the mention of Solomon's house before Yahweh's house in verse 1b as indicative of his wrong priorities. I think that is too subtle. Note, however, that Solomon had already married Naamah the Ammonitess (cf. 14:21 with 11:42-43) before this. On the historical background here, see John D. Currid, *Ancient Egypt and the Old Testament* (Grand Rapids: Baker, 1997), 162-65, and Abraham Malamat, 'The First Peace Treaty between Israel and Egypt,' *Biblical Archaeology Review* 5/4 (Sept.-Oct., 1979): 58-59.

[2] G. H. Jones (*1 and 2 Kings*, New Century Bible Commentary, 2 vols. [Grand Rapids: Eerdmans, 1984], 1:121-22) holds that the D editor responsible for verse 3 was a bit inept, necessitating a later D editor to supply verse 2; Jones also holds that verses 6-8 of our passage are an 'intrusion' and that verse 10 is an 'unnecessary insertion.' Such hack-and-slice criticism is what kills the Old Testament for many theological students, giving the impression that study of the Old Testament is both inordinately complex and certainly boring.

not end until the temple was completed'?[3] On and on we might go. However, I am compelled to take a positive view of the passage. Since Yahweh appeared to Solomon at the high place at Gibeon (v. 5), he apparently did not find this high place worship as disturbing as the imaginary Deuteronomic editors; and if there is a dark hint in Solomon's nuptials (v. 1), the clear declaration of verse 3 ('Now Solomon loved Yahweh, walking in the statutes of David his father') eclipses it.[4]

Since the theme of wisdom surfaces in this chapter, we will approach the teaching of the chapter under that rubric.

The Prayer for Wisdom (vv. 4-15)
Yahweh's invitation provides the theme for this section: 'Ask what I should give you' (v. 5). The verb *šā'al* (to ask) occurs eight times (vv. 5, 10, 11 [5 times], 13), and since Yahweh was pleased with Solomon's request (v. 10a), we may rightly take Solomon's prayer as instructive in the art of prayer. Hence we meet ...

The true incentive to prayer: the generosity of God (vv. 5b, 13-14)
Yahweh appears to Solomon in a dream in response to the latter's worship (vv. 4-5a) with his open-ended offer: 'Ask what I should give you' (v. 5b). Here Yahweh offers, as Alec Motyer says, the 'liberal fount of covenant blessings.'[5]

Now even though we are not kings, and even though we do not have the same level of kingdom responsibility as Solomon did, is not the God to whom we come the same lavish and generous God? Is this not the same God who meets us in James 1:5, where the apostle urges, 'If any of you lacks wisdom [to negotiate the trials of vv. 2-4], let him ask from the giving God, who gives to all

---

[3] R. D. Patterson and Hermann J. Austel, '1 and 2 Kings,' *Expositor's Bible Commentary*, 12 vols. (Grand Rapids: Zondervan, 1988), 4:44.

[4] Johannes Fichtner has said that so far as he could determine this was the only place in the Old Testament where it is said of an individual man that he loved the Lord (cf. Ps. 18:1; *Das erste Buch von den Königen,* Die Botschaft des Alten Testaments, 2nd ed. [Stuttgart: Calwer, 1979], 71). Such an attitude speaks approvingly of Solomon.

[5] *Expositor's Bible Commentary*, 1:270.

generously...'? It is hard to reproduce James' words exactly in English, but I like to translate his reference to God literally: the giving God. Is he not the same God we see here in 1 Kings 3, who tells Solomon to ask and then in verse 13 says, in effect, 'and all these things shall be added unto you'? Is this not the God of Matthew 7:11?

Do you see how God's generosity *lures* us to prayer? It reminds me of the New York woman who was so impressed with George Whitefield's buoyant demeanor. 'Mr. Whitefield,' she exclaimed, 'was so *cheerful* that it tempted me to become a Christian.'[6] So God *tempts* us to prayer by his eager urgency to lavish good gifts upon us. John Newton was right:

> Come, my soul, thy suit prepare,
> Jesus *loves* to answer prayer;
> He himself has bid thee pray,
> Therefore will not say thee nay.

The true foundation of prayer: the faithfulness of God (vv. 6-7a, 8)
Note where Solomon begins. He does not begin with his request. He begins with the past, with what Yahweh has done: '*You* [emphasis in Hebrew] have acted with immense covenant love with your servant David my father' (v. 6a). In verses 6-7a Solomon recounts Yahweh's faithfulness to his more recent promise, the Davidic covenant of 2 Samuel 7. He notes that the first segment of the dynasty promised to David is in place (vv. 6b-7a) – Solomon himself reigns. In verse 8 Solomon alludes to Yahweh's fidelity to his more ancient promise to Abraham (1,000 years earlier). This is clear in his reference to 'a people too numerous to be numbered or counted' (v. 8b, NJPS). Yahweh had promised Abraham & Co. that their seed would be as uncountable as the earth's dust or the sea's sand (Gen. 13:16; 32:12). And Solomon now declares that Yahweh has done it. Old promises or new promises – Yahweh has kept them.

Solomon's prayer, then, is a proclamation of the fidelity of

---

[6] J. C. Ryle, *Christian Leaders of the 18th Century* (1885; reprint ed., Edinburgh: Banner of Truth, 1978), 58-59.

God. His prayer begins with praise of Yahweh's dependability. That is proper in itself – God should be so praised. But it is also useful for the pray-er, for as we praise in prayer we are encouraged in petition, for we realize as we rehearse Yahweh's record that we are coming to a faithful God. Praise then becomes the basis of confidence.

Perhaps one doesn't realize how important that is until it is missing. One of our sons had a specific case of cynicism when he was eight or ten years old. It seems his Sunday School teacher frequently made promises or projected plans of a class swimming party or a class picnic, or a class whatever. But she never followed through. All came to naught. Hence any time he related the latest escapade Mrs. Blank (name omitted to protect the living) had proposed, it was always done with an air of disappointed disdain. He knew it was all as imaginary as Santa Claus.

Solomon, however, shares with us a faithful God. Yahweh has a record of promises kept. We can itemize them from Abraham to the empty tomb, to corporate and personal providences. That is where we begin. It is this remembering that nurtures both gratitude and confidence.

The true anxiety of prayer: the people of God (vv 7b-9)
Yahweh's word, 'Ask what I should give you' (v. 5), is both generous invitation and inevitable test. Your response to such an invitation reveals you. Once when our boys were younger we were reading 1 Kings 3 for morning devotions. Trying to press the text on my sons, I inquired what *they* would say if the Lord asked them the question in verse 5. 'Astroturf!,' the six-year-old blurted out. As you might guess, he was a baseball enthusiast, loved that uniform green stuff in professional stadiums where it destroyed knees and ravaged skin, and likely felt deprived because the grass in our back yard had been reduced to bare dirt by their incessant ball games. All the same, his reply was revealing. It revealed what mattered to him; it revealed him.

And Solomon's answer revealed Solomon. Now the text tells us the thinking behind Solomon's request. Solomon cites his own need ('I am a young lad; I do not know going out and coming in,'

v. 7b, i.e., I am inexperienced in leadership) and his huge responsibility (to rule Yahweh's chosen and vast and innumerable people, vv. 8b, 9b) and so prays: 'You must give to your servant a hearing heart to rule your people, to discern good from evil' (v. 9a). We must understand 'heart' as the whole wad of intellect, affections, and will at the center of man. The term is not primarily emotional as we tend to make it in the west (we talk of 'heart' as opposed to 'head'; biblically, our head is in our heart). Note that Solomon does not ask for a hearing or understanding heart in order to feel, but to rule and discern.

Our primary point, however, is: the welfare of the people of God drives Solomon's prayer. Not: how may I enhance my life? But: how may I make God's people secure? The king is a model here. We should not worry over how to succeed but over how we may most profit the people of God. Anxiety over the people of God controls Solomon's petition.

I think we see a moving sample of this earlier in Scripture. After Moses grew up, Exodus 2:11 tells us that 'he went out to his brothers and looked on their burdens' (no mere fact-centered observing but a sympathetic looking, as is Yahweh's in Exodus 2:25 and 3:7). What Moses did then (vv. 11b-14), whether right or, as some think, wrong, was nevertheless done to relieve God's people not to advance his career. Moses' actions were driven by Israel's need for deliverance, as Solomon's prayer was driven by Israel's need for discerning leadership.

Doesn't this 'royal' text, then, press upon us as well? I am not a king, but shouldn't I pray like one? Some anxiety is sinful, but there is a holy anxiety, a watchful worry that trembles for the welfare of the people of God and always prays with one eye open for their good. This may involve something as basic as intercessory prayer for the endurance and relief of Christ's suffering flock throughout our world where they are beaten and sold and silenced in the Chinas and Sudans and Irans of this age. Or perhaps there's an elder in a church who has no kingdom like Solomon's but who begs God for a 'hearing heart' to rule wisely among the small part of God's Israel where he serves.

The true goal of prayer: the pleasure of God (vv. 10-14)

'The Lord was pleased that Solomon had asked for this' (v. 10). The writer tells of God's pleasure, and then God expresses his pleasure to Solomon, and gives him both what he asked (vv. 11-12) and what he did not ask (v. 13). There is something so pleasing about the pleasure of someone you want to please.

I recall occasions around the supper table when I was a lad. We would eat supper, perhaps even have some dessert, and arrive at that brief moment of inertia between the end of supper and whatever came next. One is prone to reflection at such times, I suppose. And it would be then – every so often – that my father would slap his hand down on the tablecloth and declare, 'That was a good supper!' Sometimes I thought it had been a quite ordinary supper, but what I thought didn't matter. The pronouncement was his. In later years I have often thought what such a simple word must have meant to my mother. She must have been pleased to know her meal had pleased my father, who was not particularly promiscuous with compliments. In that case she had reached her goal.

I suggest that verse 10 holds out to us the goal of our praying – to please Yahweh. In fact, should this not be the intent of all our worship, private or public? The church has gone amuck by forgetting this very principle. We debate style of worship, formal or contemporary, worship teams with mike-power or choirs. We hear how worship must cater to felt needs. But it's all abortive. The goal of worship is to give pleasure to God, the only and true audience. Anne Ortlund has given us the right words to say before public worship: 'Lord, this church service is for you. I'm here to give you pleasure.'[7]

'Ask what I should give you' (v. 5). Ask, for his generosity lures you; ask, and remember his goodness to date; ask for the sake of his people; ask, above all, in order to please him.

The Proof of Wisdom (vv. 16-28)

These verses stand in close relation to verses 4-15. Solomon had asked for a hearing heart to judge God's people (v. 9); God had

---

[7] *Up with Worship* (Ventura, CA: Regal, 1982), 137.

said he had granted Solomon's petition (v. 12); and here's a court case to prove that God really had granted the king wisdom and discernment.

Two prostitutes bring their case to Solomon. The accuser rehearses the case. The narrative seems to assume the truth of her story. As she indicates, the two women gave birth three days apart; they were staying in the same house; and they were alone there. Or, as she said, 'There was no stranger with us in the house' (v. 18) – apparently no fellows hanging around for sex. Presumably they left prostitutes who were in advanced pregnancy alone. Hence the difficulty of the case: there were no other witnesses.

The accuser alleges, however, that her companion's baby died in the night because she smothered it, likely in her sleep. This woman got up, pilfered the living child from the accuser while she slept, placed her dead baby in the accuser's arms, and insisted that the pirated infant was her own (vv. 19-20).[8] Imagine my surprise in the morning, she says, when my baby wouldn't take my breast, and then, after rubbing the sleep out of my eyes, I look closer and it's not my kid at all (v. 21)! But the other woman was all denial (v. 22a).

Solomon briefly recapitulated claims and counter-claims (v. 23) and then called for a sword and ordered the living infant bisected and half of him/her given to each woman (v. 25). This order so stirred and alarmed the mother-love of the real mother that she insisted the other woman be given the living baby. If she cannot obtain justice, at least she will secure the life of her child (v. 26a). This outburst was Solomon's clue – he had detected the mother (v. 27).[9]

---

[8] One may wonder how this woman knew what took place if she were sleeping (v. 20). We should probably understand this as her reconstruction of events, though not an unlikely one, since she would surely know the identity of her own baby (v. 21) and so be able to hypothesize events.

[9] Verse 27 actually says, 'Give her the living child,' and does not actually specify 'her' as the 'first woman' as NIV and NASB do. For this reason Provan believes the text leaves us in limbo over the identity of the liar (*1 and 2 Kings*, 51-52; cf. Gary A. Rendsburg, 'The Guilty Party in 1 Kings III 16-28,' *Vetus Testamentum* 48 [1998]: 534-41, who argues that the 'other woman' of v. 22 is the true mother). I don't share Provan's skepticism. The

Israel was impressed: 'All Israel came to hear of the judgment which the king had pronounced and held the king in awe...' (v. 28, NJB). Or, let me translate verse 28 woodenly: 'Then all Israel heard the *judgment* which the king had *judged*, and they feared before the king, for they saw that the wisdom of God was in him to do *justice.*' The emphasized terms all come from the root *špṭ* and match up exactly with such use in Solomon's petition of verse 9: 'You must give your servant a hearing heart to *judge* your people, to discern between good and evil, for who is able to *judge* this vast people of yours?' Yahweh had clearly granted Solomon's request; he had assured Solomon of a 'wise and discerning heart' (v. 12) and in the prostitutes' case Israel saw obvious proof that the 'wisdom of God' (v. 28) was in him.

We should not assume that all the clear work of God is confined to the kingdom of Israel. Once when Charles Spurgeon was preaching in Exeter Hall, he suddenly departed from his subject, and pointing in a certain direction, said, 'Young man, those gloves you are wearing have not been paid for: you have stolen them from your employer.' After the service, a young man, pale and agitated, came to the vestry and begged an interview with Spurgeon. When admitted, he placed a pair of gloves on the table and through tears confessed: 'It's the first time I have robbed my master, and I will never do it again. You won't expose me, sir, will you? It would kill my mother if she heard that I had become a thief.'[10] Sometimes the way of wisdom is so uncanny that,

---

story is related from the standpoint of the accuser (the first woman) and hence NIV is likely right in its interpretation if not in its translation. As for the 'parallels' of this story, cf. the remarks of Claus Schedl (*History of the Old Testament*, 5 vols. [Staten Island: Alba House, 1972], 3:300): 'Similar stories involving quarrels over the real parentage of a child, with the truth of the matter being discovered by the willingness of the real mother to renounce her rights to the child in order to preserve his life or keep him from harm, are found in many other passages of world literature as well. Gressmann has collected 22 examples, largely from India. These examples, however, prove nothing, since they are more recent in origin than the Biblical narrative; in the whole of Asia Minor no single parallel has been discovered.'

[10] C. H. Spurgeon, *Autobiography,* vol. 2: *The Full Harvest, 1860-1892*, rev. ed. (Edinburgh: Banner of Truth, 1973), 60.

whether by Israelite king or British preacher, it is clear that *God* is there, exposing us.

The Promise of Wisdom

Solomon points beyond himself. The vocabulary of 1 Kings 3 – judge (*šāpaṭ*, and related forms, vv. 9, 11, 28), discern (*bîn*, vv. 9, 11, 12), wise/wisdom (*ḥākām/ḥokmâ*, vv. 12, 28) – recurs in the description of the coming Davidic (messianic) king in Isaiah 11:

> And the Spirit of Yahweh shall rest upon him,
> the Spirit of wisdom and discernment ...,
> and he will not judge by what appears to the eyes,
> nor will he decide cases by what he hears with his ears,
> but he shall judge the weak in righteousness,
> and he shall decide in uprightness for the downtrodden of the earth
> (vv. 2a, 3b, 4a).

Moreover, Solomon's request for a 'hearing heart' to judge and discern (v. 9) parallels the messianic king who will not decide cases merely by what he hears with his ears (Isa. 11:3).[11] Solomon's wisdom and justice then point beyond themselves to the One who was to come (see Psalm 72).

I remember an interchange when I was teaching undergraduates. It was in an upper-level Bible class, and in some jest one of the students predicted that in the future people would not refer to him as 'one of Ralph Davis' students' but would refer to me as 'one of Karl Kennard's professors' (the name is a dummy to protect the guilty). In such a manner he would eclipse me.

And that is the hint we have in 1 Kings 3. The wisdom, discernment, and justice of Solomon point to One who will outstrip Solomon, to One in whom are hidden all the treasures of wisdom and knowledge (cf. Col. 2:3). And if such a King already has begun to reign (Eph. 1:20-22), must we not assume, as his subjects, that he will never ordain or order anything in our circumstances, except what is in line with wisdom at its highest and best?

---

[11] For many of these connections see John Gray, *I & II Kings*, Old Testament Library, 2nd ed. (Philadelphia: Westminster, 1970), 125-26.

Chapter 4

The Wisdom Regime

1 Kings 4

Charles Spurgeon remembered the day he was sent to shop with a basket to purchase a pound of tea, a quarter-pound of mustard, and three pounds of rice. On his way home, however, he saw a pack of hounds and took after them over hedge and ditch but found, upon arriving home, that his spirited jostle had thoroughly mixed tea, mustard, and rice into one inseparable mess.[1] Some readers may think 1 Kings 4 meets such a description – if not one inseparable mess, at least a collection of tea, mustard, and rice brought together in one place. What is one to make of lists of cabinet officials and district officers, notes about the happiness of the populace, a tabulation of the daily dietary requirements for the royal table, along with reports about barley for horses and remarks – among other things – about hyssop shrubs?

The chapter, however, is not an unconnected basket of fragments. The wisdom-theme dominated 1 Kings 3 and that theme reappears in 4:29-34. This justifies us in assuming that chapters 3–4 stand together under the rubric of wisdom, and we may assume that the overt return to the wisdom theme in verses 29-34 is intended to wrap all the previous segments of chapter 4 within that theme.

The Order of Wisdom (vv. 1-19)
These verses contain two lists: (1) the names of those holding cabinet posts in the state department (vv. 1-6),[2] and (2) the names

---

[1] C. H. Spurgeon, *Lectures to My Students* (reprint ed., Grand Rapids: Zondervan, 1962), 131.

[2] On the function of such offices (e.g., scribe, recorder, friend of the king, palace oversight, forced labor administration), see Roland de Vaux, *Ancient Israel*, 2 vols. (New York: McGraw-Hill, 1965), 1:128-32.

of the district officers with the locales of their respective jurisdictions (vv. 7-19).[3] This latter catalog sports some difficulties, and yet the primary function of these officers is clear: 'they provisioned the king and his household; for a month in the year it was the responsibility of one to so provision' (v. 7).[4] These men made sure their districts could stock the commissary for the royal court. One catches a glimpse of their responsibility from verses 22-23, which tally the *daily* requirements for the court table.[5] At least two of these district supervisors were Solomon's sons-in-law (vv. 11, 15).

---

[3] For helpful maps sketching these districts, see *The New Layman's Bible Commentary* (Grand Rapids: Zondervan, 1979), 433, or Y. Aharoni, *The Land of the Bible: A Historical Geography*, rev. & enl. ed. (Philadelphia: Westminster, 1979), 308.

[4] Some commonly view Solomon's districts as 're-districting,' a plan to break down old tribal ties and absorb the Canaanite population into an increasingly centralized regime (e.g., W. F. Albright, *The Biblical Period from Abraham to Ezra* [New York: Harper Torchbooks, 1963], 55-56). The scheme was, on this view, a basis for taxation and revenue. Brueggemann asserts that 'the point of the list is to serve the inordinate affluence of the well-off and especially to enhance a strong defense budget.' 'That's what most of the revenue went for,' he assures us (*1 Kings*, Knox Preaching Guides [Atlanta: John Knox, 1982], 16). Never mind that you can't find that in the text as it stands. De Vries is refreshingly sane at this point: 'Since raising provisions is the only mentioned function of these prefects, we must marvel at the confidence of those scholars who assure us that Solomon made a determined, deliberate effort to slight northern traditions and wipe out every vestige of the cherished past' (*1 Kings*, Word Biblical Commentary [Waco: Word, 1985], 71).

[5] Eugene Merrill summarizes: '[T]he needs of the palace alone consisted of 185 bushels of flour, 375 bushels of meal, 10 head of stall-fed cattle, 20 head of pasture-fed cattle, 100 sheep and goats, and miscellaneous wild game *every day*' (*Kingdom of Priests* [Grand Rapids: Baker, 1987], 308). Estimates of flour and meal vary depending on the assumed capacity of the cor. Albright (*Biblical Period*, 56) thought a month's such provisions would be a terrible struggle for some districts, but Kenneth Kitchen (*The Bible in its World: The Bible and Archaeology Today* [Downers Grove: InterVarsity, 1977], 102) is not so impressed: 'Large though these quantities seem, they are in fact directly comparable with the range of supplies for other royal courts in the ancient Near East as far apart as Mari and Egypt; and one

Yet what does all this have to do with anything? What does it matter to me that Zabud is the king's personal advisor (v. 5) or that Ahinadab is over around Mahanaim rounding up royal provisions (v. 14)? Why these lists? Because they are another evidence of the wisdom God gave Solomon (ch. 3). The text implies that God's gift of wisdom extends to the ordering of life and affairs. There is a wideness in biblical wisdom. It is not only concerned with moral and accurate judgments (3:16-28) but also with efficient and orderly structure (4:1-19) that keeps chaos and waste from running life. Some of us deplore having to give attention to administrative and organizational matters, and one can so tightly structure life that one squeezes the breath out of it. Nevertheless, a few moments in a chaotic home or in a workplace lacking clear lines of authority can quickly create a thirst for order.

During the 1948 Arab-Israeli war an Israeli Palmach force had seized Kastel, an Arab village that controlled the western approaches to Jerusalem. Defense of the village was turned over to seventy men of the Jerusalem Haganah. Naturally, the Arabs regrouped and counter-attacked under Kamal Irekat, their leader. Four hundred men screaming 'Allah akhbar! God is great!' swept down on the Jewish positions, driving the Jews from their trenches, then from the quarry buildings, and eventually into the outskirts of the village itself. But then the problems began. The Arabs were exhausted. Most had been without food for twenty-four hours. Timeout while they send for village women to bring food. To the attack again. Ah, but half-way through their assault on the village they ran out of ammunition. No one had thought to procure an adequate supply. Timeout again while couriers go off to buy ammunition. But after they obtained ammunition, Jewish ammunition found Irekat, their leader. There was only one medic and one first aid kit available to the five hundred villagers. The medic insisted Irekat be carted off to Jerusalem for treatment. But Irekat knew that without his presence the assault would fizzle, for

---

month's supply of grain could be grown on about 424 acres of ground, an area some four-fifths of a mile square. Hardly an excessive area out of any one province! There is no fantasy here.' Some have estimated Solomon must have been feeding 4,000-5,000 persons.

his villagers always looked to the charismatic leader for their inspiration. There was no other leader. And Kastel remained in Jewish hands, as the Arab force gradually dwindled and left the field.[6] Wisdom, of course, would have changed everything. Wisdom would have arranged for food, amassed ammunition, secured medical supplies, trained additional leadership. One can complain that wisdom involves such tedium. I suppose so. It all depends on whether you prefer to win or lose.

— Far from being the trademark of an oppressive regime, I propose that 1 Kings 3-4 want us to see the organization of Solomon's kingdom as a reflection of wisdom from God. Does this point of view not sanctify what is frequently thought to be a most mundane ability and gift?

The Joy of Wisdom (vv. 20-28)

A colleague passed on a clip from a newspaper column. In it a man rehearsed how he had written to Procter and Gamble with a corny joke about Tide, the company's laundry detergent. He had written: My wife and I heard that Eskimos bathe in Tide. We drove to the North Pole for verification of this and found out that Eskimos do bathe in Tide because it's too cold outtide. He then received a letter from one of P & G's consumer relations representatives. After thanking him for his appreciative remarks about Tide and explaining that no one wanted to dampen such enthusiasm, she warned: 'Still, we have a responsibility to explain that Tide is not recommended for bathing.' And so on. She missed it! It was only intended as a joke, and she didn't get it.

The tone of the text

Now that can happen when we interpret Scripture. The biblical text may report something to us and because we do not catch the intention of the biblical writer we may completely miss his point. That's why it is so crucial to sense the tone of the text, the mood of the writer, in verses 20-28. We must latch on to his attitude to understand him rightly.

---

[6] Larry Collins and Dominique Lapierre, *O Jerusalem!* (New York: Pocket Books, 1972), 279-82.

Nor is this difficult. An unbiased reader can surely catch the joy of the people in verse 20 ('Judah and Israel were as numerous as the sand on the seashore – they were eating and drinking and rejoicing') and their security and contentment in verse 25 ('So Judah and Israel dwelt safely, each man under his vine and under his fig tree ...'). We hear the writer's exuberance over the scope of Solomon's rule (vv. 21, 24), over all the kingdoms from the Euphrates to the border of Egypt, with peace on every side. There is the same aura over his tally of the court's food requirements (vv. 22-23). It is as if he said, 'Get a load of this: for only *one day*, folks!' Some think the writer draws a cloud in the Solomonic sky when he tells of his stock of horses (v. 26). Is this a hint that the regime is placing its confidence in merely human military resources (cf. Pss. 20:7; 33:16-17; Isa. 31:1)?[7] Perhaps, but the predominant emphasis of verses 26-28 rests on the superb efficiency of the district officers in provisioning both the royal needs (v. 27) and the royal steeds (v. 28). What do you think of that?, our author implies. Isn't that impressive?[8]

The theology of the text
We must not simply generalize (or moralize) and say, 'Well, that shows a wise ruler makes for a joyful people.' We must go further.

---

[7] Some think so; e.g., Iain W. Provan, *1 and 2 Kings*, New International Biblical Commentary (Peabody, MA: Hendrickson, 1995), 59-60. This would be in violation of Deut. 17:16. One difficulty in verse 26 is whether to read 40,000 (Heb. text) or 4,000 (with Vaticanus mss of LXX and 2 Chron. 9:25) stalls for chariot horses. However, Yadin, considering this verse along with 10:26 (where he suggests *rekeb* may not refer to chariots but to chariot horses) and 2 Chron. 9:25, calculates that Solomon's actual chariot strength may have been closer to 500, which he calls a 'sizable figure' but 'quite realistic' (*The Art of Warfare in Biblical Lands*, 2 vols. [New York: McGraw-Hill, 1963], 2:286). So it is difficult to assess verse 26.

[8] Walter Brueggemann does not think so. He holds these verses constitute a propagandistic cover-up; they are a façade hiding 'an oppressive, self-serving regime' (*1 Kings*, Knox Preaching Guides [Atlanta: John Knox, 1982], 18). He is welcome to think so, but he hasn't heard the text. For interpretation that listens to the biblical writer, see K. C. W. F. Bähr, *The Books of the Kings*, Lange's Commentary on the Holy Scriptures, in vol. 3, *Samuel-Kings* (1868; reprint ed., Grand Rapids: Zondervan, 1960), 50-51.

And when we dig beneath the writer's joy we discover its foundation: the fulfillment of Yahweh's covenant promises. The writer alludes to three promise components in this section. The first had to do with *people* (v. 20). He says that Judah and Israel were 'many – as the sand which is by the sea.' That is an inexact census figure, but it is covenant code from the promises to Abraham (see Gen. 22:17), sometimes called the seed-aspect of the promise. The second involves *place* (vv. 21, 24). These assertions about the scope of Solomon's sway pick up the land aspect of the covenant with Abraham (Gen. 15:18-21), which was confirmed under the Sinaitic covenant (Exod. 23:31; Deut. 11:24; Josh. 1:4). The third component is *peace* (vv. 24b, 25), that is, the stability and security God designed for Israel under the Davidic covenant (2 Sam. 7:10-11), a foregleam of still future realities (Mic. 4:4). Yahweh has heaped up fulfillments to his promises under Solomon's regime.[9]

All this explains the joy that oozes out of this text, for gladness grips God's people whenever they see how firm Yahweh's word is. When Franz Joseph Haydn was setting to music the words of the Mass, Agnus Dei, qui tollis peccata mundi ('Lamb of God, who takes away the sins of the world'), he said he was seized by an 'uncontrollable gladness.' He had to apologize to Empress Marie Therese over this. Haydn explained that the certainty of God's grace had made him so happy that he wrote a joyful melody for the sober words.[10] The certainty of God's grace does that. Faith can't help but laugh when it sees fulfillments of God's word, when it becomes re-assured over Yahweh's assurances. This text is

---

[9] Paul House has rightly said: 'Students of the whole of Scripture should be cautiously optimistic after reading these chapters [1 Kings 3-4]. After all, the passage seems strategically placed to inform readers that promises made by God to Abraham about land and blessing (Gen. 12:1-9), to David about succession and peace (2 Sam. 7:7-17), and to Solomon about leadership skill have come true. Israel enjoys all the benefits that Deuteronomy 27-28 details' (*1, 2 Kings*, New American Commentary [n.p.: Broadman & Holman, 1995], 118). Obviously, 1 Kings 4 is not the final fulfillment of Yahweh's promises, but we do have realized promisology here.

[10] Patrick Kavanaugh, *The Spiritual Lives of Great Composers* (Nashville: Sparrow, 1992), 22.

ecstatic over the fidelity of Yahweh, which should stir our joy, for this interim fulfillment under Solomon provides a sample of Yahweh's dependability for all his yet-to-be-fulfilled promises.

The Excellence of Wisdom (vv. 29-34)

In this section the writer explodes with acclaim for Solomon's wisdom, using the noun 'wisdom' a total of six times (vv. 29, 30, 34), the cognate verb once (v. 31), as well as synonymous terms (v. 29). But his paean is hardly a piece of king worship, for, first of all, he insists Solomon's wisdom is excellent only because of its *source* (v. 29). God gave. God is the one (cf. Phil. 2:13). This realization (when held) keeps wisdom from transmuting into pride. There is no secret about the secret of wisdom: God gave. Grace explains wisdom.

Having confessed that, however, the writer goes on to insist Solomon's wisdom excelled in its *superiority* (vv. 30-31). It was superior to anything those bastions of wisdom, Mesopotamia and Egypt, had produced; and he was wiser than all the celebrities known to hold a corner on wisdom (v. 31; cf. 1 Chron. 2:6).

Finally, and instructively, he suggests Solomon's wisdom excelled in its *scope* (vv. 32-33):

> He also spoke 3,000 proverbs, and his songs were 1,005. He spoke of trees, from the cedar that is in Lebanon even to the hyssop that grows on the wall; he spoke also of animals and birds and creeping things and fish (NASB).

The sheer extent of Solomon's wisdom, the range of his interests, is even more impressive than the quantity of his proverbs and songs. He speaks of the moral and the material and moves between living and lyrics. He appreciates the stately (cedar in Lebanon) yet notices the trivial (the hyssop sprouting out of or on the wall). His interests include both what is in the barn and what is in the lake, what graces the skies and what slithers across the kitchen floor. How liberating wisdom can be! Wisdom, Solomon shows us, is incurably and rightly curious – it ranges over the whole domain of God's realm, joyfully investigating and describing all

God's works.[11] Nothing is hid from the sun's heat (Ps. 19:6) – nor from wisdom's interest.

Since God has left the fingerprints of his wisdom everywhere, since there is no place where God does not furnish us with raw materials for godly thinking, Christians should be seized with a rambunctious curiosity to ponder his works, both the majestic and the mundane. The task of wisdom is joyfully to describe and investigate all God's works. We may not be Solomons in insight, but we can gratefully examine the same data.

---

[11] Hence biblical wisdom is the root and womb of true science.

Chapter 5

House Plans

1 Kings 5

Even stalwart biblical readers begin to waver when they reach 1 Kings 5. They may find it hard even to feign interest in three chapters about temple construction. They look upon it as Americans view highway construction or repair: one endures however many miles it lasts simply to get beyond it. We can imagine architects or antiquarians reading on, but we might wonder if Paul was really serious when he wrote that 'whatever was written in earlier times was written for our instruction' (Rom. 15:4, NASB). Paul was right. Yet it does seem that just here inspiration by the Spirit demands more perspiration from us.

Before focusing specifically on 1 Kings 5, I want to make two remarks about the whole temple account in 1 Kings 5-9. First, this temple construction story possesses the same *structure* as a large number of extra-biblical building accounts. This pattern included: (1) decision/authorization to build (cf. 5:1-5); (2) acquisition of building materials (cf. 5:6-18); (3) actual building process with description of buildings and furnishings (cf. chs. 6-7); (4) dedication of temple, including dedicatory prayer (cf. ch. 8); and (5) divine blessing on king (cf. 9:1-9). Victor Hurowitz argues that this is the pattern of a typical ancient Near Eastern building story.[1] The biblical account fits this pattern, which tells us, among other things, that we are dealing with a coherent and orderly block

---

[1] See his *I Have Built You an Exalted House: Temple Building in the Bible in Light of Mesopotamian and Northwest Semitic Writings*, JSOT Supplemental Series (Sheffield: JSOT, 1992), esp. pp. 108-110, 126-28. Note how he shows that this pattern/structure is *not* simply the natural way to tell of building activities. For a commentary that summarizes and incorporates Hurowitz's work, see D. J. Wiseman, *1 & 2 Kings*, Tyndale Old Testament Commentaries (Leicester: Inter-Varsity, 1993), 42.

of material.[2] According to ancient standards, it is a unified account.

Secondly, archaeological evidence indicates that this description of Solomon's temple bears all the marks of *authenticity*, i.e., it fits the times. It is not that we have direct physical evidence of Solomon's temple. There are reasons why we cannot expect that: the Babylonian destruction in 587 BC; Herod the Great's complete alteration of the temple mount around 20 BC; the restriction on extensive archaeological work there due to combined Muslim, Christian, and Jewish claims on the area as a holy site. However, other Iron Age structures have been unearthed and Solomon's temple as described fits in well with these discoveries. Solomon's temple matches with other specimens in its tripartite plan, its dimensions (within range of others), its chisel-dressed blocks, its decorations and furnishings. For example, William Dever has written:

> Even the smallest details of these decorations in the biblical text now ring true. The 'gourds, open flowers, cherubs, and palm trees' (1 Kgs. 6:18, 29) can all be paralleled and were apparently favorite motifs that were carved not only on wooden wall panels, but also in masonry and especially on ivory inlays for furniture.[3]

Dever concludes his survey by observing that 'the biblical texts, at least the vivid descriptions in 1 Kings, would appear to be based on early, authentic eyewitness accounts.'[4] This doesn't solve all problems in these chapters, but it helps to know that we are dealing with the tabulations of a sober observer, rather than the fabrications of an inebriated propagandist.

Now what testimony does 1 Kings 5 give about this temple work?

---

[2] Which knocks on the head Brueggemann's allegation that the temple account is 'not very well ordered' (in his *1 Kings*, Knox Preaching Guides [Atlanta: John Knox, 1982], 22).

[3] William G. Dever, 'Palaces and Temples in Canaan and Ancient Israel,' *Civilizations of the Ancient Near East*, 4 vols. (New York: Scribners, 1995), 1:608.

[4] Dever, 'Palaces and Temples,' 1:609.

This temple preparation confirms Yahweh's promise (vv. 1-6)

Hiram, king of Tyre, sent his congratulations to Solomon on the latter's assuming the kingship of Israel (v. 1a). Hiram had had treaty relations with David and saw no reason to change course with Israel's new regime (v. 1b). Solomon responded to Hiram with both some theology (vv. 3-5) and a request (v. 6). He combines Yahweh's promise with an order for lumber.

Solomon, picking up on Yahweh's word in 2 Samuel 7:13a, tells Hiram that he is planning 'to build a house for the name of Yahweh my God, as Yahweh promised to David my father, saying, "Your son whom I will place on your throne in your place – *he* [emphatic] will build the house for my name"' (v. 5). Yahweh's providence has prepared the way for his promise: Yahweh gave military victory to David (v. 3), and he has provided political security for Solomon (v. 4). These conditions, Solomon says, give him the green light to execute what Yahweh had promised David (v. 5). So ... cut cedars (v. 6).

Yahweh's promise, then, drives Solomon's project. It is important to see this. The real foundation of the temple does not consist of huge blocks of stone; the temple rests upon the promise of Yahweh. This must be kept in mind by contemporary Christians who have a tendency to look on the temple as merely evidence for the 'externalism' of Old Testament religion, who see it as a grandiose building project that a more 'spiritual' people would have shunned. That, of course, is wrong. The promise of 2 Samuel 7:13 shows that Yahweh *wanted* the temple built in its time. It was the sacrament of his presence among his people.

Is there not, however, a principle of ministry implicit in this text for all Yahweh's servants? Does it not say that kingdom promises encourage kingdom work? It is Yahweh's clear assurance to David (v. 5) that is both the justification and stimulus for Solomon's venture. Is this not always the case? Is it not because we have – and believe – Yahweh's promises that we serve and labor for him? Let me reduce the principle to bare bones: eschatology drives ministry. It is precisely because we have these big kingdom promises like Micah 4:1-4, Habakkuk 2:13-14, Daniel 7:13-14, and Matthew 24:29-31 that we remain on our feet and do not lose heart. Where does the energy come for ministry unless from solid promises from God's own mouth? Someone will say they are very old promises. Yes, but they are like the CIA's aerial surveillance photos in the Middle East, photos that are so sharp that a viewer can read the time on a wristwatch worn by a soldier on guard duty in the Sinai.[5] So Yahweh's promises may seem very distant but they will prove very accurate. And that is the foundation of kingdom labor.

This temple preparation anticipates Yahweh's kingdom (vv. 7-11)

Hiram was willing to supply Solomon with wood, with cedar and cypress (v. 8). He may have made some counter-proposals – perhaps he preferred not to have Solomon's men working with his (v. 9; cf. v. 6); but an amicable agreement was reached. Hiram wanted food supplies for his court (v. 9b), which Solomon sent to the tune of 20,000 cors of wheat (perhaps 100,000-120,000 bushels) and twenty cors of fine olive oil (v. 11; following the traditional Hebrew text). But do we have more than a business deal here? Is Hiram more than a timber supplier?

Let's go back momentarily to 4:34 and, ignoring the chapter division, read straight on into 5:1. Hence: 'Now they came from all the peoples to hear the wisdom of Solomon, from all the kings of the earth who had heard of his wisdom. And Hiram king of Tyre sent his servants to Solomon, for he had heard that they had anointed him king....' Hiram is one of the 'kings of the earth' and as such he eulogizes Yahweh for giving such a wise son to David to rule such a vast people (v. 7). Surely the biblical writer regards this praise (whether formal or sincere, or both) in the mouth of a pagan king as worthy of note.[6] Bähr thinks even Hiram's aid in temple materials is deeply significant:

> ... so that even *heathen* nations, whether friendly or conquered, took part in the building of the house for the God of Israel, and so

---

[5] Jacques Derogy and Hesi Carmel, *The Untold Story of Israel* (New York: Grove, 1979), 293.

[6] See discussion in Johannes Fichtner, *Das erste Buch von den Königen*, Die Botschaft des Alten Testaments, 2nd ed. (Stuttgart: Calwer, 1979), 97.

contributed indirectly to the glorifying of God. It was a setting forth in act of the word: 'The earth is the Lord's, and all that therein is' (Ps. xxiv.1); 'For the kingdom is the Lord's, and He is governor among the nations' (Ps. xxii.28); and 'all the heathen shall serve Him' (Ps. lxxii.11).[7]

We are not claiming that Hiram is a blatant prophecy of Yahweh's universal kingdom, but a subtle anticipation of it. Sometimes we are given glimpses of things to come. I recall my first week in college as a typical befuddled freshman (though unaware of my condition at the time). The powers that were had arranged a series of get-togethers for new students in the homes of various faculty members. My hap was to be in a group invited to the home of an eccentric English professor, who kept chasing his uncontrollable (=uncontrolled) toddler out from under the coffee table. I began to perceive that some professors are strange. But there was more. It was on that evening that I first set eyes on a freshman co-ed, a hauntingly attractive young lady. We were even paired together in one of the games we played. But life and classes and sometimes education goes on and one does not dwell on apparently inconsequential parties. But when Providence five months later arranges another series of campus encounters with the same co-ed and these lead to over three years of courtship and over thirty years of marriage ... well, one looks back and can't help concluding that a first-week-of-college party was a foreshadowing of things to come. That's all we claim for Hiram here. His doxology and his trees are anticipations of Yahweh's firm and final decree: 'Yes, to *me* every knee will bow down, and every tongue will swear allegiance' (Isa. 45:23, emphasis in Hebrew). There is something immensely thrilling about foreshadowings – if only you have the eyes to see them.

This temple preparation exhibits Yahweh's wisdom (vv. 12-18)

A lot of 'giving' (Heb., *nātan*) is going on in verses 9-12. Hiram specifies that, per their treaty, Solomon should be 'giving' food

---

[7]K. C. W. F. Bähr, *The Books of the Kings*, Lange's Commentary on the Holy Scriptures, in vol. 3, *Samuel-Kings* (1868; reprint ed., Grand Rapids: Zondervan, 1960), 56.

for Hiram's court (v. 9b). Then the narrator begins to summarize, noting that Hiram 'kept giving' cedar and cypress wood to Solomon (v. 10), whereas Solomon 'gave' Hiram stocks of wheat and oil (v. 11a) – in fact, Solomon would 'give' like this year by year (v. 11b). Then the writer climaxes all this giving with another gift: 'And *Yahweh* [emphatic] gave wisdom to Solomon as he had promised him' (v. 12a). I agree with Keil's assessment of verse 12:

> The remark that 'the Lord gave Solomon wisdom' refers not merely to the treaty which Solomon made with Hiram, through which he obtained materials and skilled workmen for the erection of the house of God..., but also to the wise use which he made of the capacities of his own subjects for this work. For this verse not only brings to a close the section relating to Solomon's negotiations with Hiram, but it also forms an introduction to the following verses, in which the intimation given by Solomon in ver. 6, concerning the labourers who were to fell wood upon Lebanon in company with Hiram's men, is more minutely defined.[8]

Hence we are to view Solomon's raising and organizing his labor force (vv. 13-18) as evidence of Yahweh's wisdom.

This gives some scholars a case of bad nerves, for they see Solomon's labor system as a sample of what a harsh, oppressive regime does in not only enslaving Canaanite subjects (v. 15; see also 9:20-22) but impressing Israelites as well into a forced labor system (vv. 13-14). That is the way of royal repression, trampling on the rights of subjects with its policy of coercion. But I am not impressed by this hue and cry (and the sometimes Marxist mantras that accompany it). The 30,000 Israelites who were drafted served on rotation, one-third of them working in Lebanon for one month, followed by two months at home (vv. 13-14). Nor need we assume this was a permanent arrangement. The massive numbers of haulers and quarrymen (see vv. 15-16) were, if we can credit 9:20-22, supplied from the various pagan enclaves still left in Israel. In any case, such conscripted labor was common for temple building or maintenance projects.[9] Solomon was, after all, running a monarchy, not a ballot-box democracy.[10]

---

[8] C. F. Keil, *The Books of the Kings*, Biblical Commentary on the Old Testament (1876; reprint ed., Grand Rapids: Eerdmans, 1965), 61-62.

Let us return to the main point: verses 13-18 are to be seen in the light of verse 12. The administration, organization, and delegation involved in assembling and directing the temple labor force, the arrangements for obtaining stone and wood – all these flow from the wisdom Yahweh had given Solomon. Sometimes in the Bible wisdom is the skill to get things done (e.g., Ecc. 10:10). And, so the text implies, it is important to remember that it is a divine gift, not merely a human aptitude.

Wisdom is seldom flashy and so it is easily belittled. Perhaps it is only appreciated when it is absent. In 1862 the Confederacy was building a formidable ironclad called the *Neuse*, christened after the North Carolina river on which it was launched. It was finished in 1864. It sported two 6.4-inch Brooke rifled cannons, a prow for ramming other ships, and four inches of rolled iron plate over three layers of wood planking. Just one problem: her draft of eight feet was too deep for the Neuse River. On her virgin cruise she plowed less than a half-mile down the river and promptly ran aground on a sandbar.[11] A little quiet, calculating wisdom would have made such a difference.

---

[9] See, for example, for Mesopotamia, John F. Robertson, 'The Social and Economic Organization of Ancient Mesopotamian Temples,' *Civilizations of the Ancient Near East*, 4 vols. (New York: Scribners, 1995), 1:445-47. The large numbers of verse 15 are really no problem; see the succinct discussion of K. A. Kitchen (*The Bible in its World: The Bible & Archaeology Today* [Downers Grove: InterVarsity, 1977], 104-106) on this passage. Kitchen notes how pharaoh Mentuhotep IV sent 10,000 men into the wilderness of Wadi Hammamat to retrieve just one stone coffin and lid with a set of stone monuments. Transport of the coffin-lid alone was delegated to 3,000 sailors. A half century later Sesostris I (ca. 1900 BC) dispatched well over 18,000 men to the same area to 'fetch stone *not* for an entire temple (as Solomon did in Lebanon's easier setting) but just 60 sphinxes and 150 other statues' (p. 105).

[10] The basis for some of the Solomon-bashing (e.g., his harsh, repressive measures) comes from the complaint of his former subjects in 12:3-4. And scholars gullibly swallow this complaint as though it were the gospel truth, apparently not realizing that it comes from a politically-motivated opposition and is therefore likely to have as much propaganda as truth in it.

[11] Clint Johnson, *Civil War Blunders* (Winston-Salem: John F. Blair, 1997), 223-28.

Churches frequently have to be reminded that the kingdom of God is not 'bricks and mortar,' and yet this text shows us that bricks and mortar, or – to be more textual, stone and wood, can testify to the wisdom of God and instruct us not to despise Yahweh's less spectacular, more mundane gifts.

Admittedly, 1 Kings 5 is hardly electric. It only records the preliminaries. And yet in God's strange book even the preliminaries bear witness to his firm promise, his coming kingdom, his necessary wisdom.

Chapter 6

Construction Report

1 Kings 6

I suppose architects and building contractors could get hooked on 1 Kings 6. It is full of dimensions and materials and fixtures and decorations, all the stock-in-trade of such folks. Many of us, however, feel more distance from this text. We are among those who are klutzes when it comes to the least bit of such activity, who break out in hives should someone suggest we install a clothes closet or remodel a bathroom. Our lack of skill determines our lack of interest in such affairs. So 1 Kings 6 may not exactly stir our subliminal juices. But because God has chosen here to communicate his word in the form of a construction report we should pay careful heed to it. Chapters 6 and 7 could well be treated together, but since chapter 6 begins and ends with a date formula it is appropriate to take the chapter by itself. We will focus on the highlights of the text and the significance of those highlights.

A date that celebrates Yahweh's redemption (v. 1)
The chapter begins with chronology-charged-with-theology:

> In the 480th year belonging to the coming out of the sons of Israel from the land of Egypt, in the fourth year, in the month Ziv, i.e., the second month, belonging to the reign of Solomon over Israel, (then) he began to build the house of Yahweh.

And to appreciate this text we must have another landmark chronological note in front of us, namely, Exodus 12:40-41:

> And the stay of the sons of Israel that they stayed in Egypt was 430 years. At the end of 430 years – it happened on that very day – all the hosts of Yahweh went out from the land of Egypt.

These texts are frequently used for calculating chronology rather than understanding redemption. This is especially the case with 1 Kings 6:1. True, it *is* a chronological text,[1] but most discussions of it become so mesmerized with its chronology that they ignore its significance.[2] The biblical writer clearly holds the date of verse 1 as highly important, for he ties it to the exodus from Egypt and supplies us with a major numerical component (480) comparable to that of the premier Exodus text (430).[3] Moreover, he comes back to the 'fourth year' of Solomon's reign in verses 37-38, showing that the date pinpoints a landmark event for him.

Why then is this date so important? Because it marks *the inauguration of a new era*. The same is true of Exodus 12:40-41: the end of the 430 years in Egypt marked the end of bondage (see Gen. 15:13, where the period is referred to by the round number of 400 years) and celebrated the gift of freedom. First Kings 6:1 is both similar and different. The end of the 480 years since the exodus marks the end of *wandering* and celebrates the gift of *rest* (see chart).

---

[1] There is a standing debate over whether the 480 years of verse 1 are a generally symbolic number (e.g., standing for twelve generations calculated at forty years apiece) or a reasonably real number. Those who hold to the latter option calculate from the fourth year of Solomon's reign (966 BC) back 480 years and arrive at 1446 BC as the date for the exodus (the so-called 'early date'). I prefer this view because the next clause ('in the fourth year, in the month Ziv, i.e., the second month ...') is such a precise calculation that it leads me to suspect that the 480 years are of a similar ilk. But this is a matter of scholarly debate and, in my view, should be no test of orthodoxy! I simply do not want to become embroiled in it here. Those wanting to investigate the matter and the options could begin with Jack Finegan, *Handbook of Biblical Chronology*, rev. ed. (Peabody, MA: Hendrickson, 1998), 201-206, 225-49.

[2] Though Burke O. Long (*1 Kings*, Forms of the Old Testament Literature [Grand Rapids: Eerdmans, 1984], 84) catches it: 'The construction work finds its time-bound reckoning in that great rescue of the Israelites by Yahweh (6:1), as though the temple were a second mighty deed of God.'

[3] I am aware of the textual questions in Exod. 12:40, but they are not crucial to our discussion.

Text	Time	Background	Significance
Ex. 12:40-41	430 years	Gen. 15:13	End of bondage/gift of freedom
1 Kings 6:1	480 years	2 Sam. 7:10-11	End of wandering/ gift of rest

This contention is based on the Davidic covenant passage, especially 2 Samuel 7:10-11, where Yahweh declared that he intended through David's victories over Israel's enemies to end Israel's pillar-to-post, helter-skelter, up-and-down (mostly down), insecure existence. After he did that, Yahweh would permit a temple-house to be built. Yahweh would not rest (2 Sam. 7:6-7) until he had given Israel rest.[4] Now he had done so (1 Kings 5:3-5); hence Yahweh's 'resting-place' could be built. One could say the exodus was now complete.[5] Yahweh had not only intended to save Israel but to settle Israel. He shows himself as the God who both delivers and establishes.

We sometimes use the term *redemptive history* to refer to the arena in which God brings his purposes to pass. That is all right, so long as we remember that it is redemptive *history*, that is, that God's redemptive work may well cover long stretches of time. Like 480 years. That is a long time until exodus redemption is completed; yet it is so certain and definite that one can mark it on the kitchen calendar: it's the fourth year, the second month of Solomon's reign. God does his redemptive work both certainly and deliberately. Four hundred and eighty years is a long time; it's the space between the Protestant Reformation and our own day. Apparently Yahweh is in no hurry.

I remember the strategy of a basketball coach at a college where

---

[4] For more detail and argument, see my *2 Samuel: Out of Every Adversity* (Ross-shire: Christian Focus, 1999), 71-77.

[5] The old Song of the Sea seems to have the temple sanctuary in view; see Exodus 15:17 and its exposition in U. Cassuto, *A Commentary on the Book of Exodus* (Jerusalem: Magnes, 1967), 177; Nahum M. Sarna, *Exodus*, The JPS Torah Commentary (Philadelphia: Jewish Publication Society, 1991), 81-82; and C. F. Keil, *The Pentateuch*, 3 vols., Biblical Commentary on the Old Testament (1864-65; reprint ed., Grand Rapids: Eerdmans, n.d.), 2:55-56.

I once taught. These were the days before the 35-second rule had gone into effect. Hence at that time a team did not have to get off a shot within such a specified period of time. A team could control the ball on offense as long as they were able to do so. Coach Rugg would use this opportunity to slow down the game, especially if his team was facing another that had a distinct height and/or scoring advantage over our Belhaven team. The theory, I believe, was that the longer Belhaven passed and dribbled and monopolized the ball, the fewer opportunities a super-charged opponent would have to score. Coach knew how to use the clock; the slower pace was part of his design.

That seems to be the case with the God of the Bible. Here is the persevering God who slowly yet steadily accomplishes his redemptive work. We, of course, prefer a graven image: we want a microwave god. Of course, there should be an urgency about the gospel, but our chronological text implies there should never be any panic about the kingdom.

A description that reflects Yahweh's splendor (vv. 2-10, 14-36)
The writer's description seems to follow the order of exterior (vv. 2-10), interior (vv. 15-30), entrances (vv. 31-35), and courtyard (v. 36).[6] The house measures sixty cubits long, twenty cubits wide, and thirty cubits high (v. 2; approximately 90 x 30 x 45 in feet, or 27 x 9 x 13.5 in meters), with a porch ten cubits (15 feet, 4.5 meters) deep across the front and width of the house (v. 3). These dimensions obviously omit the court. Terminology for the sections of the house varies in our English versions. Perhaps the following chart will help keep all this straight:

Hebrew term	NRSV	NIV	NJPS	Text
'ulām	vestibule	portico	portico	v. 3
hêkal	nave	main hall	Great Hall	vv. 17-18, 33-35
debîr	inner sanctuary	inner sanctuary	Shrine	vv. 19-21, 23-28, 31-32

The ground plan would look like this:

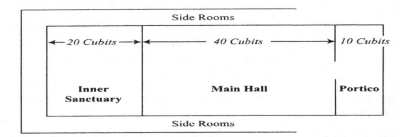

Though a number of details will remain obscure, a patient reading of the text will fix the essentials in the reader's mind or imagination. What, however, might be the reason for all this detail?

Note that the writer spends considerably more space depicting the interior of the house (vv. 14-38) as opposed to the exterior (vv. 1-10). Richard Nelson points out that the average Israelite would never have seen the interior of the temple. So perhaps we can understand the writer's focus on the interior: he gives Joe and Jane Israelite at least an 'audio tour' of Yahweh's holy place, enabling them to envisage what it is like, 'giving the reader a chance to gawk at the cherubim' in the holy of holies.[7] He describes particularly the cedar paneling in both the main hall and inner sanctuary (vv. 15-18) and then begins to inject that magic word into his description ... gold! Six times in three verses (vv. 20-22) and eleven times in total (vv. 20, 21 [3 t.], 22 [2 t.], 28, 30, 32 [2 t.], 35). Both the inner sanctuary and apparently the main hall were covered with gold (vv. 20-22a), as was the altar in front of the inner sanctuary (v. 22b). The huge cherubim made of olive wood for the inner sanctuary were covered with gold (v. 28), as were the decorated olive wood doors at the entrances of both the main hall and inner sanctuary (vv. 32, 35). Even the temple floor was decked with gold (v. 30).[8]

---

[6] Cf. Donald J. Wiseman, *1 & 2 Kings*, Tyndale Old Testament Commentaries (Leicester: Inter-Varsity, 1993), 101.

[7] Richard D. Nelson, *First and Second Kings*, Interpretation (Louisville: John Knox, 1987), 44-45.

[8] Some commentators are, of course, convinced that all this gold is a 'figment of someone's imagination' (S. J. De Vries, *1 Kings*, Word Biblical Commentary [Waco: Word, 1985], 96) and is 'an exaggeration that probably

What should we make of all this gold? Someone always bellyaches about 'such needless extravagance.' Their question is always, 'Why this waste?' (cf. Matt. 26:8). 'Imagine,' they say, 'what social services could have done with all that revenue.' But why must we gag on the gold? There is no negative tone in the text about it. If anything, a sense of wonder pervades the passage. Moreover, we must remember that many an ancient temple functioned as a national treasury, as a repository of national assets (cf. 2 Kings 18:14-16).[9] Why should such assets be stashed away in a dark storeroom when they could be part of a splendid décor? Above all, I suggest that the splendor of the temple is meant to reflect the splendor of Israel's God, that the temple's gold points to Yahweh's glory. It was a world in which kings built or refurbished lavish temples as appropriate tributes to their gods and goddesses. In such a world why should Yahweh look like a discount store deity with a government loan house? If there is an indulgence that is sinful (cf. Luke 12:17-21), there is an extravagance that is godly (cf. Mark 14:3-9). And perhaps the message of temple gold is that nothing cheap should be offered to Yahweh but only what is a tribute commensurate with his splendor, whether, for example, in formal worship, biblical scholarship, or quality of daily work.[10]

---

originated from a later tradition about the splendour of Solomon's Temple' (so G. H. Jones, *1 and 2 Kings*, New Century Bible Commentary, 2 vols. [Grand Rapids: Eerdmans, 1984], 1:169, in reference to v. 21). But Alan Millard cites comparative Near Eastern data to show that the biblical record is certainly plausible ('Does the Bible Exaggerate King Solomon's Golden Wealth?,' *Biblical Archaeology Review* 15/3 [May-June 1989]: 21-34).

[9] See ABD, 6:361, 371, 375-76.

[10] Church building committees should not use lavish temple construction as leverage for obtaining donations to a church building fund. There is no one-for-one correspondence between the temple and our contemporary church buildings. There was only one legitimate temple in Israel; buildings for church assemblies are many. One might say a more direct analogy exists between synagogue buildings and our church edifices, but not between the temple and the latter.

An intrusion that underscores Yahweh's priority (vv. 11-13)

Take a good look at verses 11-13:

> (11) The word of Yahweh came to Solomon: (12) 'As for this house you are building – if you walk in my statutes and will do my ordinances, and if you shall guard all my commandments to walk in them, then I shall carry out my promise with you, which I spoke to David your father, (13) and I shall dwell in the midst of the sons of Israel, and I will never forsake my people Israel.'

These verses are obviously different from the surrounding text. Before and after we have reports of various aspects of temple construction, but here we meet a revelation from Yahweh given to Solomon, a word of promise and of admonition. Yahweh must have communicated this message to Solomon while the temple was being built if verse 12a means anything. There is a sense in which any reader can see that verses 11-13 seem 'intrusive.'

Critics, of course, believe this is a sure sign that verses 11-13 constitute a later insertion into the text, usually a 'deuteronomistic' insertion (J. Gray), or, more precisely, a squib from the special group of law-oriented deuteronomistic editors (G. H. Jones). You can see yourself how such assertions thrill the mind and warm the soul. Sometimes appeal is made to the LXX, which does not have verses 11-13; hence they may be 'secondary,' and so on.[11]

My problem with such critics is that they never get to the claim of the text itself. They seem to suppose that once they label a text 'deuteronomistic' they have done their work and don't need to listen to or explain its claims. So what if a text is deuteronomistic? What does it demand from us or give to us? But the critics never arrive at these questions. By dubbing a text 'secondary,' they emasculate its authority and so have no need to pay further heed to it. They may deny this, but read their scintillating comments for yourself.[12] When they see an 'intrusive' text, they don't ever

---

[11] However, since the LXX text of *all* of 1 Kings 6 is so confused, it is foolhardy to base any conclusions on the fact that the LXX omits verses 11-13; see S. J. De Vries, *1 Kings*, Word Biblical Commentary (Waco: Word, 1985), 87, 89-90.

[12] E.g., G. H. Jones, *1 and 2 Kings*, 1:167 (for help with the critical terminology, see pp. 42-46).

seem to ask why this intrusion intrudes. We must not ignore purpose or intention in the present form of the text.

Now clearly verses 11-13 are distinct in style and concern from the surrounding text. If they *were* omitted one could read from the end of verse 10 to verse 15 and following and never miss our verses. And yet these verses are placed at a natural transition point in the chapter, for verses 1-10 focus on the exterior of the temple, while verses 14-38 are concerned with the interior.[13] So verses 11-13 interrupt at a natural division in the text.

Why the interruption however? I suggest the analogy that interruptions signal priorities. On a given evening the emergency room of the county hospital may be populated with a two-year-old who fell out of her top bunk with a broken arm to show for it, a self-styled artisan whose thumb cuddled too closely with the blade of his table saw, and a woman suffering from mysterious abdominal or intestinal pain. But let the ambulance arrive with a young man who's been in a highway pile-up, with some broken limbs and internal bleeding, and all attention, effort, and activity zeroes in on him while other cases take second place. A more extreme emergency rates a higher priority. Hence the interruption of the previous pattern of care.

I propose verses 11-13 function in that way in 1 Kings 6. It is all very well to describe the temple under construction. But there is a far more crucial matter that pre-empts this description: there must be, so verses 11-13 demand, personal royal obedience to Yahweh's commandments if Israel is to enjoy all that the temple signifies. If the king and his people do not see this, the temple will be useless, a mere building minus the benefit. Yahweh alludes to his promise to David (v. 12b; see 2 Sam. 7:12-16), but verse 13 shows the boon he promises goes beyond establishing David's dynasty and is expressed in both positive and negative terms: 'And I shall dwell in the midst of the sons of Israel, and I will never forsake my people Israel.' The message of this literary intrusion is clear: you must live faithfully under the covenant of God (v. 12a) if you are to enjoy the promise of God (v. 12b) and the

---

[13] Bezalel Porten, 'The Structure and Theme of the Solomon Narrative (I Kings 3-11),' *Hebrew Union College Annual* 38 (1967): 104.

presence of God (v.13). As goes the dynasty-house (2 Sam. 7:11ff.), so goes the temple-house. How heavy those second-person, singular pronouns in verse 12a are as they come tumbling down on Solomon's shoulders! Solomon's personal fidelity to Yahweh's covenant law is the condition for Yahweh's gracious presence among his people through the temple. How critical one man's obedience will be. And one must interrupt a construction report to underscore it.

Verses 11-13 present a case of the-one-affects-the-many. And that can be for good or ill. On July 2, 1863, General G. K. Warren went to the crest of a knoll called Little Round Top, outside Gettysburg, Pennsylvania, where a classic battle of the War between the States was erupting. He was chief engineer of the Federal Army. The spot was only used as a signal post and stood undefended. Warren discovered Confederate troops were forming in the woods to take Little Round Top and thus outflank and roll up the left wing of the Union lines. Immediately he sent for troops to hold Little Round Top. One man's vigilance saved a whole army from disaster. But then there is a Joe Stalin, who fancied he had mastered military affairs, and so imposed stupid and impossible orders on his field commanders in the Second World War. In 1941 he refused to allow the evacuation of Kiev and so the Germans took half a million prisoners. In May 1942 Stalin ordered a major offensive in the Ukraine, again refusing to listen to his commanders' objections. His attacking armies were surrounded and, since Stalin forbade retreat, another massive horde of Soviet soldiers were carted off to German POW camps. One man is a blockhead and tens of thousands suffer for it.[14]

Though we are not covenant kings, there is a proper principal application to all leaders in Christ's church. My obedience or faithlessness can bring blessing or bane to a whole people. Robert Murray M'Cheyne grasped this perfectly in his one-liner compendium of pastoral theology (repeated without apology): My people's greatest need is my personal holiness.

---

[14] For these instances, see Clarence Edward Macartney, *Highways and Byways of the Civil War* (Pittsburgh: Gibson, 1938), 137-38; and Robert Conquest, *Stalin: Breaker of Nations* (New York: Viking, 1991), 240, 254.

The living God is not ashamed to speak to us about cubits and cherubim, about store rooms and cedar, but does it in such a way that we understand his redemption, see his splendor, and feel our responsibility.

Chapter 7

Interior Decorating

1 Kings 7

I cannot explain it. I have only observed it. Whenever our family is about to move, we know we will end up in different quarters, whether a rented townhouse, a church manse, or a house we have purchased. In spite of the drudgery and work such change involves, the favorite (and only) female in our household is stricken with an energetic fever. The thrill of anticipation attacks my wife (even if the housing prospect is not that attractive) because she knows she will have another 'world' to shape, a wilderness to conquer. The sheer joy of tape measures, drape selection, color coding, and furniture arranging! A man – at least this one – finds it difficult to engage in animated conversation about the colors of a bathroom. He certainly thinks there should be a plastic shower curtain on the shower stall or tub. But, no, there is also a decorative curtain in front of that, and it should in some way match or pick up the color(s) of the wallpaper, and, of course, the bath towels and washcloths should coordinate with all of the foregoing. A wife can't help it if interior decorating stirs all her juices.

Now 1 Kings 7 is mostly concerned with interior decorating, i.e., with the furnishings that went into the temple building of chapter 6. And I think the writer's attitude is very close to my wife's when we move to a new home. But more on that later. For the present we must recognize that it's far easier to be excited over interior decorating than it is to decipher someone else's written description of *their* interior decorating, especially when it pre-dates you by almost three thousand years and contains no pictures or diagrams. For a start I would suggest reading the chapter in the NIV, which in its footnotes provides approximate equivalents in feet and meters for measurements in cubits.

Since the chapter is lengthy a map of its contents may be useful:

Vv. 1-12   Royal Complex

       House of the Forest of Lebanon (2-5)
       Hall of Pillars (NIV: colonade; 6)
       Hall of Justice (7)
       House of Solomon (8a)
       House for Pharaoh's daughter (8b)
       Construction notes (9-12)

Vv. 13-51   Temple Furnishings

       Hiram's work in bronze (cf. 13-14):
       2 bronze pillars (15-22)
       the sea (23-26)
       10 movable stands (27-39)
       summary (40-47)

       Solomon's provision of gold (48-51)

Since we do not have exhaustive detail in the text, we cannot be sure of the exact configuration of the royal buildings (vv. 1-12) and their position in relation to the temple. Readers, however, will likely find helpful the discussion and reconstruction in, e.g., William LaSor's article, 'Jerusalem,' in ISBE, 2:1007-1008. In what follows I have chosen to focus on the significance of the text rather than on the details of the material. Readers wanting the latter have plenty of resources.[1] Ours is a broader approach that begins with the question, What do we find when we come upon 1 Kings 7?

---

[1] Check most multi-volume biblical encyclopedias (e.g., IDB, ISBE, ZPEB) under 'Temple,' especially the Solomon section. For a lucid discussion of the text of 1 Kings 7, see R. D. Patterson and Hermann J. Austel, '1, 2 Kings,' *Expositor's Bible Commentary*, 12 vols. (Grand Rapids: Zondervan, 1988), 4:69-78.

A Matter of Emphasis

First, we discover a matter of emphasis. Of course, verses 1-12 describe the palace complex – and that in impressive terms.[2] And yet the reader who steps back from verses 1-12 realizes immediately that these verses are scrunched and sandwiched between extended sections on the temple building (chap. 6) and the temple furnishings (7:13-51). Now verses 1-12 are perfectly in place: after the reporting on the temple's external building in chapter 6, 7:1-12 continues with the royal buildings before going on to the interior furnishings of the temple (7:13ff.).[3] Yet there is a matter of emphasis: there is very cursory attention paid to the

---

[2] Note, e.g., the mention of the hefty foundation stones of twelve or fifteen feet in length in verse 10. Some of these would be longer than my seminary office space. John Gray points out that these are not excessive; he alludes to the stones of Herod's vintage in the western wall, some measuring over 16 feet by 13 feet (*I & II Kings*, Old Testament Library, 2nd ed. [Philadelphia: Westminster, 1970], 181).

[3] Some hold that the juxtaposition of the seven years Solomon took to build the temple (6:38) with the thirteen years he took to build his palace complex (7:1) reflects Solomon's skewed priorities – more concerned with his comfort than with Yahweh's worship. See Iain W. Provan, *1 and 2 Kings*, New International Biblical Commentary (Peabody, MA: Hendrickson, 1995), 69-70, who seeks to argue this exegetically; cf. also Paul R. House, *1, 2 Kings*, New American Commentary (n.p.: Broadman & Holman, 1995), 130. I do not think there is enough evidence to justify this inference. I think Alfred Hoerth is right: 'The temple took seven years to complete, but sometimes Solomon is faulted for spending about twice that much time to build his palace. This is hardly a valid criticism because the Bible makes it quite clear Solomon did his best to make God's temple the finest structure in the world and that God was pleased with the results (1 Kgs. 8:10-11). Certainly Solomon spared no expense on the precious woods and gold overlay used in building and outfitting the temple. Moreover, the structure was not large (temple size was not necessarily an indication of devotion to deity), the main building measured only ninety feet long by thirty feet wide by forty-five feet high. Seven years seems a generous length of time to build such a small edifice' (*Archaeology and the Old Testament* [Grand Rapids: Baker, 1998], 283). Moreover, as Patterson and Austel point out, in the case of the temple, 'there had been extensive advanced planning and acquisition of materials. This was not the case with the palace' ('1, 2 Kings,' 69).

House of the Forest of Lebanon *et al*. These government buildings are dwarfed by the massive blocks of temple material on either side of them, as if the writer says, 'This [= vv. 1-12] doesn't matter too much.'

De-emphasis is a perfectly legitimate ploy. Franklin D. Roosevelt used this technique politically. He told his associates never to mention the name of the opponent. One could call him 'our opponent' or 'the gentleman from Indiana,' but never mention his name. His rationale was that if people 'don't hear the opponent's name, that is a clear gain for us.' He didn't 'want to do anything to advertise the name of the opposing candidate.'[4]

Now I hold that our writer is engaging in de-emphasis here in 1 Kings 6-7. By minimizing the space given the government buildings he magnifies the importance of the temple.

If that is what he is doing, however, is there any significance to it? I think so, but we must be careful not to press the matter out of proportion. But let me put it in crassest form. If the temple structures are magnified and the royal complex minimized, is the writer implying that worship is more important than government? Remember that the temple does not stand for any worship but for the way of public worship revealed by God. Even more: the temple is the place of sacrifice, where atonement is made. Hence, in New Testament terms, the temple would stand for public worship that is centered upon the cross. I do not mean that 1 Kings 7 implies some dichotomy between sacred and secular. Obviously the governing of the king stood under Yahweh's sway and standards as well. But when the writer shrinks the press time given to fascinating structures, which took far longer than the temple to construct, is he not making a point? To put it in very western terms, again: worship is more important than government. And do not Christians in the west need to hear this? We who live among deity-swaggering welfare states that are always trying to convince us that government *cares*? Do we not need a fresh reminder that the massive reality that matters is that God dwells among his people?

---

[4] Paul F. Boller, Jr., *Presidential Campaigns* (New York: Oxford, 1985), 256-57.

A Word of Testimony (vv. 15-22)

Secondly, we may discover a word of testimony in this chapter. Take a look at the two bronze pillars Hiram made to stand in front of the temple. They are about 27 feet high (8.1 m.), 18 feet in circumference (5.4 m.; v. 15), about three inches thick (metalwise) and hollow (see Jer. 52:21). The capitals atop the pillars added over seven feet (2.3 m.) to their height (v. 16); thus the pillars stood about 34 ½ feet high (10.5 m.) and were likely free standing.[5] This much is relatively clear, though the technical details of verses 17-20 are torturous to follow. Hiram erected the two pillars in front of the temple, naming the one on the right Jachin, the one to the left Boaz (v. 21).[6]

Since the pillars are likely free standing and not weight-bearing (functional), they are probably symbolic. Clearly, the names given them are significant or symbolic: Jachin, Boaz.

One of our sons coaches high school girls' basketball. Such teams have certain plays for all kinds of situations. Let's say my son's team gets to take the ball in-bounds under their own basket. Just as one of the girls is going to take the ball from the referee to throw it in-bounds, Seth may holler out, 'Five!' That's all. Five. It's code for a particular type of in-bounds play that his girls will immediately recognize but the other team (hopefully) will not. One word, but it conveys a whole scheme of movements and assignments.

I suggest that 'Jachin' and 'Boaz' are like that: single words meant to conjure up a whole piece of (previous?) communication. Jachin means 'He [Yahweh] will establish' (or, it could be construed as a prayer, 'May he establish'). The name comes from the verb *kûn*, used three times in Yahweh's covenant promise to

---

[5] The latter is somewhat debated, but see Carol Meyers, 'Jachin and Boaz,' ABD, 3:597-98, for discussion, as well as C. F. Keil, *The Books of the Kings*, Biblical Commentary on the Old Testament (1876; reprint ed., Grand Rapids: Eerdmans, 1965), 102.

[6] Since the temple faced east (see Ezek. 8:16 and Josephus, *Antiquities*, 8.3.2), one assumes that we are to imagine ourselves facing east at the erection of the pillars, so that Jachin, on the right, is to the south (as in NIV) and Boaz, on the left, is to the north (also NIV). Cf. the ground plan in IDB, 4:536.

David in 2 Samuel 7:12, 13, 16 (e.g., 'Your throne will be established [*nākôn*] forever,' v. 16) and four times in 1 Kings 2 with particular reference to securing Solomon's hold on the kingdom (1 Kings 2:12, 24, 45, 46; see our exposition there). Jachin, I hold, means to encapsulate Yahweh's promise that David's dynasty would be the vehicle through which he would bring his kingdom on earth. Yahweh will establish that royal line.

Boaz seems to mean 'In him [Yahweh] is strength' or 'By him [Yahweh] he [the king] is mighty.' One writer connects this name with Psalm 21, where the king rejoices 'in your [Yahweh's] strength' (v. 1, and cf. v. 13).[7] This name implies the dependence of the king and accents his only viable recourse in all situations.[8]

Here then are 'He will establish' and 'In him is strength' serving as sentinels in front of the temple proper. The first highlights the promise of Yahweh, the second the power of Yahweh. The first recalls what Yahweh has said, the second suggests what Yahweh can do. Jachin points to the original anchor of Yahweh's word; Boaz points to his ongoing adequacy to bring that word to pass (cf. Rom. 4:21, '[B]eing fully assured that what God had promised, He was able also to perform' [NASB]). Or one could say that Jachin emphasizes the foundation on which the king and the people are to rely, while Boaz signifies the resources upon which they must draw. Jachin then would highlight Yahweh's gift, while Boaz would point to their task (cf. Ps. 105:4, 'Seek Yahweh and his strength; seek his face continually').[9]

None of us likely sees bronze pillars outside our place of public worship. We may dispense with the pillars but must retain their

---

[7] For a summary of diverse views on these pillars, see G. H. Jones, *1 and 2 Kings*, New Century Bible Commentary, 2 vols. (Grand Rapids: Eerdmans, 1984), 1:182-83. R. B. Y. Scott (in an influential 1939 article) takes the names as being the first words of inscriptions on the pillars. Though one can't prove this particular of his view, I tend to agree with the substance of it (see his article in IDB, 2:780-81).

[8] Some may object that these chapters are about the temple rather than kingship. True, but they were bound up together (cf. 2 Sam. 7:13). As goes the kingship, so goes the temple.

[9] One finds the same pattern of divine initiative and human response in the dual inscription of 2 Timothy 2:19.

testimony. Don't Christian believers still need to be freshly gripped with kingdom assurance (Jachin) and newly impressed with their own implicit helplessness (Boaz)?

A Delight in Detail

Finally, we discover in 1 Kings 7 – obvious even to the casual reader – a delight in detail. The detail, however, can be deceptive. We may think as we plod through the various descriptions line by line that the writer has simply put intricate blueprints into semi-understandable prose. But we would be wrong, for de Vaux is right:

> The editor did not have the interests of an architect or an archaeologist and he has omitted details which would be essential for a reconstruction (*e.g.*, the thickness of the walls, the layout of the façade, the way in which it was roofed).[10]

So the writer has omitted much. And yet he has described much. And he seems to have pleasure in doing so. One senses this, for example, in his depiction of the bronze 'sea' (vv. 23-26), with its diameter of 15 feet (4.5 m.) and half that in height, its circumference of 45 feet (13.5 m.), its three inch thickness, and its capacity of some 11,000 gallons, all resting nicely on the haunches of twelve bulls.

One can see how much the Kings writer relishes this temple detail by comparing his account with that in 2 Chronicles 3–4. The Chronicler has an intense interest in the temple and yet

> Chronicles' account of the temple's construction is actually much briefer than in Kings. Seventy-seven verses in 1 Kings 6-7 (omitting the account of the royal palace, 7:1-12) have been condensed into forty verses in 2 Chronicles 3:1–5:1.[11]

---

[10] Roland de Vaux, *Ancient Israel*, 2 vols. (New York: McGraw-Hill, 1965), 2:313. Cf. some of the observations of Roger Tomes, '"Our Holy and Beautiful House": When and Why was 1 Kings 6–8 Written?,' *Journal for the Study of the Old Testament* 70 (1996): 39-41.

[11] Martin J. Selman, *2 Chronicles*, Tyndale Old Testament Commentaries (Leicester: Inter-Varsity, 1994), 303.

All this is very clear. Chronicles takes less than half the space Kings does to describe the bronze pillars (2 Chron. 3:15-17; cf. vv. 15-22 here), while it gives one verse (2 Chron. 4:6) – as opposed to the thirteen in Kings (vv. 27-39) – to the bronze stands and basins (actually, Chronicles only alludes to the basins).

This section (vv. 27-39) is a premier example of our writer's enthusiasm for describing liturgical equipment. Hiram makes ten bronze stands, each six feet square (1.8 m.) and four and a half feet (1.3 m.) high (v. 27). Each stand has four wheels of 27 inches in diameter (vv. 30, 32-33). Resting on supports on the top of each stand is a basin or laver six feet (1.8 m.) in diameter (apparently – NIV's 'across' in v. 38 is not in the Hebrew) with a capacity of 40 baths, or over 200 gallons. One writer estimates these stand-basin combinations must have been over seven feet high. And don't let the wheels or NIV's 'movable' (not in the Hebrew) in verse 27 fool you; each stand with its bronze and 200+ gallons of water probably weighed in at about a ton. Not likely that a lone Levite would budge it.[12] All this, not to mention the panels, supports, and decorative work.

Why such intricate description? Western Bible readers at least don't seem to have the patience for it. Isn't it tedious? You may wonder why you should care how many pomegranates are on the top of that pillar or how many baths those ten basins/lavers contain. Why do we need to print the inventories of the bronze and gold artifacts (vv. 40b-50)? But these questions are all wrong-headed. Does *the writer* find it laborious and tedious? That is the proper question. And the answer is, Not likely, or he wouldn't have gone into such detail. Item by item he sees science and art in the service of Israel's God.

Ronald Allen and Gordon Borror pass on the story of a European craftsman who traveled to America to give his life to some of the most intricate work in one of its grandest places of

---

[12] See the useful survey in William Sanford LaSor, '1 and 2 Kings,' *The New Bible Commentary: Revised* (Grand Rapids: Eerdmans, 1970), 331; cf. also John Gray, *I & II Kings*, 193. For a sample of a mobile temple laver from Cyprus, see the 1962 edition of *The New Bible Dictionary*, p. 1244, fig. 205.

worship. A tourist was viewing the edifice one day and noticed this craftsman doing meticulous work high up near the ceiling, focusing his skill on some symbol all but invisible from the floor. In fact, he was occupied with a detail that faced the ceiling, out of view of any worshiper. So the sightseer asked, 'Why are you being so exact; no one can even see the detail you are creating from this distance?' The busy artist shot back, 'God can!'[13]

Is that not the position of the writer of 1 Kings 7? Is he not suggesting that intricate, carefully wrought *beauty* is most fitting for the God of the Bible? Is he not implying that nothing can be too good, too lavish, too well done for such a marvelous God? We must never offer slop to him. Who would have thought that the Holy Spirit might use 1 Kings 7 to convict us of the flippant and casual procedures we sometimes call 'worship'?

---

[13] Ronald Allen and Gordon Borror, *Worship: Rediscovering the Missing Jewel* (Portland: Multnomah, 1982), 29.

Chapter 8

What God Has Joined Together

1 Kings 8

The theological institution where I now serve has three distinct campuses. One of these has just moved into newly constructed facilities and yesterday they held the dedication ceremonies with all the flair and celebration proper to such occasions. They featured two prominent outside speakers; as we say, they had the whole shooting match. Such ceremonies are a normal and recurring feature, especially in ecclesiastically-loaded situations. I have even been present when newly donated pew cushions have been dedicated. Though one can be grateful for added comfort, it is admittedly more difficult to enshroud pew cushions in an aura of sanctity and do so with a straight face! But you get the point: dedications are proper and fun and Solomon's temple was no different on this score. So in 1 Kings 8 we have the celebrating and dedicating of the temple. Indeed, as a reader you would be angry if you did not have this – after all the rigorous detail you've waded through in chapters 6 and 7, you would be furious if there were not a party at the end of it all.

Let us take care of a few matters of introduction. First, the *setting* for this occasion: it occurred in the seventh month (its Canaanite name is Ethanim, later known as Tishri, our September/ October) at the festival (vv. 2, 65), apparently the Feast of Tabernacles (see Lev. 23:33-43), the celebration that recalled Israel's wanderings in the wilderness. Now, however, the temple is a sign of the rest Yahweh has given (v. 56), putting an end to Israel's wanderings.

Secondly, let us observe the *structure* of the chapter. Here I have found Porten's work most helpful,[1] though I have altered

---

[1] Bezalel Porten, 'The Structure and Theme of the Solomon Narrative,' *Hebrew Union College Annual* 38 (1967): 107.

his scheme a bit. Hence the overall order of chapter 8 falls out like this:

Celebration and sacrifice, vv. 1-13
   Blessing Israel and Yahweh, vv. 14-21
      Solomon's prayer of dedication, vv. 22-53
   Blessing Israel and Yahweh, vv. 54-61
Celebration and sacrifice, vv. 62-66

One might conclude that Solomon's prayer carries special importance since it stands at the center of this sandwich. I think this is the case and will allude to this matter in the exposition.

Thirdly, the *teaching* of the chapter can be developed largely from this structure. Each primary segment carries its own distinct focus, as our outline suggests:

I. Setting of the prayer, vv 1-13
    Focus: the presence of God (note: the ark)

II. Framework of the prayer, vv. 14-21, 54-61
    Focus: the fidelity of God (to his promise)

III. Content of the prayer, vv. 22-53
     Focus: the grace of God (need for forgiveness)

For the present exposition, however, I want to follow a somewhat different approach. As one reads 1 Kings 8 one notes a number of fascinating combinations which, I think, will prove a fruitful way to hear the theology of this chapter. Hence I propose we look at 1 Kings 8 under the rubric of 'what God has joined together.'[2] What then has God joined together?

---

[2] Be warned! My approach flies in the teeth of current critical orthodoxy since I assume that the text reports faithfully, if in summary, what Solomon did and said, and that, therefore, Solomon was capable of sophisticated theological expression. But this is not so in current criticism. Rather, 1 Kings 8 is the end product of theological wars and counter-attacks. Solomon received much help from Deuteronomic ghost-writers and priestly redactors

God has joined together clarity and mystery (see vv. 1-13)
Let us take the mystery first. We run into it in verse 10; when the priests come out after installing the ark of the covenant in the sanctuary, 'the cloud filled the house of Yahweh.' The priests had to postpone their service because of that. In verse 11 the writer makes a parallel statement to that in verse 10: 'the glory of Yahweh filled the house of Yahweh.' Thus he equates the cloud with the glory. (We find this very same phenomenon at the inauguration of the tabernacle in Exodus 40:34-35). The cloud is visible and so is a sign of God's presence, yet the cloud also conceals – they do not see Yahweh in the full blaze of his presence. God is clearly there, but they do not see him in – shall we say? – a bare-faced way. Solomon's words in verse 12 pick up this cloud event: 'Yahweh has chosen to dwell in the thick cloud' (JB; Solomon uses the word *ărāpel*, the same word used in Exod. 20:21 when Moses approached the 'thick cloud' or 'thick darkness where God was').[3] The cloud both is Yahweh's glory and covers Yahweh's glory; it both reveals and conceals. The cloud and thick darkness signify that there is a certain *hiddenness* about God; there is much we cannot see and do not know.

But now notice verse 9, the climactic reference to the ark of the covenant in these verses (the ark is mentioned eight times in vv. 1-9): 'There was nothing in the ark – only the two stone tablets

---

and creation-oriented theologues, all of whom he never had the pleasure of meeting. Everyone's inserting his own pet theological notes is what accounts for the astute theology. One can find this tracking of various 'voices' in the text in Walter Brueggemann, *1 Kings*, Knox Preaching Guides (Atlanta: John Knox, 1982), 27-35, and in Richard D. Nelson, *First and Second Kings*, Interpretation (Louisville: John Knox, 1987), 49-52. If one prefers all the tedious detail, it is available in G. H. Jones, *1 and 2 Kings*, New Century Bible Commentary, 2 vols. (Grand Rapids: Eerdmans, 1984), 1:191-209, where we are even assured that kneeling in prayer (v. 54) probably belonged to a later period than Solomon. The only hard datum one has to expound is the biblical text as we have it. When critics reconstruct what they think is the process behind the text, they frequently end up expounding just that—a reconstruction, but not the text.

[3] The word used in vv. 10 and 11 is *'ānān*, a more common word for 'cloud.'

which Moses had placed there at Horeb, where Yahweh cut (a covenant) with the sons of Israel, when they came out of the land of Egypt.' The covenant stipulations, the ten words (commandments), were inscribed on those two tablets (see Deut. 10:1-4). What does this imply but that the people of God live under the word of God, under his will expressed in commandments? This is the clarity.

Put all of this together. Yahweh has made his word clear, his will obvious. The ark of the covenant holds the transcript of his will in legibly inscribed Hebrew words. Yet he veils his presence in a cloud, hides the full beauty of his being. As noted, the cloud both displays and conceals Yahweh's splendor. Though Yahweh does not show himself in a totally transparent way, he has made his will clear in the tablets of stone. The cloud points to Yahweh's obscurity, the ark to his clarity; the former suggests we cannot know him exhaustively, though the latter testifies that we can know him adequately. He satisfies your need for clarity but not your passion for curiosity. Mystery and clarity.

A few years ago I was pastor of a small congregation. Our design was to purchase land and eventually to build a church structure. We were alerted by our bank that an anonymous gift of $10,000 had been deposited in our account. Now there was much mystery about that. No one knew where it came from or who had given it. The tracks had been covered. And yet the funds were real and clearly resting in state in our account! Mystery and clarity side-by-side.

So it is in the life of the people of God. And this episode of cloud and ark at the temple dedication carries practical import. It implies that you do not live from the sight of God but from the speech of God. You are content with God's hiddenness because you know 'the will of God for your life.' Christians often use that last phrase to refer to God's *circumstantial* will, i.e., whether God would have me be a teacher or politician or auto mechanic or whatever, or whether he would have me matriculate at this or that university, or marry this or that or the other fellow or girl.[4] But

---

[4] For good sense in this area, see Garry Friesen (with J. Robin Maxson), *Decision Making and the Will of God* (Portland, OR: Multnomah, 1980).

the phrase better describes God's *central* will, that is, what's written on the tablets of stone in the ark of the covenant (= Exodus 20:1-17). Relatively speaking, I don't think God cares much whether I teach in a seminary or remodel homes (if I could), or whether I'm accepted at Princeton University or attend Dumpsville Junior College, but he intensely cares that whatever I am, wherever I am, with whomever I am, that I do not worship any other gods, that I keep the Sabbath day holy, that I do not commit adultery or bear false witness.[5] That is clear. I cannot penetrate secrets God has kept to himself, but I can seek to obey commandments that he has given to me. The Christian will usually find much about God that is obscure and baffling – but he has given us all the direction we need for godly living in Christ Jesus.

God has joined together fidelity and expectancy (vv. 14-21, 22-26)
Let us pick up with the opening lines of Solomon's prayer in verses 23-24:

(23) Yahweh, God of Israel,
   there is no God like you
      in heaven above or on earth below
      – keeping covenant and covenant love
         to your servants who walk before you
         with all their heart;
(24) You have kept to your servant David my father
   what you promised him,
   so that you promised with your mouth
      and with your hand you have fulfilled (it),
      as it is today.

---

[5] I am writing all this with a straight face. I know some Christians have allergic reactions when told they are subject to Yahweh's moral law in Exodus 20. This, they fear, is legalism and an effort at salvation by works. But that fear misunderstands the function of the ten commandments. The law (Exod. 20:3-17) comes in the context of grace (Exod. 20:1-2). Yahweh lays down his pattern in the Book of Exodus: he *delivers* his people (e.g., chs. 1-15), then he *demands* (10 commandments); he works his *redemption* before he sets down his *requirements*. He first sets Israel free and then tells them how that freedom is to be enjoyed and maintained. Glad obedience to Yahweh's moral law is simply our 'logical' act of worship (cf. Rom. 12:1).

Solomon begins with the incomparability of Yahweh: 'there is no God like you.' How is Yahweh incomparable? 'Keeping covenant and covenant love to your servants....' Yahweh is incomparable, without parallel, in his fidelity to his covenant promises. Which promises, for instance? Those to David, Solomon's father (v. 24). Aye, and what were they? Here we hark back to the 'blessing Israel and Yahweh' section of verses 14-21,[6] especially verses 19-20. There Solomon specifies Yahweh's promise that David's son would build a house for Yahweh (v. 19; see 2 Sam. 7:12-13), and he affirms that Yahweh has fulfilled that promise in two particulars (v. 20): (1) 'I rose up in the place of David my father and I sat upon the throne of Israel as Yahweh had promised,' and (2) 'I built the house for the name of Yahweh, God of Israel.' This is the fidelity Solomon has in mind in that marvelous line: 'So you spoke with your mouth and with your hand you have fulfilled (it)' (v. 24, picking up the phrase from v. 15). With Yahweh there is no truth gap. What his mouth speaks, his hand does.

Now note what Solomon does with Yahweh's previous Davidic fidelity (vv. 19-20, 23-24):

> Now then, Yahweh, God of Israel, keep to your servant David my father what you promised him, saying, 'A man belonging to you will never be cut off from before me, sitting upon the throne of Israel; only your sons must keep their way, to walk before me as you have walked before me' (v. 25; see too v. 26).

Yes, there is a condition for Solomon & Co. to fulfill, but do you see the prime line of logic here? 'You have been true to what you promised David to this point, Yahweh; now then, let that same faithfulness govern the future.' In short, act in the future as you have acted to date. Yahweh's fidelity in the past becomes the basis for expecting the same in the future. God has joined fidelity and expectancy.

---

[6] Though David is the primary focus of verses 14-21, the temple is not lost to view: building the house for Yahweh's name is mentioned five times in the section (vv. 16, 17, 18, 19, 20).

Sadly, Christians today may not feel the punch of this. We may appreciate Yahweh's faithfulness but we might not think him incomparable for it. That, however is Solomon's point: Scour the nooks, crannies, corners, and galaxies of the universe and you will find no God like Yahweh, who 'keeps covenant and covenant love' to his servants (v. 23). But what is so incomparable about that?

When perplexed, try a little paganism. Ancient Near Eastern deities did not receive high grades for fidelity. They were notoriously – as current slang has it – flaky. In the Babylonian *Gilgamesh Epic* the young king Gilgamesh, having vanquished the villain Humbaba, cleans up and decks himself out in festive duds and thereby attracts the admiring eye of the goddess Ishtar. The divine lady offers to become Mrs. Gilgamesh, but Gilgamesh rejects her proposal in the most scathing terms, itemizing her infidelities to a whole series of her previous favorites.[7] Divinity and fidelity were not natural bedfellows in paganism. Indeed, even if a pagan deity assured you of blessing, you could not be sure of that assurance, for some other deity might exercise his/her veto power and cancel the benefit thought to be guaranteed. Such is the liability when the world is run by a committee (sometimes called a pantheon). That is why pagans kept their trump card, magic, up their sleeves: it, hopefully, gave them access to power beyond the gods, so that they were not completely victims of their collection of fickle divinities.[8]

Yahweh is not like any of these. He is incomparable; he always 'keeps covenant and covenant love' for/to his servants. In a word, he keeps promises. That's why his people are such hopeful hombres. His to-date fidelity breeds future expectancy. That is the theology you meet in Romans 8:32. Or in Yahweh's simple but compound sentence of Isaiah 46:4, 'I *have* made, and I *will* carry.'[9] Where can you find a God like that? Because he has held

---

[7] Alexander Heidel, *The Gilgamesh Epic and Old Testament Parallels,* 2nd ed. (Chicago: University of Chicago, 1949), 7, 50-52.

[8] See briefly, Walther Eichrodt, *Theology of the Old Testament,* 2 vols. (Philadelphia: Westminster, 1961), 1:234-35.

[9] Emphasis mine; I wanted to show the distinction between the first verb

you in the past, you do not fear for the future. God has joined
fidelity and expectancy.

God has joined together immensity and intimacy (vv. 27-30)
Let me at least put verses 27-28 in front of us:

> (27) But, will God really dwell upon the earth? Why, the heavens
> and the highest heavens cannot contain you – how much less this
> house which I have built!

> (28) But you must turn to the prayer of your servant and to his plea
> for grace, O Yahweh, my God, to hear the cry and the prayer which
> your servant is praying before you today.

In verse 13 Solomon had referred to the temple as 'a place for
Your dwelling forever' (NASB). But in verse 27 Solomon acknowledges that that was only 'relatively speaking.' Here he confesses
the uncontainability, the unboxability, of God. Here is the God
who bursts all our categories and frustrates all our attempts to
surround his majesty. Here is the immensity of God. Will God
really dwell upon earth, let alone in a temple? Why, the heavens,
even the highest heavens, cannot contain him! The words drip
with our happy failure to get a grip on the massive majesty of
God.

But conjunctions provide some of our most astounding
theology. Follow Solomon's verbal tracks. No sooner does he
confess God's immensity in wonder and praise (v. 27) than he
walks right into verse 28: 'But [conjunction] you must turn to the
prayer of your servant and to his plea for grace.' What an audacious
assumption! The true God is as described in verse 27, but you can
talk to him with prayers, pleas for grace, and cries. Solomon teaches
us that *transcendence does not destroy intimacy* (though it does
give intimacy goosebumps). Yahweh is transcendent yet available.
This intimacy is an intimacy of the ear (v. 28) and of the eye (v.

---

in the perfect state, focusing on God's work in the past, and the imperfect
verb, anticipating what comes in the future. In the Hebrew text, the personal
pronouns ('I') are emphatic.

29) and that constantly ('night and day,' v. 29a). Note how verse 30 contains both sides of this paradox: Solomon and Israel pray toward 'this place,' the temple, and God will hear 'in heaven [his] dwelling place.' The latter (heaven) acknowledges that Yahweh is uncontainable, while 'this place' shows he is accessible. The temple is a sacrament of God's true dwelling. Indeed verse 27 suggests that even heaven is too confining for this God whose immensity leaves the boundaries of the universe in tatters. Yet (v. 28!) you can speak with him.

We can have difficulty holding immensity and intimacy together. We can ponder one or the other but the combination stretches our theological elastic. Tom Gibson, a friend and Presbyterian pastor, once highlighted the unusual career of General Joseph Wheeler. Wheeler served the Confederacy during the War between the States. After the war he was serving as a congressman from Alabama. During this latter period he was commissioned as a major general in the United States Army to serve in the Spanish-American War, commanding volunteer forces (and referring to Spanish troops as 'Yankees'). Wheeler was the only man to serve as general in the Confederate army and subsequently to hold that rank in the Federal forces. It sounds contradictory, mutually exclusive, that one man could be both a Confederate and a Federal general. Yet it is so. And perhaps we cannot imagine how the living God could be both immense and intimate; and yet it is delightfully so.[10]

Here is reason for both trembling and joy. Yahweh's people can never *comprehend* him in all the fullness of his being, but they can *apprehend* him in the place of prayer. I cannot encompass God in his grandeur but I can engage him in his grace (cf. Isa. 66:1-2). His majesty dwarfs our universe yet his ear receives our prayers (note the use of the verb 'hear/listen,' Hebrew *šāmaʿ*, five times in vv. 28-30).

---

[10] If this piece of Old Testament theology grabs hold of us, we are not really shocked at the incarnation. It is, simply and miraculously, 'vintage Yahweh.'

God has joined together severity and mercy (vv. 31-53)
Solomon's prayer now surveys seven scenarios, potential need-situations in Israel, five of which will be due to Israel's sin. Fodder for Solomon's petitions comes from the covenant curses in Leviticus 26 and Deuteronomy 28. Note the following:

Text	Item	Curses
Vv. 31-32	Sin against neighbor/oath	
Vv. 33-34	Defeat by enemy	Lev. 26:17 Deut. 28:25
Vv. 35-36	No rain	Lev. 26:19-20 Deut. 28:23-24
Vv. 37-40	A collage: famine, pestilence, blight/mildew, locust/grasshopper, besieging enemy, plague, sickness	Lev. 26:25 Deut. 28:21-22, 38-39, 42, 58-61
Vv. 41-43	Foreigner	
Vv. 44-45	Going into battle	
Vv. 46-50	Captivity/exile	Lev. 26:33 Deut. 28:36-37, 41, 49-50, 64ff.

Take stock of what we have here: the house of Yahweh is now built; this constitutes the supreme privilege for Yahweh's people; but, at the same time, the supreme fact about Yahweh's people is that they are always in sin-situations (vv. 31, 33-34, 35-36, 38-39, 46ff.). Not all their circumstances are sin-infected (vv. 41-43, 44-45), but most are. They are forever in need of forgiveness (vv. 30, 34, 36, 39, 50).

The assumptions in Solomon's prayer stand in sharp relief to utterances in contemporary public celebrations. In my own country

I think of those annual high school and college graduation ceremonies, each of which seems to require a 'commencement address'. Though I myself have heard significant exceptions, any number of such addresses are full of flattery and foolishness, implying that the assembled institutional exit specimens are the hope for our world, wholly aside from the fact that they may not be able to read beyond the sixth grade level. None of that hype at the temple dedication. There is a cold, hard realism in Solomon's prayer that faces squarely the sinfulness of God's people.

And yet there is not despair. Look at the worst case scenario in verses 46-53. Suppose Yahweh casts Israel off for her sin – her people are carted off to a foreign country and languish in exile. Yet suppose they repent and plead for grace:

> And they shall turn to you with all their heart and with all their soul in the land of their enemies who have taken them captive, and they shall pray to you toward their land which you gave to their fathers, toward the city which you have chosen, and toward the house which I have built for your name, then you must hear in heaven your dwelling place their prayer and pleading for grace... (vv. 48-49a).

There is a way to restoration and forgiveness (vv. 49b-50).

Now this is not some novel idea of Solomon's. This is old stuff. He is simply praying out of the Pentateuch. Verses 46-53 are simply Leviticus 26:40-45 and Deuteronomy 30:1-10 in the form of prayer. Yahweh had already promised the sort of thing Solomon asks for here. And other Israelites believed this! There was more going on in Daniel's pre-lion days than simply his refusal to skip personal devotions. He was praying with his windows open 'toward Jerusalem' (Dan. 6:10) – the land, the city, and the house 1 Kings 8:48 specifies. Daniel 9:1-19 gives us a sample of the prayers Daniel prayed at his window – prayers of repentance seeking restoration. Nehemiah follows suit. His prayer in Nehemiah 1:4-11 specifically rests on the threats of Leviticus 26 and the promises of Deuteronomy 30: God had said, If you are unfaithful, I will scatter; if you return, I will gather (see Neh. 1:8-9). Solomon's prayer unites both the threats (Lev. 26:14-39; Deut. 28:15-68) and promises (Lev. 26:40ff.; Deut. 30:1-10) of Yahweh and draws the pattern for later biblical pray-ers (like Daniel and Nehemiah) to follow. No wonder the writer placed Solomon's prayer as the centrepiece in the structure of 1 Kings 8 (see introductory comments at beginning of this chapter). Solomon holds together Yahweh's severity and mercy.

Do you see the realism and yet the hope here? Sinful Israel will suffer God's severity (v. 46), but that severity may bring them to repentance (vv. 47-48) and to restoration (vv. 49-50). The sins of God's people will not maroon them in a hopeless cul-de-sac of guilt, but even in their sins there is a future and a hope, because the God of the Bible brings his severity upon his people in order to lead them back into his mercy.

I like Spurgeon's anecdote about the premier painter who was working in St. Paul's high up on a platform. He was sizing up his work and its proportions, stepping backward inch by inch as he made his careful assessment. His feet, however, were at the very edge of the platform, a fact one of his assistants noted with proper alarm. Yet his worker knew that if he shouted, 'Sir, you are in danger,' the start and tendency to look back meant a fatal plunge into the pavement below. Instead (how many thoughts rush into the mind in mere seconds) his aide grabbed a brush, dipped it in a paint pot, and flung the stuff on the picture. The painter bolted forward in rage to chew out his worker, and then saw that the ruin of his work had been the saving of his life. Severity and mercy.

Have you not found this God to act this way in your case? Can you not tell stories in which with you he has united judgment with kindness, distress with deliverance, chastisement with consolation, wounding with healing?

God has joined together particularity and universality (vv. 41-43)
Most all Solomon's prayer scenarios focus, as expected, on Israel's difficulties, Israel's sins, disasters, and needs. But in verses 41-43 Solomon prays for the fellow who comes from over the border, for the outsider, the foreigner, the pagan who is attracted to Yahweh.[11] 'He shall come from a far-off land because of your

---

[11] Solomon speaks of the *nokrî*, the foreigner from outside the land, not of the *gēr*, the resident alien who lives among Israel. Verse 41 makes this clear.

reputation' (v. 41b). Solomon assumes that such individuals at least will come because of the testimony which the nations will hear about Yahweh's deeds ('For they will hear about your great name and your strong hand and your stretched-out arm,' v. 42a). So it will not be surprising to have a foreigner come and pray toward Yahweh's temple (v. 42b), and Solomon begs Yahweh to hear and act in accord with the foreigner's request in order that international missions may explode with such converts (or, as Solomon put it, 'In order that all the peoples of the earth may know your name [reputation], to fear you, as your people Israel do,' v. 43b).[12]

Solomon did not expect the temple to remain Israel's best-kept secret. He expected it to be a kind of mission station. In Solomon's prayer for the foreigner we may see a foregleam of that day when 'all the nations shall flow' to Yahweh's house and 'many peoples' flock there to be taught torah (Isa. 2:1-4). Indeed Yahweh encourages the 'sons of the foreigner [*nēkār*] who join themselves to Yahweh' by promising 'I shall bring them to my holy hill, and I shall make them glad in my house of prayer' (Isa. 56:6-7).[13] The temple was God's gift to Israel, but it was intended to draw those far beyond Israel into the joy of atonement and prayer.

Now God is still doing this particularity-universality act. Some of you see it within the relatively small orbit of your own lives or in the families of others. Sometimes the Lord delights to start a

---

[12] On the last clause of verse 43 (usually translated, 'this house is called by [or, bears] your name'), see the commentaries of Keil and Bähr; it does not merely mean the temple is associated with Yahweh but that he possesses it and people encounter *him* there.

[13] Jesus went ballistic in Mark 11:15-18 because the wheeling and dealing of the cattle bazaar and money exchanging had been set up in the Court of the Gentiles in Herod's temple. How could gentile proselytes enjoy their designated area as a house of prayer (Isa. 56) amid bleating livestock and blabbering customers? See William Lane, *The Gospel According to Mark*, New International Commentary on the New Testament (Grand Rapids: Eerdmans, 1974), 402-408. Note that in 1 Kings 8 *prayer* is the premier activity associated with the temple; on this see the fine remarks of Ronald S. Wallace, *Readings in 1 Kings* (Grand Rapids: Eerdmans, 1996), 58-59.

new covenant connection where there's never been one. He brings one in a family (a parent, son, or daughter) to know and confess Jesus as Lord. By faithful living, quiet testimony, and the Spirit's work another family member comes into the kingdom of God; then, another. Perhaps two or three friends savingly come to Jesus. That is not invariably the case; sometimes a new believer has to stand alone within his/her own household. But frequently we see God operating as Solomon hopes he will in this prayer. God begins by bringing a particular one to his Son because he has designs on a whole family, or on a whole office crew. Yahweh is still joining together particularity and universality.

Solomon assumes this in his prayer. He expects foreign gentiles to come and share in Israel's privilege. Yahweh, then, is no back-alley, museum-piece god, no mascot of an Israelite suburb but the Lord of all the earth who will draw all kinds of non-kosher types to himself.

God has joined together eschatology and practicality (vv. 54-61)
By this heading I do *not* mean that eschatology (study of last things) is not practical. I do want, however, to pick up the dual note in Solomon's blessing of the people, especially in verses 56-60. Solomon's whole prayer, of course, presupposes God's redemptive scheme, especially the Davidic covenant. In verse 56 he alludes to the rest which Yahweh had brought about for Israel through David's victories (1 Kgs. 5:3-5; 2 Sam. 7:10-11); and his prayer-blessing for Yahweh's presence (v. 57), enabling (v. 58), and support (v. 59) has in view the grand finale: 'that all the peoples of the earth may know that Yahweh – he is the real God; there is no other' (v. 60).

But if Solomon has last things in view he has not forgotten daily things. In verse 59 he asks that the words he has used in pleading for Yahweh's grace might be 'near to Yahweh our God day and night.' Solomon asks that his prayer remain 'on record' (we might say 'on file', but that is too office-sounding) with Yahweh and that, in line with Solomon's prayer, Yahweh would 'maintain the cause of His servant and the cause of His people Israel, as each day requires' (NASB). The last phrase reads, literally, 'a matter of a day in its day.' It is the very same phrase used in Exodus 16:4, where Israel was to gather the manna 'a day's portion every day' (NASB) or, as the NIV has it, 'enough for that day'. So there is the covenant scheme and the ultimate view of all peoples acknowledging Yahweh, and yet there is also the regular, mundane, bump-a-long day-to-day need that Solomon and Israel have to be supported by a God who keeps the words of Solomon's prayer under his constant eye.

Occasionally in academia one bumps into students who structure marvelous overall plans for completing a whole term's work. A student like this carefully works out all deadlines and every bit of work to be done by certain junctures, so that all will be finished when required. But a student may work out his grand plan (or an alternate grand plan after the original grand plan has not been met) and yet fail, for whatever reason, to do the day to day grunt work of reading, research, and writing to bring his plan to pass. Somehow it is easier to conceive than to deliver.

But Israel's God is not like that. There is the grand scheme of Yahweh's redemptive work and there are the daily needs of his people. And the latter do not get lost in the former. Yahweh has joined together eschatology and practicality. Yahweh is Lord of the last day but also of every day. He will bring the consummation of his kingdom at the last, but he will not forget you in the third week of September. He cares about what 'each day requires' for you. How you should adore this God.

Closing word

'What therefore God hath joined together, let not man put asunder' (Matt. 19:6, KJV).[14] This maxim of Jesus was spoken in support of the sanctity of the marriage union. But does this principle not properly apply to the study and expression of theology, especially to our teaching about God's character and ways? Do we not have

---

[14] I am sure my memory of Graham Scroggie's sermon ('Inseparable Things') on Matthew 19:6 has suggested my approach in treating 1 Kings 8. His approach was topical; mine is confined to the chapter expounded. Scroggie's sermon can be found in Robert J. Smithson, ed., *My Way of Preaching* (London: Pickering & Inglis, n.d.), 146-53.

a tendency to stress one aspect of Yahweh's character at the expense of another and so risk ending up with a distortion of the true God? With a doctrinal graven image? Is not Solomon's prayer then a theological corrective, showing us how we must hold the truth about God in a holy tension? In a different connection John Bright once wrote that when sallying forth in the morning he did not have to choose between wearing his trousers *or* his shirt.[15] Decency has joined together trousers and shirts. So too we must keep together what God has joined together as he has revealed himself to us in the Scriptures. Is it not precisely in what God has 'joined together' that we see the 'beauty of the Lord' (cf. Ps. 27:4)? And does not the fact that all this is expressed in the form of prayer teach us that our finest theology will be done on our knees?

---

[15] John Bright, *The Authority of the Old Testament* (Nashville: Abingdon, 1967), 75-76.

Chapter 9

Surveying the Construction

1 Kings 9

Not long ago I enjoyed northern Louisiana hospitality, staying with people who had planned and built their own home and who obviously had gotten great pleasure from the process. Every piece of their home had a history, whether flooring, cabinets, doors, or columns. There was no flimsy material in the whole place. How fascinating it was to hear them tell where they had obtained various materials. Flooring or paneling had come from shelving in an 1880-vintage building in town that was being torn down; or heart cypress pillars came from beams beneath an abandoned home. The cedar closets smelled so good one wanted to sleep in them rather than in bed. What a delightful home, and what a pleasure it was to enjoy the family's proper pleasure in it simply from surveying again what they had built.

That is the background of 1 Kings 9. Of course it doesn't seem to be. It looks like a coherent piece of text (vv. 1-9) followed by a rag bag of snips and pieces all the way from miffed kings to the high seas (vv. 10-28). But the verb 'build' (*bānāh*) occurs nine times (vv. 1, 3, 10, 15, 17, 19, 24 [twice], 25) and holds the whole chapter together. Both major sections begin with a reference to Solomon's building Yahweh's house and the king's house (vv. 1, 10). We seem to have a survey that, from a mid-reign perspective (cf. v. 10), looks back over his construction that had been completed to date. The building terminology does not tightly control the chapter but loosely holds together a highly directive (vv. 1-9) and a mostly descriptive (vv. 10-28) section, which suggest two primary emphases.

The urgent need for faithfulness (vv. 1-9)

This was a signal occasion – 'Yahweh appeared to Solomon a second time as he had appeared to him at Gibeon' (v. 2; cf. 3:4-5). This was not something that occurred every other Wednesday. Hence this episode must be as crucial as Yahweh's first appearance in 3:4-15. The content of Yahweh's communication can be summarized as consisting of:

Privilege, v. 3
Assurance, vv. 4-5
Warning, vv. 6-9

In verse 3 Yahweh, per Solomon's dedicatory prayer, authorizes the temple as a means of grace where Israel will have access to his sovereign – and caring – presence,[1] and in verses 4-5 he assures Solomon that he will enjoy Davidic covenant blessing so long as he lives a Davidic-like life. But verses 6-9 turn more ominous: if Solomon and/or his successors prove faithless, the people will lose their place in the land and the temple will become exhibit A of the disaster. Royal faithlessness (v. 6) will bring judgment on the people (v. 7) – though the people will certainly ape royal apostasy (v. 9).

Yahweh's 'second advent' to Solomon is sobering. Over half of his words constitute warning (=vv. 6-9). Yahweh wants to impress Solomon with the high cost of apostasy. Infidelity will bring the loss of *turf, temple,* and *throne.* The first involves the loss of the land (v. 7a) and the eclipse of the Abrahamic covenant (Gen. 15); the second involves the loss of the sanctuary and the visible means of grace just climaxed under Solomon's regime (vv. 7b-8a); and the third (implicitly from vv. 4-5) will entail the loss of kingship and the eclipse of the Davidic covenant (2 Sam. 7). Only a fool would flirt with faithlessness.

Red Army troops were going berserk as they zeroed in on Berlin in 1945. Dr. Georg Henneberg was aghast when he found Russians had broken into his test laboratories at the Schering chemical plant.

---

[1] 'Heart' occurs 51 times in 1-2 Kings; of these verse 3 has the only reference to God's 'heart.'

Why so upset? The Russians were in there playing catch with laboratory eggs that had been infected with typhus bacteria. Who knows what might have happened had Henneberg not laid hold of a Russian colonel who ejected the soldiers and locked up the building?[2] Those troops had no idea of the trouble they could have let loose.

But Solomon did – because Yahweh told him precisely what the price-tag of infidelity would be. Yahweh is so kind, isn't he? He spells it all out, he warns clearly, so we'll understand the urgent need for faithfulness. Nor has he changed. There is a whole New Testament book in which he calculates for us the high stakes of apostasy: he begins in Hebrews 2:1-3 and continues throughout the epistle (3:12-13; 6:1-8; 10:26-31; 12:25-29) scaring the liver out of us, all to the praise of his grace and the safety of his people.

The ongoing business of kingship (vv. 10-28)

Now we meet a summary piece of various activities in Solomon's reign, apparently at about its midpoint (cf. v. 10). It is loaded with the stuff of kingship and breaks down into four primary sections:

1. Politics, vv. 10-14
2. Defense, vv. 15-24
3. Religion, v. 25
4. Commerce, vv. 26-28

What a note of realism in diplomatic relations! Not everyone comes up smiling in such affairs – certainly not Hiram. Hiram furnished Solomon with construction materials and gold (v. 11a) – in fact over four tons of it (v. 14).[3] Apparently Solomon ran up more debt than he could pay in foodstuffs (cf. 5:9, 11) and so ceded twenty border towns to Hiram. If these towns were around the *town* of Cabul (cf. Josh. 19:27), then they were in the territory of Asher near the border with Tyre. Hiram toured the area and

---

[2]Cornelius Ryan, *The Last Battle* (New York: Simon and Schuster, 1966), 494.

[3] The NIV is correct to translate the verb of verse 14 as a pluperfect, explaining how much gold Hiram 'had sent' to Solomon.

was unimpressed. Not much he could do about it but object. He could tell Solomon he thought they were sorry samples of towns.[4] But Hiram is no dunce. He's not about to be so upset that he would boycott joining Solomon in a lucrative sea trade (vv. 26-28).

The writer also clips a piece for us (vv. 15-24) from a document dealing with the forced labor Solomon used. Most of the building described is defense work, putting key military sites into a proper state of preparedness.[5] One often meets a hue and cry among commentators about how oppressive Solomon's regime was – witness the forced labor. True, Solomon was not particularly nice to the Perizzites, for example. But the writer's point in verses 20-23 is not to damn Solomon with innuendo but to defend Solomon's policy: those who were permanent state slaves were from enclaves of subject peoples, but no Israelites were reduced to such status. More than anything the writer intends a Solomonic apologetic.[6]

And orthodoxy seemed to be thriving. Apparently Solomon saw to that, as the three annual festivals were regularly celebrated

---

[4] Some (e.g., BDB, 459) suggest the name 'Cabul' (v. 13b) might reflect a Hiramian wisecrack that the towns were 'as good as nothing' (we might say 'Zerosville'), but we cannot be sure of this.

[5] Both Hazor and Megiddo (v. 15) were primary fortresses at strategic points on the interstate highway between Mesopotamia and Egypt. Hazor was the massive site between Lakes Galilee and Huleh that guarded the northern entrance into Israel; Megiddo controlled one of the passes on the southwest edge of the Plain of Esdraelon, at the point where, if one were traveling up from Egypt, the international highway swings east to cross northern Israel. Gezer (vv. 15-17a) stood on the edge of the Judean foothills, a bit to the east of that main north-south highway and guarding the route through the Valley of Aijalon on up to Beth-horon and so to Jerusalem. Cf. John Gray, *I & II Kings*, Old Testament Library, 2nd ed. (Philadelphia: Westminster, 1970), 244-46. Tamar (v. 18 – I prefer this reading to 'Tadmor') was likely southwest of the Dead Sea on the road between Hebron and Elath (the port on the Gulf of Aqaba), perhaps fortified to protect the trade with S. Arabia via Elath (cf. F. C. Fensham, 'Tadmor,' NBD, 3rd ed., 1149-50; and J. T. Butler, 'Tamar,' ISBE, 4:725). On Solomon's storage cities (v. 19), see Alfred Hoerth, *Archaeology and the Old Testament* (Grand Rapids: Baker, 1998), 284-86.

[6] Solomon needed a large work force because he had building in his blood. Verses 1 and 19 use the noun *ḥēšeq* (and 19 adds the cognate verb)

(v. 25; see Exod. 23:14-17). The last part of verse 25 is difficult. The NIV may be correct in its rendering of the last clause ('and so fulfilled the temple obligations'); if so, it means 'Solomon met all religious obligations set by the Mosaic law and implied by the building of the central sanctuary.'[7]

Then the writer takes us from sanctuary to shore to get a glimpse of shipping and commerce on the Red Sea and beyond (vv. 26-28). They would set out from the Gulf of Aqaba south of Edom and go, wheeling and dealing, all the way to Ophir – wherever that was.[8] Hiram's Phoenician mariners supplied the naval expertise and both Israel and Tyre raked in the profits. When Hiram's sailors brought Solomon imported wealth we can be sure Hiram didn't suffer in the deal. Indeed, we must remember that Solomon's united kingdom sat on the transportation crossroads of the Near East and his fortified cities controlled (and, no doubt, collected duty on) all the major overland arteries. Hence Aharoni and Avi-yonah can say that

> when a strong power such as the united monarchy of Israel, controlled all the caravan routes connecting the main markets with one another, it was possible to reap vast profits from the flow of goods being shipped between the sophisticated societies of Egypt, Mesopotamia, South Arabia, Anatolia and Greece. The partnership between Solomon and Hiram king of Tyre guaranteed an abundant financial harvest for both nations.[9]

---

of Solomon's 'desire' to build. It is a strong word; we would say he had a 'passion' for building (see Patterson and Austel, '1 and 2 Kings,' *Expositor's Bible Commentary*, 12 vols. [Grand Rapids: Zondervan, 1988], 4:94, and David Talley, NIDOTTE, 2:318-19).

[7] Paul R. House, *1, 2 Kings*, New American Commentary (n.p.: Broadman & Holman, 1995), 159.

[8] For the possibilities (S or SE Arabia, Somalia, India), see D. J. Wiseman, 'Ophir,' NBD, 3rd ed., 849-50. On the site of Ezion-geber (v. 26), see the convenient summary in Walter C. Kaiser, Jr., *A History of Israel from the Bronze Age through the Jewish Wars* (Nashville: Broadman & Holman, 1998), 277-80.

[9] Yohanan Aharoni and Michael Avi-yonah, *The Macmillan Bible Atlas*, 3rd ed. (New York: Macmillan, 1993), 88.

I have called this segment the 'ongoing business of kingship.' I do not see here explicit signs of Solomon's foolishness (as, e.g., Provan does).[10] Most such summary sections (ch. 4 and 10:14-29 are the others) seem to have a generally positive tone. So here is Solomon: engaging in politics but unable to keep Hiram smiling (vv. 10-14); giving free rein to his love for building – much of it for defense purposes (vv. 15-24); maintaining orthodoxy in all its liturgical regularity (v. 25); and venturing and profiting in world economy and trade (vv. 26-28). My point is that all this is not particularly objectionable; it's simply what kings do.

It all reminds me of the father of one of my boyhood friends. Tom, my friend, and I would play 'cars and trucks', and as Tom would play with his toy truck, driving it along with the appropriate oral sputtering sound one makes when playing with toy trucks, he would claim he was going 'honeydipping.' That's because Tom's father was a 'honeydipper.' My mother never seemed to like my saying I was going honeydipping when I drove my toy trucks. Then I came to understand why. You see, honeydipping had nothing to do with bees or food processing. Around 1950 in our little western Pennsylvania town there were still some people without indoor plumbing and who still used outhouses or outdoor privies. Now Tom's dad cleaned out the pits under those outhouses for people. That was 'honeydipping.' Which explains, I suppose, why I would regularly see Tom's father hauling a large tank on his truck, heading up the lane past our house toward the town dump, where he would deposit his treasure. But my mother needn't have been so repulsed. Honeydipping was proper work; it was simply what honeydippers do.

In the same way these activities highlighted in verses 10-28 are, on the whole, legitimate concerns of kings. They are simply what kings do. Perhaps they seem a bit too 'secular' for us, but that is the case with most of our daily callings – we find ourselves doing what electricians or paralegals or accountants or welders or real estate agents do. Such activities are perfectly proper and should not be viewed as somehow sub-covenantal.

---

[10] However, I admit that ceding covenant turf to a foreign ruler (v. 11) is hardly kosher.

And yet.... Yet what? Yet we must not forget that verses 6-9 stand like a Mt. Rushmore peering down over verses 10-28. One may be enjoying a thoroughly successful kingly (or financial or professional or ministerial) career and yet end in utter ruin unless one takes obedience to the first commandment as his very highest calling.

Chapter 10

A Light to the Nations

1 Kings 10

A couple of years ago our city hosted an exhibit called 'The Palaces of St. Petersburg'. Patrons could enjoy a well-spent two hours, seeing and hearing about the opulent surroundings of some of Russia's czars. And 1 Kings 10 is like that. In case you've missed it, the writer wants you simply to stand there and gaze at magnificence. Why don't we allow him to take us on his tour? We can sit down and talk about how we are to understand it all afterwards.

Data

The Queen of Sheba was no slouch – witness the inventory of her wares (v. 2a).[1] She found Solomon fully up to his reputation in wits and wisdom (vv. 1-3), but she found Solomonic style literally breath-taking (vv. 3-5). Such class she had never seen.

The narrator pushes us on. In verses 14-22 his operative word is 'gold' (ten times). On the way to the shield exhibit he informs us that Solomon takes in up to twenty tons of gold in a year (v. 14)[2] – though, of course, that figure doesn't include it all (v. 15). Ah, here we are at the House of the Forest of Lebanon. Look at these shields – two hundred body-sized shields (v. 16), three hundred smaller, hand-carried shields (v. 17). Gold-plated – with about seven and a half pounds of gold per body shield, three and three-fourths for a smaller one.[3] Look awfully spiffy on state

---

[1] Most locate Sheba in S. Arabia, present-day Yemen, over 1,000 miles below Jerusalem.

[2] The figure is not ludicrous; see discussion in K. A. Kitchen, *The Bible in its World: The Bible & Archaeology Today* (Downers Grove: InterVarsity, 1977), 101-102.

[3] Richard D. Patterson and Hermann J. Austel, '1, 2 Kings,' *Expositor's Bible Commentary*, 12 vols. (Grand Rapids: Zondervan, 1988), 4:103.

occasions. Now this throne (vv. 18-20) – ivory inlay, gold overlay; note the steps, the lions. Nothing like it anywhere.[4] As we pass one of the storage rooms our host points out the gold drinking containers. Note (he says), no silver – it doesn't amount to anything in Solomon's regime (v. 21). He concludes the tour with a few remarks about Solomonic commercial ventures. Joint Israelite-Phoenician shipping periodically returns laden with gold, silver, ivory, and even apes and baboons (v. 22, NJB, NIV). (The latter specimens shouldn't surprise us – apparently Solomon simply had a passion for zoology very like some Assyrian kings of the 12th–9th centuries B.C.)[5] Moreover, Solomon through his merchants acts as middleman in a thriving import-export trade in chariots and horses (vv. 28-29). Egypt in the south and Kue (Cilicia) in the northwest are his sources, while Hittite groups in the north and Aramaeans to the northeast constitute his market.[6] (Solomon was not abetting the arms trade. These chariots were likely deluxe models for royal, ceremonial [not military] use – hence the relatively high prices [v. 29]).[7]

The tour ends. Of course there was no e-mail or fax machine in all Solomon's kingdom. But no matter – it was massively impressive. Folks walked away from tours exclaiming (like the Queen of Sheba), 'Well, I never...!'

---

[4] 'The throne was probably made of wood, partly overlaid with sheets of gold and partly decorated with carved panels of ivory, often elaborately carved, veneered to the wooden parts' (W. J. Dumbrell, NIDOTTE, 1:1030-31).

[5] See Yutaka Ikeda, 'Solomon's Trade in Horses and Chariots in Its International Setting,' *Studies in the Period of David and Solomon and Other Essays* (Winona Lake, IN: Eisenbrauns, 1982), 219-20. In any case, one is tempted to say that few kings aped Solomon.

[6] On the Hittites at this time, see Harry A. Hoffner, Jr., 'Hittites,' *Peoples of the Old Testament World* (Grand Rapids: Baker, 1994), 131, 152; on Solomon's commercial interests, cf. Yohanan Aharoni and Michael Avi-Yonah, *The Macmillan Bible Atlas*, 3rd ed. (New York: Macmillan, 1993), 88.

[7] See the fascinating discussion in Ikeda, 'Solomon's Trade,' 221-38.

Perspective

How are we readers to regard all this grandeur and luxury? That is, how does the writer want us to think about it? Does he describe Solomonic splendor with cautious reluctance or with grateful enthusiasm? Clearly, I would say, the latter.

All of chapter 10 can be divided into two major sections, verses 1-13, where the Queen of Sheba says, 'This is unreal!,' and verses 14-29, where the narrator exclaims, 'And get a load of this!' Does that sound like too much hype? Then let me simply point out that within each of these two primary divisions the writer places a testimony section: verses 6-9 contain the testimony of the Queen of Sheba and verses 23-25 the testimony of the narrator himself. These testimonies are important for communicating the writer's intended perspective. The queen exudes that the reality she sees is even truer than all the fantastic reports she had heard (vv. 6-7). Her commendation climaxes in a note of praise to Yahweh (v. 9):

> May Yahweh your God be blessed,
> who has delighted in you
>> to place you upon the throne of Israel;
> it's because Yahweh loves Israel forever
>> that he placed you as king
>> to carry out justice and righteousness.

But some may object that verses 6-9 are only what the Queen of Sheba said. How do we know the writer agrees with her view? After all, surely she felt the pressure to make a politically correct press release. And one senses that some commentators and historians are secretly disappointed with the queen and wish they could have drafted her speech. They would have her say with dripping irony in verse 8, 'Happy are your slaves, who sweat and toil and work and bleed and die in order to build your monuments!'

But back to the main concern. The writer shows he himself agrees with the queen's assessment when he so much as seconds her sentiments in his own testimony (vv. 23-25), the aside he inserts into his description of the royal magnificence:

(23) Now King Solomon became greater than all the kings of the earth with respect to wealth and wisdom. (24) And all the earth kept seeking Solomon's presence to listen to his wisdom which God had placed in his heart. (25) And they kept bringing each one his tribute, items of silver, and items of gold, and robes, and weapons and spices, horses and mules – what was due each year.

In verse 23 he shows Yahweh had indeed fulfilled his promise of 3:12-13 regarding wisdom and wealth. Indeed, by his notes or reports, he clearly holds that Solomon's wealth and wisdom flow from Yahweh's reputation (v. 1), Yahweh's love (v. 9), and Yahweh's giving (v. 24). In the main, then, I think Wallace has sized it up well:

It seems obvious that throughout this chapter the writer himself is inspired by the same kind of enthusiasm about Solomon as was caught by the Queen of Sheba. He has seen in the grandeur of Solomon a preliminary earthly sketch of the Messianic kingdom promised by God. This is why he tends in his account to resort to the use of superlatives and to lapse into exaggeration in order to give an understandable emphasis to his point. Of course he is recording the facts of history, but at this crucial point in his description of Solomon's kingship he gives us no hint that there were more sombre and threatening aspects of his kingship of which he had to take account. He will deal honestly with these as his account goes on. At the moment they are kept out of sight. His purpose is to fix in our minds a specially impressive picture of the actual climax of Solomon's rule.[8]

Assuming now the writer's positive perspective let us sketch out the significance of this text.

---

[8] Ronald S. Wallace, *Readings in 1 Kings* (Grand Rapids: Eerdmans, 1996), 69. (I do not think that the writer 'lapse[s] into exaggeration.' One could speak of hyperbole in verses 23 and 27, but exaggeration would have undercut the value of the writer's testimony). One might ask, however, if Deuteronomy 17:16-17 does not cast a shadow over 1 Kings 10? Probably not; see the discussion in Patterson and Austel, '1, 2 Kings,' 104.

Significance

In light of what we have just said in the preceding section, we can say that 1 Kings 10 speaks *a word of testimony*, namely, that the prosperity of the people of God is always a gift of Yahweh's goodness, which (I would think) demands of us both gratitude (lest we idolize the gifts in place of God) and joy (lest we despise God's gifts as though they were sinful). Some have difficulty with the latter response in 1 Kings 10. In spite of the positive tone of the writer commentators seem convinced that all that gold can't be good and so feel impelled to emphasize the clouds on the horizon for Solomon's kingdom. It reminds me of what missionary Don McClure once told about the Nuer people in the Sudan: 'The Nuer believes that milk is a beverage for women and children, but he likes it so well that he cannot bear to see it all go to the women, so he makes a cocktail with a bite by adding cow urine, which makes it a man's drink.'[9] That is, he can't enjoy it unless he ruins it first. I wonder if we don't do that with 1 Kings 10 – feel obligated to moan over 'materialism' and all that could possibly go wrong with such bounty rather than acknowledging that it is the blessing of the Lord that makes rich (cf. Prov. 10:22) and being content to enjoy that should he give it. Must we, to stretch illustration into analogy, pour cow urine over the text in our panic to stay out of bed with the whore we call the health-and-wealth gospel?

Secondly, there is a sense in which 1 Kings 10 is *a word of prophecy*, for the attraction that Solomon's kingdom held for the nations of his day is a foregleam of the destiny of the kingdom of God on earth. The Queen of Sheba is simply a sample of the future homage the nations will bring to Yahweh's covenant King. Indeed Solomon himself[10] seems to have previewed the future of the covenant king when he prayed in Psalm 72:

May he have dominion from sea to sea,
     and from the River to the ends of the earth!

---

[9] Charles Partee, *Adventure in Africa* (Grand Rapids: Zondervan, 1990), 144-45.

[10] See the superscription to the psalm.

> May his foes [?] bow down before him,
>> and his enemies lick the dust!
> May the kings of Tarshish and of the isles
>> render him tribute,
> May the kings of Sheba and Seba
>> bring gifts!
> May all kings fall down before him,
>> all nations serve him!
>
> Long may he live,
>> may gold of Sheba be given to him!
>>> (Ps. 72:8-11, 15, RSV)[11]

Isaiah is burning the same fuel when he depicts Zion's splendor in the coming age:

> [B]ecause the abundance of the sea shall be turned to you,
>> the wealth of the nations shall come to you.
> A multitude of camels shall cover you,
>> the young camels of Midian and Ephah;
>> all those from Sheba shall come.
> They shall bring gold and frankincense,
>> and shall proclaim the praise of the LORD
>>> (Isa. 60:5b, 6, RSV).

Isaiah's camels are not creating a traffic jam but transporting wealth and tribute to Zion, and Isaiah reads off the names from his map (see also 60:7) to 'create the sense of a world-wide surge to Zion.'[12] And there are those camels from Sheba swaying along with all that gold (just as in 1 Kings 10). As it was in 1 Kings 10, so it shall be.

When our youngest son was two or three years old he was already into baseball and acting the part of a left-handed pitcher. I would squat as his 'catcher' at one end of the family room, and he would wind-up and throw his southpaw pitches to me using a

---

[11] NIV takes verses 8-11 as statements; they are better taken as requests as in RSV and NASB.

[12] Alec Motyer, *The Prophecy of Isaiah* (Downers Grove: InterVarsity, 1993), 495.

harmless plastic ball. His passion for baseball continued through the years into his university days. All four years of college he was a starting left-handed pitcher – and a first-class one at that – on his team. His college pitching was in no way an exact duplicate of his two/three-year-old performance. But, looking back, we can say we saw it all coming years before in his family room workouts. Those were a foregleam of what was to come.

That is the way 1 Kings 10 functions as 'prophecy.' The trek of the Queen of Sheba (vv. 1-13) and others (vv. 24-25) is a preview of the future flow of gentiles to Zion (Isa. 2:2-3).[13] Already in 1 Kings 10 Solomon's prayer (8:41-43, 60) was beginning to be answered.

But this is not merely a matter of grasping a biblical concept; it is our very hope. Most of us reading these pages are probably not ethnic Israelites; hence how ought we to lay hold of this picture of gentiles being drawn to the covenant kingdom? By rights we have no claim to it, no place to stand in it. I recall a get together several churches in our community had when I was about six years old. We were in the basement of the local Methodist church and some visiting musician was leading us in songs as he played his accordion. (Why did they always have accordions?) At that time in my life, I must confess, I liked Methodist songs far better than the psalms we tended to sing; the Methodists' fare was more spritely. Our accordion friend played through a new song and then asked if anyone knew it. I raised my hand to say, 'I'm a United Presbyterian, but I know it.' Wonder of wonders! Who would have thought? A U. P. knowing a song like that. And yet I did – surprising as it was. That is the sense we must have as gentiles

---

[13] Bezalel Porten ('The Structure and Theme of the Solomon Narrative [I Kings 3-11],' *Hebrew Union College Annual* 38 [1967]: 111) points out that the Queen of Sheba story 'is part of the recurrent biblical theme of the pagan admiring, or acknowledging, the achievement of Israel and blessing or praising its deity: Melchizedek (Gen. 14:18ff.), the Hittites (Gen. 23:6), Pharaoh's magicians (Exod. 8:15 [19]), the Egyptians (9:20), Pharaoh (9:27), Jethro (18:9ff.), Balaam (Num. 23-24), the nations (Deut. 4:6ff.), Rahab (Josh. 2:9ff.), the Midianite soldier (Judg. 7:13f.), Naaman (II Kings 5:15), etc.' We might add Ruth (Ruth 1:16-17), as well as the clips in Daniel when pagan kings praise Israel's God (2:46-49; 3:28-30; 4:34-37; 6:25-27).

reading our Hebrew Bible: Look at that! Gentiles coming to Jerusalem. It must be possible. Isn't grace grand?

Lastly, 1 Kings 10 speaks *a word of criticism.* We may finish 1 Kings 10 but Jesus tells us we haven't seen the last of the Queen of Sheba.

> The queen of the south will be raised at the judgment with this generation and will condemn it; because she came from the ends of the earth to hear the wisdom of Solomon, and look! – something greater than Solomon is here (Matt. 12:42).

Jesus' statement comes near the end of two chapters that highlight the unbelief of Israel and her leadership (Matt. 11-12). The latter had asked for a stark-raving indisputable sign to prove Jesus' claims; this he basically refused (12:39-40). But he did give them a couple of snapshots of the resurrection and last judgment. And there she is! And perhaps her mere presence is enough to condemn Israel.

Jesus' argument is that the queen had both less truth and less privilege. She had only Solomon's wisdom and was not one of Solomon's people – yet she came to hear Solomon's words. Not bad for a gentile apparently out of the covenant loop. But now Israel faces something greater than Solomon – Jesus himself in his word and works, and she refuses to hear. Israel's greater privilege will not secure her immunity but will aggravate her responsibility (v. 42). That is Jesus' point.

Of course we tend to assume that increased privilege somehow negates responsibility. For example, Rose Kennedy seemed delighted in her role as top mother after Jack Kennedy had been elected President of the United States. She would be reading newspapers as Frank Saunders, her chauffeur, drove her around. Whenever she finished reading a paper, Mrs. Kennedy would pitch it out the car window. Saunders warned her that they could be fined for littering. Rose's response? 'Oh, Frank. They know who we are!'[14] Translation: Our position and privilege puts us above all that.

---

[14] Ronald Kessler, *The Sins of the Father* (New York: Warner Books, 1996), 395.

But Jesus says no. And we must heed him because most of us stand in Israel's sandals; indeed we have even more light than Israel had during Jesus' tenure on earth. And whether we are viciously resistant or merely casually indifferent to him makes no difference. So don't you dare read 1 Kings 10 and pat the Queen of Sheba on the head. You can do that, you know. You view this regal story in 1 Kings in the same way you do an old classic movie – it has entertainment value but no serious relevance. But you don't dare patronize this royal lady or look on her as a fascinating literary cipher; because unless you bow before the Son of God you will see her striding into the judgment hall and pointing her finger at you.

Chapter 11

You Have Left Your First Love

1 Kings 11

In one of Charles Schulz' *Peanuts* cartoon strips he depicts Lucy and Linus sitting together while Lucy reads a story. Lucy from the book: 'And so the King was granted his wish – everything he touched would turn to gold! Now, the next day....' At this point Linus jumps to his feet and exclaims: 'Stop! You don't have to read any further! I know just what's going to happen.' He walks away bemoaning, 'These things always have a way of backfiring!'

That is the impression one receives when reading 1 Kings 1–11. It sounds as if everything Solomon touches turns to wisdom, buildings, and gold. Then: 'Now King Solomon loved many foreign women...' (v. 1). These things always have a way of backfiring. Chapter 11 is the dull thud after the high hopes of chapters 1-10.[1]

This is a long chapter (43 verses), but I think we will do better to swallow it whole than to fragment our treatment. What highlights are we meant to see here?

The Heart that Yahweh Desires (vv. 1-13)
Before we get to the heart of Solomon's fall, let us be very clear about the *character of the offense*. Verse 2 picks up Yahweh's previous rationale (Deut. 7:1-4; Exod. 34:11-16) against intermarriage with pagans: 'Surely they will turn away your heart after their gods.' Willy-nilly it happened with Solomon in his later

---

[1] Cf. Johannes Fichtner, *Das erste Buch von den Königen*, Die Botschaft des Alten Testaments, 2nd ed. (Stuttgart: Calwer, 1979), 177-78. Cf. Paul R. House: 'After the glowing report in 10:14-29, these verses [11:1-13] are the literary equivalent of a blow to the face' (*1, 2 Kings*, New American Commentary [n.p.: Broadman & Holman, 1995], 166).

years: 'His wives had turned away his heart after other gods' (v. 4).² The result was predictable: 'So Solomon went after Ashtoreth the goddess of the Sidonians' *et al.* (v. 5). Then Solomon built cozy chapels for his pagan wives, so they could carry on their (literally) damned worship, burning incense and sacrifices to Chemosh, Molech, or whatever (vv. 7-8).

I have belabored this point because some writers moan so much over what they divine of Solomon's affluence, indulgence, excesses, extravagance, exploitation, and oppression, that one can be duped into thinking that such items are the principal trouble. That's why it's so important to notice that 1 Kings 1–10 are almost wholly positive toward Solomon and then to hear chapter 11 clearly, for the latter trumpets that the problem is not wealth or luxury or high-handedness or wisdom or popularity or renown or splendor or achievement but *other gods*. First commandment stuff.

Now we can notice the *subtlety of the sin*. How is it so subtle? Because it is internal; it is, to use the key word of our passage, a matter of the 'heart.' This term occurs five times in verses 2-4: 'they will turn away your heart,' (v. 2); 'then his wives turned away his heart,' (v. 3b); 'his wives had turned away his heart,' (v. 4a); 'his heart was not completely with Yahweh his God, as the heart of David his father was,' (v. 4b). The Bible, however, does not use 'heart' as does contemporary western culture merely to denote emotions or feelings.³ That's part of it, but the Bible has a bigger heart; it means the willing, loving, thinking centre of the person.⁴ The Bible does not separate the head (or brains or mind) and heart; rather the head is in the heart. The fixation on the heart in this text does tell us we are dealing with the invisible and the

---

² Remember that according to Deut. 17:17 the king was forbidden to 'multiply wives to himself,' even if they were orthodox Israelite women. Solomon's 700 + 300 harem (v. 3) clearly violated this. In 1 Kings 11 Solomon's is a compound offense: his wives are *both* many and pagan.

³ The climactic scene of a recent movie featured an attorney pleading with the jury not to decide with their respective minds but with their hearts, i.e., by feeling rather than by thinking.

⁴ See Edmond Jacob, *Theology of the Old Testament* (New York: Harper & Row, 1958), 163-66; and William Dyrness, *Themes in Old Testament Theology* (Downers Grove: InterVarsity, 1977), 89-91.

internal. Let me remind you that this is the *Old* Testament. Do you see how internal Old Testament faith is? Like Jesus (Mark 7:21-23) it cares about the root of it all. But that is what makes infidelity so subtle – it begins in the hidden depths of a man. Long before you see a new Chemosh chapel going up outside Jerusalem a royal heart had taken a turn.

This infidelity is also subtle because it is gradual. Verse 4 has a scary line: 'When Solomon was old, his wives had turned away his heart after other gods.' It was not some sudden attack or irresistible assault that explains Solomon's plunge into pagan ecumenism. No, it took years – the result of the creeping pace of accumulated compromises, the fruit of a conscience de-sensitized by repeated permissiveness. The process is like what happens with one's eyeglasses. We may wear our glasses constantly, or at least repeatedly, and subject them to frequent cleanings; but unless we happen to be toying with them or, uncharacteristically, inspecting them, we likely do not notice whether the minute screws that keep the frames securely around the lenses might be getting a bit loose. One might almost thoughtlessly check and find a screw has loosened up a couple of turns. It's more probable, however, that a lens simply pops out when we are in the middle of something. We were completely unaware that the frame was loose. It happened gradually, slowly, imperceptibly.

We must take a moment to be frightened. 'When Solomon was old....' How that text ought to goad older believers to pray the last petition of the Lord's Prayer (Matt. 6:13a). Is there not a warning to churches as well, who have a fixation on youth ministry and a love affair with young marrieds and/or young families? Need we not exercise far more vigilance over our over-sixties crowd, many of whom will doubtless meet the major troubles of their lives in their final years?

Now let us make what has been implicit explicit: the *tragedy of the story*. Chapter 11 cues us that we must look at this episode in light of the whole Solomon story. Observe the love terminology in 11:1-2: 'Now King Solomon loved many foreign women...; to them Solomon clung in love.'[5] This calls to mind the narrator's

---

[5] 'Them' in 11:2b is masculine and could refer to the nearest antecedent,

comment from the beginning of Solomon's reign: 'So Solomon loved Yahweh, walking in the statutes of David his father' (3:3).

Of course, it is common to qualify the 'love' of 11:1-2. Many sources will point out that the huge harem (v. 3) does not mean that Solomon hovered around slobbering with lust. Rather, many of these marriages were political, meant to cement alliances concluded with other nations or groups. I see no reason to dispute this; but the text says more. The text is not interested in Solomon's politics but in his affections. Solomon clung to these women in love, it says. Whether many marriages were political does not matter. We must not allow the possible background of a text to overthrow the clear claim of the text.

So there is the tragedy: a story that begins with 'Solomon loved Yahweh' (3:3) and ends with 'King Solomon loved many foreign women' (11:1). How these 'book end' texts should sober us. Where are my affections? Has an imperceptible drift taken place in them over the years? Am I headed for tragedy because I have left my first love?

Solomon did not officially renounce Yahweh, but 'his heart was not completely with' Yahweh (v. 4) and he 'did not follow Yahweh fully' (v. 6). Apparently his offense was not limited to building shrines for his wives; verse 5 suggests at least some degree of participation on Solomon's part. What happens when one makes first commandment compromises? One meets the *anger of the Lord* (vv. 9-13).

We will focus on verses 9-10 (vv. 11-13 will surface with a later section). As Bible readers we are not shocked to read, 'So Yahweh was angry with Solomon because his heart had turned away from Yahweh' (v. 9). Yahweh is simply following his declared policy (Deut. 6:14-15) toward those within the covenant. His anger flows out of his jealousy for supreme place in his people's worship and affection (and jealousy is simply the character of any love that is worth its salt when that love has an exclusive claim). But our culture *is* shocked by the Lord's anger, for he does not conform to canonical human expectations. And –

'their gods.' However, I take the masculine plural pronoun as alluding comprehensively to the women from the various nations.

as we've said before – Yahweh is unique among ancient Near Eastern gods, goddesses, and godlets. No pagan deity demanded exclusive devotion of his/her worshipers. And the anger of the biblical Yahweh bothers contemporary man because it clearly tells him that the God of the Bible is not a pluralist. He does not fit our times and mentality. Why should he be so irate because someone (like Solomon) wants to spread his liturgical devotion around, to expose himself to other religious traditions, or to broaden one's horizons by investigating alternate forms of human spirituality? Folks in our time want no truck with a God who will brook no rival, nor do they want to face Yahweh-in-the-flesh who sits on Galilee's shore, peers across the fire, and assumes he has the right to keep probing us about our love for him (John 21:15-17).[6]

The History that Yahweh Controls (vv. 14-43)
Since this section of text is so long, we can make our discussion more manageable if we break it down into two divisions.

---

[6] It is interesting to note the assumptions 1 Kings 11:1-10 overthrows (by implication). One sometimes reads Christian writers who bemoan the current lack of 'heroes.' There is such a dearth, they claim, of suitable models for youth. But the text says Solomon had a fine model – David his father (vv. 4, 6). (The idea is not that David was Simon-pure, but that he was first-commandment faithful). Yet that did not keep Solomon from folly. This exposes the *example* fallacy. Yahweh's anger in verse 9 is 'because his heart had turned away from Yahweh, the God of Israel, who had appeared to him two times' (see 3:4-15 and 9:1-9). Note the inference: even the most privileged, intimate experiences with God do not guarantee immunity from infidelity – undermining the *experiential* fallacy. Verse 10 affirms that Yahweh had clearly warned Solomon about this other-gods seduction, yet Solomon 'did not keep what Yahweh had commanded.' How often socio-political groups assume that if people are only informed about some danger they will then avoid it. If only youth know that drugs will fry their brains like an egg in a skillet, well, then, they will 'just say no' to drugs. Or even Christians can assume that if only they indoctrinate their children in biblical doctrine and with a biblical world view, then they will not fall away. But Solomon did – with Yahweh as his teacher; and that exposes the *educational* fallacy.

History and Sovereignty (vv. 14-26)

In three key verses this section tells us what Yahweh was doing on the historical scene circa 950 BC:

(1) 'Then Yahweh raised up an adversary to Solomon, Hadad the Edomite...' (v. 14)
(2) 'Then God raised up to him an adversary, Rezon son of Eliada...' (v. 23)
(3) 'Now Jeroboam son of Nebat ... he lifted up his hand against the king' (v. 26)

The last example differs in form from the other two, but the rest of the chapter will make clear that Yahweh also raised up Jeroboam.

Newspapers do not report events that way, i.e., telling Yahweh's role in them. Historians do not write history that way; rather they look for cause-and-effect relationships, for various 'factors,' for explanations and motives. This is not merely because news reporters and historians are secularists. Granted, many of them are; but even believers are baffled to understand exactly what God is doing in any given historical situation. The latter may claim to know but frequently have no more sure light than anyone else. Historical events, in one sense, are opaque; it's difficult to figure out what God may be doing at any given point.

That's why the Bible is so different. The biblical writers have light from 'the outside.' Without batting an eye one of them will tell you, 'Yahweh raised up an adversary for Solomon – Hadad the Edomite' (v. 14). We may be so accustomed to reading that kind of line in the Bible that it fails to surprise us. You will not read anything like this in your newspaper or history books. But here in 1 Kings 11 the Bible writer is saying, 'Yahweh did this here and here and here.' Hadad, Rezon, and Jeroboam are not accidental blobs that happened to appear in the historical menagerie; rather their place, their time, and their impact took place at the beck of Yahweh's sovereign finger. One could assume the same for other petty rulers – Hitler, Stalin, and Franklin Roosevelt, to name several.

Though other details clamor for discussion,[7] we must underscore one central contention: when Yahweh acts sovereignly in history he always does so by means of a *faithful* sovereignty. What do I mean by that? I mean that Yahweh's work in history is in accord with his previously stated principles, his covenant policy. What covenant policy? In this case, Davidic covenant policy, and the applicable section is found in 2 Samuel 7:14: 'Should he [any covenant king descended from David] commit iniquity, I shall punish him with the rod of men and with blows from the sons of men.'[8] Yahweh is simply carrying out his previously announced measures in case Davidic royalty proved unfaithful. In Solomon's case the rod and the blows came from Hadad, Rezon, and Jeroboam. First Kings 11 simply depicts Yahweh's faithful application of Davidic covenant principles to a particular historical situation. Yahweh is so consistent.

---

[7] For example: (1) Apparently the roots of the Hadad and Rezon trouble began in David's time (vv. 15-17, 21, 24) but came to fruition in the latter part of Solomon's reign; (2) Of the two external enemies, one was in the south/southeast (Hadad in Edom), the other to the northeast (Rezon in Damascus) – both potential threats to Solomon's control of caravan routes to/from the Red Sea and the Euphrates respectively; cf. John Bright, *A History of Israel*, 3rd ed. (Philadelphia: Westminster, 1981), 214; and (3) Why all the detail about Hadad's escape from Joab's clutches and especially his hobnobbing in Pharaoh's court (vv. 15-22)? Note Eugene Merrill's suggestion (*Kingdom of Priests* [Grand Rapids: Baker, 1987], 299):

> Traveling through the desert by way of Midian and Paran, Hadad and his protectors eventually reached Egypt where they found sanctuary, probably under Pharaoh Amenemope (993-978). Hadad likely did not reach a marriageable age until the reign of Siamun (978-959), and so it was probably Siamun's sister-in-law whom Hadad wed (1 Kings 11:19). If this is correct, one cannot help noting the irony of Siamun's having given his daughter to Solomon and his sister-in-law to Solomon's mortal enemy.

Could the writer be hinting at the futility of political alliances? As if to say, 'Pharaoh rides again! He gives his daughter to cement an alliance with Solomon (3:1) and then mollycoddles Solomon's enemy and ties a marital knot with him as well. Why bother politicking with such snakes?'

[8] See my *2 Samuel: Out of Every Adversity* (Ross-shire: Christian Focus, 1999), 77-80, for discussion of this premier passage.

We are not so used to that sort of thing. Once in the U.S. House of Representatives, Nelson Dingley from Maine was speaking in favor of a tariff bill, for he was an ardent supporter of protectionism. In his speech he scourged Americans who shirked the rigors of the custom laws by making their purchases overseas. While he continued to harangue, Jerry Simpson from Kansas quickly reached under Dingley's desk, pulled out Dingley's silk hat, and held it up for all to see the label: 'Made in London.'[9] It is one thing to have a distinct policy and another to apply it consistently. Yet that is precisely what Yahweh is doing in this text. But in doing so he is being faithful in a way we do not usually consider. He is faithful in his judgment, faithful in chastisement, faithful in wrath, in jealousy, in severity. And yet is he not deserving of praise for all this, that is, for being – whatever men prefer – a *true* God?

History and Prophecy (vv. 27-40)

Jeroboam had success written all over him – seemed to be an energetic worker and natural leader (vv. 27-28).[10] Maybe he was heading north out of Jerusalem for the weekend when Ahijah, the prophet from Shiloh, made a point to bump into him and urge him off the road for a word in private. Prophets can be curious characters, and, if Jeroboam expected the unusual, he was not disappointed. Ahijah was sporting a new cloak,[11] and no sooner were they out of sight than he whips it off and tears it to shreds. Jeroboam couldn't figure why Ahijah was counting. Apparently the number of pieces he tore up was important. Ahijah stops at twelve, holds them out to Jeroboam with the brusque order: 'Take

---

[9] Paul F. Boller, Jr., *Congressional Anecdotes* (New York: Oxford, 1991), 202.

[10] He is dubbed a $\bar{g}ibb\hat{o}r$ $h\bar{a}yil$ in verse 28 (traditionally translated 'a mighty man of valor'; so NKJV); here it probably means he is exceptionally capable or industrious; see Robin Wakely, NIDOTTE, 1:810-11, and cf. 2:119-20.

[11] I assume Ahijah tore his own cloak, the more natural view in my opinion. However, verses 29-30 are rather ambiguous; hence H. L. Ellison, e.g., thinks Jeroboam's finery was destroyed (*The Prophets of Israel* [Grand Rapids: Eerdmans, 1969], 18)!

ten!' Now it's Jeroboam's turn to count (vv. 30-31a). The explanation follows: 'Here's what Yahweh the God of Israel says: "See! I am going to tear the kingdom from the hand of Solomon, and I shall give you ten tribes"' (v. 31).

Here we encounter some common features of prophetic methodology. The first is *suddenness*. Ahijah simply drops into the story from nowhere (v. 29). Well, not exactly.

We're told he's from Shiloh. But he just appears. We've never heard of him before. We know nothing about him – wife? children? hobbies? Nothing. Because it doesn't matter. The Lord's word, not the prophet's biography, is crucial. The second feature is *action* (vv. 29b-30). The prophetic word is often both verbal and visible – an action accompanies the word that depicts – or embodies – what the word declares.[12] Then there is *interpretation* (v. 31b), else the action does not speak definitively. If Ahijah had given no verbal declaration with his visible action, what was Jeroboam to make of it? Did it mean the textile industry was headed for ruin? Was Ahijah wanting Mrs. Jeroboam to make his wife a quilt? So this explanatory word about the torn kingdom keeps the prophetic action from being a mystifying charade.

Our concern, however, is history and prophecy. Here Ahijah announces beforehand[13] what direction history will go under Yahweh's design. Indeed prophecy functions within sovereignty (see last sub-point). By prophecy Yahweh simply indicates the path his sovereignty will take in any segment of history. Now he is going to tear[14] the kingdom; he announces that through his word; and we can watch that word, as it were, bring that history to pass.

---

[12] On this, including more instances, see Alec Motyer, *Look to the Rock* (Leicester: Inter-Varsity, 1996), 103-106.

[13] One often hears the predictive element of biblical prophecy played down. Introductory lectures on the prophets often stress that the biblical prophets were primarily forthtellers rather than foretellers, perhaps due to a paranoia of encouraging eschatological kooks. But the kooks will always be with us, so why justify distorting the character of prophecy by our panic? Biblical prophecy is primarily not tangentially predictive. Anyone who doesn't think so should spend an afternoon with Isaiah 40-48.

[14] One can't read the 'tear' (*qāra'*) terminology in verses 30-31 (see also vv. 11-13) without remembering its use in 1 Samuel 15:27-28.

Some may be bothered by the fact that Jeroboam seemed to find Ahijah's prophecy strangely moving. It stirred him to rebel. If Jeroboam had done nothing post-Ahijah, why would Solomon seek to execute him (v. 40)? He must have used Ahijah's prophecy to justify an assault on the throne (though Ahijah had plainly said that the 'tearing' would only occur in the reign of Solomon's son, vv. 34-35). He would not wait for Yahweh to give him the kingdom as David did (1 Sam. 24, 26); rather he will seize it for himself. But this is hardly news; Yahweh has often bent human selfishness and greed to serve his word.

The main point for the church, however, is that what we see particularly in 1 Kings 11 is true universally: History is in Yahweh's control. Mesopotamian paganism paints a different picture of its gods. No sooner had they brought the flood on mankind than

(Even) the gods were terror-stricken at the deluge.
They fled (and) ascended to the heaven of Anu;
The gods cowered like dogs (and) crouched in distress (?).
Ishtar cried out like a woman in travail;
The lovely-voiced Lady of the g[ods] lamented:
'In truth, the olden time has turned to clay,
Because I commanded evil in the assembly of the gods!
How could I command (such) evil in the assembly of the gods!
(How) could I command war to destroy my people,
(For) it is I who bring forth (these) my people!'[15]

Everything veered out of control. Ishtar and her gang are like teenagers who get drunk, joy-ride, and are surprised to wake up in traction in the emergency room. Yahweh is not like that. Oh, to be sure, 1 Kings 11 is sad. After all, he's tearing his own kingdom to bits just when it reached the apex of its earthly success. But Yahweh is not paranoid. Hadad and Rezon rage at his command, and he knows the plan Jeroboam is forming as he walks away from Ahijah flexing his grip on ten pieces of cloth. So true saints can rest in this God even when he is ripping apart his own people.

---

[15] Alexander Heidel, *The Gilgamesh Epic and Old Testament Parallels* (Chicago: Phoenix Books, 1965), 85.

The Hope that Yahweh Sustains (vv. 11-13, 31-39)

Can God preserve what he is destroying? That question presses on our minds when we hear Ahijah's prophecy of the torn kingdom. Does his threatened judgment negate the sure promise to David (2 Sam. 7:12-16), laced as it was with that deliberate power-word 'everlasting'? And we must answer, 'No,' based on the clear qualifiers that Yahweh includes in his word to Solomon (vv. 11-13) and to Jeroboam (vv. 31-39).

Clearly the principle is: Yahweh's judgment does not involve cancellation of Yahweh's promise. When Yahweh announced his judgment to Solomon he placed two restrictions on it: not now (v. 12) and not all (v. 13). Ahijah underscored these same qualifications to Jeroboam (vv. 32, 34, 36). The judgment will be delayed in time (in the days of Solomon's son) and restricted in extent (Solomon's son gets one tribe).[16] And why these restrictions? Because Yahweh has made previous commitments, previous choices. Yahweh has an elect person (David, v. 34) and an elect place (Jerusalem, vv. 32, 36); covenant king and covenant worship are non-negotiables. They cannot be completely obliterated. Jeroboam's rule must take place within these confines (vv. 35, 37-38).[17] Verse 39 implicitly suggests the restoration of David's line to full strength: 'So I will afflict the seed of David because of this – but not all the days.' Yahweh's promise then may be eclipsed but not eliminated. Verse 39 states the principle in a nutshell: affliction but not abandonment.[18] The rays of hope flicker from behind the clouds of judgment.

---

[16] The implicit math of this chapter, $10 + 1 = 12$, is puzzling for most. Some look upon Benjamin being the one tribe while Judah is assumed (cf. 12:20-21, 23). However, cf. Leon Wood's position, which brings Simeon into consideration; R. D. Patterson and Hermann J. Austel, '1, 2 Kings,' *Expositor's Bible Commentary*, 12 vols. (Grand Rapids: Zondervan, 1988), 4:108.

[17] I do not think Yahweh is making a 'phony' offer in verse 38; he offers him a stable (*ne'ĕmān*) dynasty if he is faithful but not an everlasting one (cf. 2 Sam. 7:13, 16). Note that Ahijah holds up David as Jeroboam's model ('to keep my statutes and my commandments as David my servant has done'); if he would enjoy David-like benefits he must walk in David-like ways.

[18] Note the beauty of the paradox: Yahweh does not deny his word – he

Can you imagine how this ray of hope must have sustained remnant believers as time wore on? I remember dating a young lady (who later became my wife) during college days. In our junior year, when the relationship was relatively serious, we had some disagreements and spats and broke up. The semester wore on toward Christmas break. We were to have a special assembly in the chapel led by the German Club. O Tannenbaum and all the trimmings. It so happened that Barbara was in the German Club and was to lead a couple of segments of the program. I was in my assigned seat, slouched in postureless comfort. Naturally I watched her above all creatures on stage, though discreetly. One didn't want to appear overly-interested. After all, we had broken up. It was just near the end of the program after Barbara had made some German or English statement – who can recall? – that she looked at me in the audience. Our eyes met – just momentarily. We mustn't draw attention to ourselves. But I remember her look. My roommate happened to observe it all, and he helped interpret it for me. It was as if she said, 'This relationship isn't over yet.' It was only a look. It took barely a second. But you can think about it for hours. And its meaning! In a very disheveled relationship there was a mere glance that spoke all kinds of hope.

That is the sort of effect Yahweh's hints should have carried to believers in Israel and Judah. 'I will afflict ... but not forever' (v. 39, NKJV). Do you see how Yahweh's assurances build a bottom in the pit of his scourging? Granted it's no fun to go from living in the Golden Age to surviving under the Torn Kingdom, but one can endure with Yahweh's anchor, 'but not forever.'

---

remains faithful to his promise to David (2 Sam. 7:12-13, 16); yet Yahweh does not deny his holiness – he is faithful to his threats (2 Sam. 7:14); and it is dogged grace (2 Sam. 7:15) that fuels hope.

Part 2
The Torn Kingdom
1 Kings 12–2 Kings 17

Chapter 12

Kingdom Crud

1 Kings 12:1-24

Last summer several of our family traveled through the Dakotas. There I came upon a tourist's blurb telling how smallpox once devastated the Mandan Indians. In 1837 an epidemic broke out among the white traders on the boat *St. Peters*. While the boat was docked at Fort Clark a chief stole a blanket from an infected deck hand. Officers tried to obtain the blanket by offering a new one but the chief refused. He insisted on keeping 'his' blanket. In about three days the Mandans began to get sick. Things progressed until hundreds were dying each day. Some of them preferred suicide. When all was over, only thirty Mandans remained of a tribe once numbering 1,700. All because a blanket was stolen.

The situation in 1 Kings 12 is like that. Huge repercussions came from what might have appeared minor matters – a political discussion and a press conference. Pig-headedness split a kingdom. One can imagine with some reason that Rehoboam looked on the Shechem assembly as largely a formality. He must not have recognized a crisis when he saw it: even after the first waves of revolt he sent Adoram on his fatal mission (v. 18). One supposes even Rehoboam wouldn't have done that had he really been clued in to the true state of affairs.

The narrative is easy to follow. There are two major sections (vv. 1-15 and 16-24), each of these ending on the same theological note (vv. 15, 24). One could set it out like this:

Assembly (vv. 1-15)
    Appeal to the king, 1-5
    Consultation with advisors, 6-11
    Declaration to the people, 12-14
    Explanation of the event, 15
Aftermath (vv. 16-24)
    Rebellion, 16-20
    Restraint, 21-24

Stupidity under the Sovereignty of God (vv. 1-15)

This is an interesting episode in spite of the fact that it's a political story. There is ferment for change among the northern tribes. They make their confirmation of Rehoboam's kingship contingent upon his granting concessions – he must give relief from the harsh policies of the previous regime. Solomon's measures had been too severe (v. 4).[1] Rehoboam wants time to confer with his advisors; on the third day he'll announce his decision (vv. 5, 12).

The story of the double consultation (vv. 6-11) is fascinating. It takes only two verses to relate Rehoboam's query and the advice of the older men (vv. 6-7). They counsel that a little restraint 'today' (v. 7a) will win the dissidents' allegiance 'all the days' (lit., v. 7b). In short, concessions will conquer complaints. But the writer immediately gives you a news reporter's scoop: 'Now he forsook the counsel of the older men' (v. 8a). So you already know where Rehoboam's head is and where his mouth will go. Rehoboam gives himself away when he consults the younger fellows who grew up with him: 'What do you advise that we [note the first person plural] return as an answer to this people?' (v. 9). The king's 'we' shows with whom he identifies.

These younger bucks believe that nothing impresses like

---

[1] Some Old Testament historians make verse 4 bear tremendous weight. There is a tendency to take the northern tribes' words here as gospel truth. Result? See there – Solomon's regime was *so* oppressive! Seldom does anyone stop to consider the source. Verse 4 is not necessarily the narrator's view. It is the view of Jeroboam and the northern tribes. There had already been rumblings of revolt – that's why Jeroboam had vamoosed to Egypt (11:40). Now they press their case for 'change' with Rehoboam. They must have had some plausible ground for complaint in order to use this plea, but readers must be astute enough to recognize that they *need* an argument to justify the direction in which they are already leaning. Verse 4 is at least as much political propaganda as it is historical truth. Some scholars seem highly suspicious when reviewing Solomon's reign in 1 Kings 4-5 and 9-10, finding oppression and high-handedness lurking under every Solomonic success, and yet are incredibly naïve when they arrive at Shechem, sucking up the sentiments of 12:4 as if they were – of course – the unadulterated truth. Rehoboam's reply (v. 14) seems to concede Solomonic severity, though whether as accurate or only for argument is difficult to say. In short, more balance is needed in this matter. Israel came to Shechem without halos.

intimidation, nothing tames like threatening. So they give Rehoboam a memorable one-liner to use: 'My little one is thicker than my father's waist' (v. 10b).[2] In case that baffled anyone they furnished an addendum (v. 11): 'My father imposed a heavy yoke on you, and I will add to your yoke; my father flogged you with whips, but I will flog you with scorpions' (NJPS).[3] That is relatively clear. In their view this is no time to give the proverbial inch but to impose the royal weight. They would have agreed with James I's instruction to his son, that God had made the young prince 'a little God to sit on his throne, and to rule over other men.'[4]

The rest is history. Oh, the writer doesn't tell you what the people did until verse 16, but as soon as you hear the surly, heavy-handed announcement in verses 13-14, you know the glue has gone out of the kingdom.

One almost instinctively wants to moralize this text. One could launch into the folly of refusing to listen to wiser, more experienced folks. One could gather proof texts from Proverbs. Or, at a bit of a stretch perhaps, we could carry on about the 'perils of peer pressure' and harangue youth over that. But the text forbids you. You are not free to make anything you want out of this story because the text itself explains why what happened happened.

In verse 15 the writer gives you the lens through which you are to view this episode:

---

[2] Most translations understand 'little one' as the little finger. That is, of course, a reasonable guess. Some interpreters, however, noting the reference to 'waist/loins,' referring to the middle of the body, suggest that the 'little one' was meant as a reference to the penis. See Iain W. Provan, *1 and 2 Kings*, New International Biblical Commentary (Peabody, MA: Hendrickson, 1995), 107; and NIDOTTE, 3:911. One might imagine the younger set taking delight in crafting such a coarse rejoinder.

[3] Patterson and Austel explain 'scorpions' here as referring to 'many-tailed whips armed with barbed points or hooks that, when lashed against the intended victim, felt like a scorpion's sting' ('1, 2 Kings,' *Expositor's Bible Commentary*, 12 vols. [Grand Rapids: Zondervan, 1988], 4:116).

[4] J. D. Douglas, *Light in the North* (Grand Rapids: Eerdmans, 1964), 17.

And the king did not listen to the people, for it was a circumstance
coming from Yahweh, in order that he might make his word stand,
which Yahweh had spoken by the hand of Ahijah the Shilonite, with
reference to Jeroboam son of Nebat.

The focus is on divine sovereignty not human stupidity. Don't
read this story, says the writer, and bemoan how headstrong youth
seem to be or how older folks tend to be ignored. Let's say one
morning you tell a friend what happened at home the night before:
'I went into the kitchen and saw a zebra washing dishes at the
sink!' As you speak the words, will you stress 'kitchen,' 'dishes,'
or 'sink?' Would that really be proper? Doesn't 'zebra' stand out
(one might say, in black and white)? Shouldn't the emphasis fall
on that strange culinary assistant? So with biblical narrative. When
a writer so much as says, 'Now here's what you need to understand
about this story,' or, 'Here's the explanation behind this whole
event,' we should pay primary attention to *his* emphasis – if we
want to get it right.

What does verse 15 tell us? It tells us the *end* Yahweh had in
mind in this whole affair: 'in order that he might make his word
stand, which Yahweh had spoken by the hand of Ahijah the
Shilonite.' The text refers to the prophecy of Ahijah in 11:31-39,
that, among other things, ten tribes would be given to Jeroboam;
the text underscores the certainty of the word of God. What
happened at Shechem that day happened because Yahweh wanted
to make his previous word come to pass.

That's the end. What about the *means*? How did he bring it
about? It was a 'circumstance coming from Yahweh.'
'Circumstance' is *sibbāh*, a term used only here (cf. 2 Chron.
10:15), though the root occurs often. Versions frequently translate
it as a 'turn of affairs.' That's good. Or one might simply say 'a
twist from Yahweh.' In any case, the term suggests the subtlety
by which Yahweh's sovereign design goes into effect. Nothing
mechanical here. Yahweh's sovereignty did not violate
Rehoboam's free decision; rather it came about through that
freedom.[5] Sovereignty seems so ... natural. Here is Rehoboam,
unsatisfied with the moderating, conciliatory stance of his father's

advisors, but his blood gets up when his peers do their wordsmithing. He likes the concepts they throw around, the new terminology they float: assertive leadership; power-rule; ultimatum. No doubt about it. That's the way they should go. That's what Rehoboam *wants* to do. Yet it was a twist from Yahweh.

This story filtered through verse 15 should prove a massive encouragement to Christ's flock. Is kingdom division a sad affair? Yes, but Yahweh had already predicted it and is here bringing his word to pass. Are Rehoboam and his favorites arrogant, cocky, and stupid? Probably. But verse 15 testifies that human hubris never catches Yahweh by surprise. He *uses* it. Big men (especially royal, arrogant ones) are simply little servants of Yahweh's word. Contrary to our fears, human stupidity is not running loose but is on the leash of God's sovereignty. I think that bears a relation to my sanity.

Tragedy in view of the Promise of God (vv. 16-20)

Rehoboam's stupidity was not an episode; it was a pattern. Perhaps 'stupidity' is too strong. In any case, Rehoboam repeatedly gets it wrong. First, he accepts and spouts surly and arrogant counsel (vv. 1-15, esp. 8, 13). Second, still suffering from royal density, Rehoboam sends Adoram on a northern mission, apparently to show that the king meant to 'walk the talk' (cf. v. 14) and to impose forced labor on (some) northern subjects.[6] No one was going to push Rehoboam around. Adoram, however, met with a rocky – and fatal – reception (v. 18b). Third, after Rehoboam came to his wits and had hightailed it back to Judah (v. 18c), he amassed his

---

[5] Cf. R. S. Wallace: 'Rehoboam is fatally responsible even for what God is seen to have already decreed' (*Readings in 1 Kings* [Grand Rapids: Eerdmans, 1996], 80).

[6] Donald Wiseman implies that Adoram's mission was an effort at diplomacy (*1 & 2 Kings*, Tyndale Old Testament Commentaries [Leicester: InterVarsity, 1993], 142), but Provan (*1 and 2 Kings*, 107) is likely nearer the mark in proposing that this was Rehoboam's attempt to make good on his word to outstrip Solomonic severity (vv. 13-14). He would impose forced labor on free Israelites and treat them like Canaanites (cf. 9:20-22). Hence the reminder that Adoram was 'over the forced labor.'

troops to attack Israel and force them into submission (v. 21). The prophet Shemaiah stamped this scheme as wrong-headed (vv. 22-24).

Even though stupidity is under sovereignty (v. 15) it is still sad. And verses 16-20 highlight that sadness. Note the four-fold 'David' references. The rebels ask their rhetorical question ('What portion do we have in *David*?,' v. 16a)[7] and offer their defiant advice ('Take care of your own house, *David*,' v. 16b). The narrator summarizes that 'Israel has revolted against the *house of David* until this day' (v. 19) and reminds us that 'no one went after the *house of David* except the tribe of Judah alone' (v. 20). The repeated mention of David and the house of David cannot help but dredge up the memory of 2 Samuel 7, the Davidic covenant passage, where Yahweh had assured David

You will always have descendants,
and I will make your kingdom last forever.
Your dynasty will never end (v. 16, TEV).[8]

There is nothing that can overthrow the Davidic covenant, nothing that can falsify the Davidic promise, nothing that can prevent the certain coming of the greater (messianic) David (cf. Hosea 3:5; Ezek. 34:23-24). What a grand covenant with David and his seed!

The good news is that Rehoboam cannot nullify it; the bad news is that he can besmirch it. He cannot destroy the covenant, but he can derail it. So, under Rehoboam, instead of seeing the Davidic covenant exemplified, we see it eclipsed; we find it mangled rather than modeled.

Colonel Bonner Fellers, military secretary to General MacArthur, has left a sobering account of the events leading up to Japan's surrender in 1945. Emperor Hirohito and prime minister Suzuki were desperately trying to work out arrangements for Japan's surrender early in 1945. The emperor could not communicate directly with the United States because the militarists

---

[7] Cf. the vivid NLT: 'Down with David and his dynasty!'

[8] On the Davidic covenant, cf. my exposition in *2 Samuel: Out of Every Adversity* (Ross-shire: Christian Focus, 1999), 69-89.

controlled all the communications. He tried to contact the Allies through the Soviet government, but the Soviets proved strangely cool to the matter and would either delay or give no response. All the time Japan was withering; she suffered 185,000 casualties in a B-29 attack on Tokyo. Then came August 6 and 9. Atomic bombs. Then the strangely silent Soviets spoke up and declared war on Japan. Fellers claimed that the facts

> show indisputably that the U.S.S.R. repeatedly smothered Japanese overtures for peace with the Allies for six months before Japan's surrender. The U.S.S.R. was determined to obtain a dominant position in the Orient, both territorial and political, and therefore planned to enter the war at a time most favorable to Russia's interest.[9]

Japan's defeat was not in doubt at that point; her surrender would have to come. The emperor knew it. Yet here is another 'if only' of history that casts a sad shadow. What destruction might have been prevented, how many lives might have been spared. So with Rehoboam. He can in no way dissolve Yahweh's David Plan, but he certainly demeans it – and that's sad. Neither can any of us prevent God's kingdom from coming in power and great glory but we can tarnish its luster today by our folly and faithlessness. And that's sad.

Humility before the Word of God (vv. 21-24)

Back in Jerusalem, Rehoboam, still operating in knee-jerk mode, re-institutes the draft and calls up the troops 'to fight with the house of Israel to bring back the kingdom to Rehoboam son of Solomon' (v. 21). He feels forced to use force. However, the word of God comes to put a stop to Rehoboam's words and plans, a word coming through Shemaiah:

> Here's what Yahweh says,
> 'You are not to go up

---

[9] *Secrets and Spies: Behind-the-Scenes Stories of World War II* (Pleasantville, NY: Reader's Digest Assoc., 1964), 556.

and you are not to fight with your brothers,
> the sons of Israel;
Return, each man to his house,
for this affair has come *from me*' (v. 24a).[10]

I find the response mildly amazing: 'And they listened to the word of Yahweh, and they turned to go away, according to the word of Yahweh' (v. 24b). It was Rehoboam's first wise move in the whole chapter.

One must confess the divine initiative here. Yahweh intervenes with his word to cut off Rehoboam's further folly. That is clearly a footprint of grace.[11] And yet one must also acknowledge that Rehoboam and Judah have gained wisdom here: they listened to the word of Yahweh. I am so used to the prophets' scoring Israel or Judah for *not* heeding Yahweh's word that this little notice rather surprises me. Yet here they submit. Yahweh insists this whole affair is *his* doing. And both king and militia give it up.

Sometimes it is right to give it up. After William Jennings Bryan's third defeat (in as many bids) for the U. S. presidency, he would tell the story of the fellow (apparently under the influence) who tried three times to get into a private club and was thrown downstairs each time. When he landed on the street after his third attempt, he picked himself up, dusted off his clothes, and said reflectively, 'They can't fool me. Those fellows don't want me in there!'[12]

Is that perhaps a proper point of counsel from verses 21-24 for Christ's people? Are there some times when we should acquiesce to our mucked up circumstances or resign ourselves to the hard providences Yahweh has imposed? That is not a welcome word to contemporary men and women, at least in the west. For some reason we think there must be some way to 'fix' everything, a Band-aid for every dilemma. But most sinful and thoughtful believers know that sometimes their choices, their folly, their

---

[10] Emphasis in the Hebrew.

[11] My thanks to James Hakim, one of our students, for underscoring this point to me.

[12] Paul F. Boller, Jr., *Presidential Campaigns* (New York: Oxford, 1985), 190.

bullheadedness or their hard-heartedness have landed them in a network of circumstances they simply cannot undo. Their lives are riddled with gaping cracks that can't be caulked or with irreversible consequences that can't be righted. What can one do but listen to the word of Yahweh at that point and go on living in the kingdom as grace enables to do so? Is that mere weakness or is it finally wisdom?

Chapter 13

Bootleg Religion

1 Kings 12:25-33

During the 1920s in the United States the law forbade the manufacture, transportation, and sale of alcoholic beverages. This was the Prohibition Era. Some folks, refusing to give up their toddies, decided to make their own. These bootleggers engaged surreptitiously in bootlegging and so produced bootleg, their own home-brewed elixir. That's what Jeroboam does with religion in this text; he makes his own – bootleg religion.

Ah, but a significant hunk of Old Testament scholarship insists that that is *not* what Jeroboam did. He is frequently tooted as St. Jeroboam who was advocating a sort of liturgical renewal rather than bastard religion.[1] Moreover, we are told, you must realize that this text was written/edited by Judeans (Jerusalem-based southerners) who obviously wanted to depict Jeroboam and northern religion in the most lurid tones. You must reconstruct the text to get at the real truth; if you merely read the text you will obtain a completely naïve and wrong impression.[2] Then, too, you must reckon with the probability that Jeroboam's bulls (the word in v. 28 is masculine, hence bull calves) were not meant to represent other gods or even Yahweh. Rather, Near Eastern iconography sometimes depicts a god standing on the back of a bull. In Hebrew religion, however, Yahweh is invisible. So, when Jeroboam produces bare bulls – or, should we say, vacant bulls? – he may only have intended them as pedestals for an invisible Yahweh, in the same way the ark of the covenant in the Jerusalem temple was

---

[1] I exaggerate little; see the succinct and lucid discussion of 'Jeroboam's Reform' in B. W. Anderson, *Understanding the Old Testament*, 4th ed. (Englewood Cliffs, NJ: Prentice-Hall, 1986), 259-61.

[2] Analyze the comments of G. H. Jones, *1 and 2 Kings*, New Century Bible Commentary, 2 vols. (Grand Rapids: Eerdmans, 1984), 1:256-59.

a footstool for Yahweh – and no one viewed the ark as idolatrous. This view of Jeroboam's bulls has nearly become a sacred cow to judge from its prevalence in Old Testament histories and handbooks.

I cannot accept this reconstituted Jeroboam. Let's start with the bulls. Near Eastern iconography bears a double witness; it sometimes depicts bulls as themselves symbols of deity and objects of worship, and sometimes portrays them as supports for a deity.[3] With Jeroboam we may prefer the latter option, the pedestal theory. But that lands us in trouble because it cannot be falsified or even tested. Pagan deities can be visibly pictured riding on the back of a bull, but if that paradigm is used for Jeroboam's bulls and if they are claimed to be pedestals for an *invisible* Yahweh, how can one know that? Yahweh is invisible, so when you look at that Bethel bull how do you know an invisible Yahweh is meant to be there or whether you're simply looking at a lot of bull? The theory is so safe it's suspicious.

And then there is this thing called the text. Whether one hears Jeroboam's call to worship in verse 28 ('Look! Your gods, O Israel, who brought you up [the verb is plural] from the land of Egypt') or reads the narrator's remark in verse 32 ('Thus he did in Bethel to sacrifice to the calves which he had made'), one doesn't dream these are mere divine pedestals. Nor did Ahijah the prophet see pedestals. He passed on Yahweh's accusation of Jeroboam in 14:9: 'You made for yourself *other gods* [emphasis mine], even molten things, to aggravate me, but *me* [emphatic in Hebrew] you have thrown behind your back.' If anything, these gods had more connection with Canaanite fertility worship than with Yahweh (note the 'Asherim' in 14:15).[4] I hold then that in 12:25-33

---

[3] See, e.g., Amihai Mazar, 'The "Bull Site" – An Iron Age I Open Cult Place,' *Bulletin of the American Schools of Oriental Research* 247 (1982): 30-32.

[4] See the superb remarks of Iain Provan, *1 and 2 Kings*, New International Biblical Commentary (Peabody, MA: Hendrickson, 1995), 111-12, on this matter; cf. also John N. Oswalt, 'The Golden Calves and the Egyptian Concept of Deity,' *The Evangelical Quarterly* 45/1 (1973): 13-20. Hosea (ca. 740 BC) didn't seem to treat the calves as liturgical aids; otherwise why did he insist 'a craftsman made it – it's not God' (Hos. 8:6; cf. 10:5-6;

Jeroboam is instituting false religion in Israel.[5] Let us go on to the witness of the text.

Security: The Need for False Religion (vv. 25-27)

Jeroboam's passion for security was not all wrong. He was likely wise to refurbish (I take 'build' in v. 25 to mean 're-build' or 'outfit') Shechem and Penuel for defense purposes. Fortified Penuel, a little east of the junction of the Jabbok and Jordan rivers, was likely meant to guard Jeroboam's kingdom from incursions from the east. But Jeroboam got into trouble when he began talking to himself: 'Then Jeroboam said in his heart...' (v. 26). Nothing wrong with such self-conversation in itself – it all depends on what one says to oneself. But as readers it makes us jittery, for we have come fresh from chapter 11 where we ran into a huge heart problem – Solomon's heart had turned away from Yahweh (11:2, 3, 4, 9). Now Jeroboam speaks 'in his heart' and within two verses religion has gone bovine. You see then where false religion begins? Calvin was right: 'man's nature, so to speak, is a perpetual factory of idols.'[6] How crucial to guard one's heart. And, quite naturally,

---

13:2)? On Hosea 8:5-6, see Duane A. Garrett, *Hosea, Joel*, New American Commentary (n.p.: Broadman & Holman, 1997), 182-84. It may be that Jeroboam's intent was syncretistic rather than idolatrous, i.e., to worship Yahweh by means of bull worship, breaking the second commandment rather than the first. But to worship the true God in a false way (second commandment) inevitably leads to worshiping a false god (first commandment). The word through Ahijah (14:9) labeled it 'other gods' not 'enriched Yahwism.'

[5] The problem with my view is that I have taken the testimony of the text at face value. Obviously, this is not good, furrow-browed scholarship. Many would hold that I fail to understand that the viewpoint in the text comes from later Judean editors who held an extremely anti-Jeroboam bias – hence one cannot depend on such texts. I don't mind if they think such. If they do, they should be faithful agnostics, i.e., they should deny that they can know anything accurate about Jeroboam's cult since the evidence is tainted. This they do not do; they deny the reliability of the texts yet proceed to do plastic surgery on Jeroboam. If the texts are unreliable, they should shut up. Instead they proceed to reconstruction based upon (essentially) re-written texts. This yields both bad history and perverse theology.

[6] *Institutes*, 1.11.8.

it is the *Old* Testament that underscores such internal concerns.

But what was Jeroboam so afraid of? Orthodoxy. Listen to his heart-talk:

> Now the kingdom will return to the house of David. If this people go up to make sacrifices in the house of Yahweh in Jerusalem, then the heart of this people shall return to their master, to Rehoboam, king of Judah, and they shall kill me and shall return to Rehoboam king of Judah (vv. 26-27).

His problem was not that orthodoxy was dull or boring, but that it was unnerving. But of what did this Old Testament orthodoxy consist? Clearly, of David's dynasty ('the house of David,' Rehoboam being the current representative) and Yahweh's temple ('the house of Yahweh in Jerusalem'). That is, orthodoxy focused on a royal person and on an atoning place.[7] Now Yahweh through Ahijah the prophet had promised Jeroboam a ten-tribe kingdom (11:31, 35, 37-38). But that word, that promise, was not enough for Jeroboam. He must have something more secure than Yahweh's word.

Jeroboam then turns away from orthodoxy, not because it is no longer true but because it is no longer useful. He does not find it false but fearful. You see his thinking then. He must hold on to 'his' kingdom, and, since he cannot simply trust Yahweh's word for that, he must make himself secure. That is the stimulus here for false religion. *If you cannot trust God, you will use religion.* In Jeroboam's case, what matters is not truth but position – his position.

---

[7] We rightly trace this person-place scheme straight into New Testament orthodoxy. David's dynasty reaches its crescendo in that rascal Rehoboam's premier descendant, Jesus the Messiah (hence Christology is at the heart of orthodoxy); and Yahweh's temple, where, as Jeroboam stated, they 'make sacrifices,' was therefore the place where atonement was made and reaches its fulfillment in the cross. Orthodoxy revolves around person and place, around the Christ and the cross, or, as we might put it, around the person and work of Christ. It is this area of belief that false religion invariably skews.

Politicians, of course, are especially adept at using religion so long as it serves them.[8] Yet I must confess Jeroboam is not alone in this guilt. I haven't the authority to use religion as blatantly as he did, yet basically and subtly I share his sin: security is my god. I am frequently quite happy to be a disciple of Jeroboam, walking by logic and not by faith, by calculation and not by commitment.

Appeal: The Subtlety of False Religion (vv. 28-30)

Jeroboam came out of the strategy room with a new policy: 'You have been going up to Jerusalem long enough' (v. 28, NJPS). Of course, there were new artifacts (the bull images) to go with the new policy, but more on those below. Many versions translate Jeroboam's announcement as 'It is too much for you to go up to Jerusalem,' which implies Jeroboam is appealing to convenience. 'You needn't bother with the Jerusalem Connection, and all the distance and expense; we can make religion much handier for you than that.' That, however, is probably not the sense the grammar intends. The Hebrew idiom borders on our English 'That's enough of that,' and so should be taken as NJPS does (cited above).[9] As Lumby puts it, 'Jeroboam's argument was "You have chosen a new king, choose also new places of worship."' Jeroboam does not announce the real reason for the change (fear, vv. 26-27); he is, after all, a politician and deals in propaganda rather than candor.

What about the geography? Why were the bulls placed at Bethel and Dan? Some say because of location, Bethel at the southern and Dan at the northern end of the ten-tribe turf. Accessibility, you see. Probably not. More likely, tradition and associations were

---

[8] Witness the solemn oaths Charles II was willing to take in order to gain Scotland – and his frivolous perfidy afterwards; cf. Thomas M'Crie, *The Story of the Scottish Church from the Reformation to the Disruption* (1825; reprint ed., Glasgow: Free Presbyterian, n.d.), 232-38.

[9] The phrase is *rab-lākem;* use of the same idiom in Deut. 1:6, 2:3, and 3:26 clearly supports the 'long enough' rendering. For the data, see Gesenius-Kautzsch, *Hebrew Grammar*, 133c; J. R. Lumby, *The First and Second Books of the Kings*, Cambridge Bible for Schools and Colleges (Cambridge: CUP, 1909), 143; and Joseph Hammond, *I. Kings*, Pulpit Commentary (Chicago: Wilcox & Follett, n.d.), 270-71.

decisive. Bethel had sacred links to the patriarchs, Abraham (Gen. 12:8; 13:3-4) and especially Jacob (Gen. 28:10-22; 31:13; 35:1-16). How can Abraham's and Jacob's descendants go wrong worshiping in a place where their ancestors worshiped and encountered God (cf. also Judg. 20:26-28)? And what of Dan? Alternative worship had been established there in the time of the judges, with no less than a grandson (or descendant) of Moses as presiding priest (Judg. 17-18, esp. 18:30-31).[10] Bethel and Dan had worn halos for some time.[11]

Notice particularly Jeroboam's call to worship: 'Look! Your gods, O Israel, who brought you up from the land of Egypt' (v. 28). It is important to remember that Jeroboam's liturgical cry is a quotation; it regurgitates the cry of the apostate Israelites in post-exodus time who embraced the worship of the bull calf they had pressured Aaron to make (Exod. 32:4).[12] Herein is the subtlety of it all. Jeroboam may be suggesting that this bull-assisted worship is not so wild, not so off the wall, as Israel might think. He is rather merely picking up on a different 'tradition,' which was held in the past but, sadly, buried from view. Jeroboam is not some radical innovator; rather he only fears Israel is ignoring the 'richness of her heritage.' Time was, he could suggest, when the stream of faith in Israel was broader and more inclusive, when matters of faith and faithfulness were not construed so narrowly.

Whether apostasy stinks depends on how it's pitched. In the 1930s, a horse liniment named Absorbine was plummeting in sales. An advertising man named Obie Winters had the liniment lab tested, and they found that it would work on ringworm of the foot. With a stroke of genius, however, Winters conjured a whole new name for such ringworm – athlete's foot.[13] There is such a

---

[10] On 'Moses' in Judges 18:30, see my *Judges: Such a Great Salvation* (Ross-shire: Christian Focus, 2000), 203-204n.

[11] For this position, see C. F. Keil, *The Books of the Kings*, Biblical Commentary on the Old Testament (1876; reprint ed., Grand Rapids: Eerdmans, 1965), 199; and Carl D. Evans, 'Jeroboam,' ABD, 3:744.

[12] Whether we translate 'gods' or 'god' here and/or in Exod. 32:4 makes no difference for the point under discussion.

[13] Eric Clark, *The Want Makers* (New York: Viking, 1988), 54.

difference in the way the malady is marketed. Who would want to admit having ringworm even if there was a cure? But 'athlete's foot'? One would almost be disappointed if one didn't suffer from it periodically! It carries such positive associations.

That was, tragically, Jeroboam's genius. Linking his new cult with the bull worship at Sinai seems to have cast a mantle of legitimacy over his innovation. It was not apostasy but diversity. It was not novel but historical; it had roots, precedence. So much depends on how it's pitched. False religion majors in such subtlety. It will use terms like redemptive, reconciling, atoning, etc., for their positive, emotive value but without their proper biblical content. Mormons won't approach you averring that Jesus was born from sexual relations between God and Mary, that Jesus is Lucifer's spirit brother, or that Jesus himself celebrated his own marriage to both Marys and to Martha. No, they will run cute commercials on your local radio station, urging fathers to spend requisite time with their families. False religion almost always wants to appear both congenial and justifiable.

One footnote. This text breathes such an air of tragedy, for it shows us that the deviation of Israel and Aaron in Exodus 32 and that of Micah and of the tribe of Dan in Judges 17-18 gave the excuse to someone (Jeroboam) years later to advocate falsehood, and in such a way that finally destroyed a nation. We may think our infidelity is our own business, but, sadly, it may be embraced by those who come after and damn a whole generation. A little covenant-breaking at Sinai, a deviant cult at Dan – and a future in ruins.

Invention: The Stupidity of False Religion (vv. 31-33)

So Jeroboam inaugurated his deviant religious cult. The new 'church year' scheduled the Feast of Tabernacles in the *eighth* month, a date Jeroboam 'invented from his own heart' (v. 33). That clause could describe all the trappings of Jeroboam's cult.

Jeroboam clearly rejected revelation governing Israel's worship, for Yahweh had prescribed the *personnel* (the priests were to come from the Levites, vv. 31b, 32b), *periods* (e.g., the festival in the seventh month, vv. 32a, 33b), and *place* (Jerusalem, not Bethel, v. 33a) for public worship. Jeroboam violated all these stipulations. Religion for Jeroboam was not a 'given,' but something pliable to be massaged and shaped as one prefers.

Our writer, however, is no detached historian content simply to describe Jeroboam's religious ingenuity for your enlightenment; he is rather a disciple of Yahweh who mocks the king's cult even as he depicts it. The writer says that Jeroboam's cult is both different and stupid. He does this, I suggest, in a subtle but telling way. In verse 28 he had informed us that Jeroboam 'made two bull-calves of gold.' The verb is '*āśāh*, to make or to do, as common in Hebrew as its equivalent in English. However, when we come to verses 31-33 the writer piles up this verb, using it eight times in three verses. A quick survey: Jeroboam '*made* houses on high places and *made* priests' from the whole run of the people (v. 31); he '*made* a festival in the eighth month' (v. 32a) and he 'went up upon the altar – this is what he *did* ['*āśāh*, but cannot translate 'made' here] in Bethel, to sacrifice to the bull-calves which he had *made*' (v. 32b); he also installed 'priests for the high places which he had *made*' (v. 32c); so he 'went up upon the altar which he had *made*' (v. 33a), and 'he *made* a festival for the sons of Israel' (v. 33b).

One must be cautious, for '*āśāh* is a common verb, but when the writer uses it with repetitive overkill one can't help but ask the reason. I propose he is not merely reporting but ridiculing. He made high places, he made priests, he made a festival, he made bulls, he made an altar. Don't you see it? The writer has dipped his pen in acid. Jeroboam's religion, he says, is Jeroboam's concoction. Concoctions should not be taken seriously.

On the night of August 31, 1939, Polish soldiers and guerrillas stirred up incidents along the Polish-German border – attacking a forestry station, destroying a German customs building, and occupying the German radio station at Gleiwitz. The Poles shouted anti-German slogans into the microphone and littered the place with the dead bodies of their German victims. No wonder Nazi Germany invaded Poland the next day.

Do you believe that? I hope not. German SD (Security Service) detachments were disguised as Polish soldiers and created all the mayhem. And the German corpses strewn around? They were 'canned goods,' specimens furnished compliments of German concentration camps. Reinhold Heydrich had concocted the scheme to provide justification for Hitler's long-planned attack on Poland.[14] There was no truth to it.

That is the writer's point about Jeroboam's religion: it is sheer invention – why lend it any credence at all? Worship either rests on the prescriptions of divine revelation or on the preferences of the human heart. It sounds simplistic, but it's scriptural. Our current western culture may not be enamored with gold bulls but is deeply in love with its own religious subjectivism. It could be epitomized in a woman named Sheila interviewed for Robert Bellah's *Habits of the Heart*. She described her faith: 'It's "Sheila-ism." Just my own little voice.'[15] It's bootleg religion. Invention. Hence stupid.

---

[14] John Toland, *Adolf Hitler* (New York: Ballantine Books, 1977), 567-68.

[15] Cited in Charles Colson, *Against the Night* (Ann Arbor: Vine Books, 1989), 98.

Chapter 14

A Tale of Two Prophets

1 Kings 13

By using the term 'tale' in the chapter title I am not denying the historicity or having-happenedness of this story but am merely underscoring the strangeness of it. The story has a bizarre ring to it. One wonders if a slight smile idled on the sacred writer's face as he wrote it up, since he had determined not to answer all the questions of the curious and so knew how elusive later readers might find his narrative. Biblical writers are no mean artists; this one has made history as teasing as parable.

Story

The story is gripping in its own right. One must ignore the chapter division – chapter 12 flows right into chapter 13. Here is King Jeroboam standing beside or having ascended the altar, officiating at a solemn 'bull session' at the Bethel sanctuary. One can imagine the aura of sanctity that must have hung in the air. The assembled worshipers parted here and there as a man 'excused-me' his way to the front, where he suddenly launched into a tirade against the altar, prophesying that a coming descendant of the house of David by name of Josiah would slaughter the new breed of priests upon it and profane it by offering human bones on it (v. 2). Not content to interrupt a perfectly solemn worship service the man announced an imminent sign that would authenticate his predicted threat: the altar would be torn apart and the ashes spilled out (v. 3). Looks of exasperation spread over the assembly – they knew he was a southerner, from Judah (v. 1). Naturally he would have a jaundiced view of the new wave in the north.

But Jeroboam was a take-charge type. The king would handle this interloper. The royal index finger targeted the man of God.

147

Jeroboam's lackeys jumped to seize him. But the authority and anger on Jeroboam's face turned to confusion and fear: try as he might he couldn't draw his hand and arm back to his body. They were frozen. Paralysis (v. 4). But the altar's ashes eclipsed Jeroboam's ashen face – the altar *did* split, the ashes were poured out, just as that aggravating Judean preacher had predicted (v. 5).

Jeroboam had no choice but to change his approach. Paralysis makes kings do that. He pleads with the man of God to intercede for him with 'Yahweh your God' (v. 6 – Is the pronoun significant?) that his limb might be restored. He did so and the royal hand returned to normal use. Jeroboam is more than mollified. Instead of arresting him for disturbing the peace, the king now offers a reward for services rendered. How about coming home for lunch (v. 7)? Perhaps Jeroboam hoped diplomacy could tame the prophetic vigor. The man of God bluntly repudiates the invitation. He is under Yahweh's orders to do no socializing in Bethel; he was to have no truck with the place (vv. 8-9). Off he went, like the later Magi, by another way (v. 10).

An old prophet lived in Bethel and his sons came home with one of those you'll-never-believe-what-happened-in-church-today stories. For some reason their father wanted to chase down the Judean preacher. It so happened – and the whole story rests on this puny item – that his sons had seen the return-route the man of God had taken (v. 12b). Their father ordered the donkey saddled, started off, and actually discovered the fellow, apparently enjoying a rest stop on his journey home (v. 14). He invited him to lunch and received the same rejection as did Jeroboam and for the same reason. But the old prophet flashed his own clergy credentials and claimed that he had received a word from the Lord commanding him to bring the Judean home for hospitality. It was a pure lie, but the man of God fell for it (v. 19).

Suddenly in mid-meal the old prophet received a real word from Yahweh and announced judgment on the man of God because the latter had 'rebelled at the mouth of Yahweh' (v. 21) by agreeing to lunch when he had been ordered by Yahweh not to do so. Because of this, the man of God would not enjoy a peaceful death (v. 22). After this strange outburst, the fulfillment begins. The man of God sets out on a loaned donkey, a lion meets him, kills the man of God, but suddenly loses his appetite for both men and asses (vv. 23-25). Word filters back to town. The old prophet makes a second trip, retrieves the corpse, performs burial rites, and assures his sons that the word the disobedient man of God had spoken would certainly come to pass (vv. 27-32). Lions may liquidate Yahweh's disobedient prophets, but nothing can derail Yahweh's sure word. And Jeroboam continues as before (vv. 33-34).

Questions

We read 1 Kings 13 and repeatedly ask, 'But why...?' Our question marks litter the margin of our Bible page. Why was the man of God to refuse any hospitality (vv. 8-10)? We can reasonably well guess, but the writer does not inform us. Nor does he enlighten us about why the man of God must return home by a different route.

The most perplexing items arise in verses 11-32. What were the sons of the strange prophet doing at Jeroboam's church service (v. 11)? Were they in sympathy with the bull cult the king had instituted? Or only curious? Why was the man of God sitting under a tree still north of the border (v. 14)?[1] Were we wrong to infer there was a certain urgency about his return to Judah? Since the border was not far from Bethel, was such a rest that necessary?

What are we to make of this old prophet (vv. 11, 15ff.)? Why is he so weird? Why did he lie to the man of God (v. 18)? What could be his motive? Could he have been guilt-ridden, sensing that he himself should have had the gumption to denounce Jeroboam's cult? This is guesswork. The text gives us no clues. Why does the man of God though having clear orders (vv. 8-9, 16-17) go back with the old prophet without engaging in any debate or registering any suspicion (v. 19)? How is it that a true word of God comes to a prophet that lies (vv. 18, 20)? Why is there no protest recorded (after v. 22) from the man of God regarding his doom? Why no sudden anger? Why does he not verbally abuse the old prophet for the scoundrel he was in tricking him? Why is he mute? Why was his punishment so severe? We even begin to

---

[1] The man of God's allusion to 'this place' in verse 16 makes it clear that he had not gone far from Bethel.

wonder if the lion left the scene peaceably (v. 28). Did the old prophet, upon arriving, simply tell the lion to 'Shoo!'?

Welcome to the strange world of Hebrew narrative. Notice all the answers the writer refuses to give us. It is a revealing reticence. It must mean that such data do not matter and that what really matters lies elsewhere.

Teaching

If our writer tantalizes and frustrates our curiosity with non-answers, at least he is clear about his theme. We are clueless about many details but we are clear about the matter that matters. Nine times either the writer or one of the characters refers to the 'word of Yahweh' (vv. 1, 2, 5, 9, 17, 18, 20, 26, 32). The phrase may refer to orders given the man of God (vv. 1, 5[?], 9, 17), to the content of his preaching (vv. 2, 32), to an alleged word of God (v. 18), or to a true word given or spoken by the old Bethel prophet (vv. 20, 26). We may add to these the numerous references to what Yahweh 'spoke' (vv. 3, 26), to what he had 'commanded' (vv. 9, 21), to the formula 'Thus says Yahweh' (vv. 2, 21), and to 'the mouth of Yahweh' (vv. 21, 26). The word of Yahweh is the theme of the story. If we keep that as our compass point we can't go astray no matter how many unanswered questions litter our study.

To expose the teaching of this text I want to focus on each of the three main characters in the narrative, not out of some 'biographical' interest but because each typifies a specific relation to the word of God, which, after all, is the theme of the text.[2]

---

[2] On the structure and literary art of 1 Kings 13, see James K. Mead, 'Kings and Prophets, Donkeys and Lions: Dramatic Shape and Deuteronomistic Rhetoric in 1 Kings XIII,' *Vetus Testamentum* 49 (1999): 191-205. He divides the narrative into two main sections (vv. 1-19 and 20-32) with a total of four scenes. Note his footnotes for bibliography on the passage. As an aid in reading and remembering one could divide the story into five scenes plus postscript:

By the altar, vv. 1-10
Under the tree, vv. 11-19
At the table, vv. 20-23
On the road, vv. 24-28
In the grave, vv. 29-32
Postscript, vv. 33-34

Jeroboam: The word of God was his mercy – and he despised it (vv. 1-10, 33-34)

It didn't seem like mercy. More like mayhem. Had a perfectly fine church service going when, all of a sudden, here is this uninvited guest, front and center, ranting against the altar (vv. 1-2). Sometimes God simply irrupts, perhaps to show what liars those are who yawn and blabber how 'everything goes on as it has since the beginning of creation' (2 Pet. 3:4, NIV). Something different happened at Bethel that day. A divine word shattered a smooth liturgy. If it was mercy, it was a *sudden* mercy.

And it was a *severe* mercy. Jeroboam, fuming over the audacity and message of this unwelcome apostle, pointed at him and snarled for the ushers to grab him (v. 4). Instantly, he knew something was wrong – he couldn't bring his hand back to his body. Even kings can be fast learners – Yahweh was obviously strong-arming Jeroboam and thereby protecting his servant from Judah. It was as if Yahweh was whispering in the royal ear, 'Keep this up if you like, Jeroboam, but think: How many limbs do you want to keep?' Jeroboam understood and asked for a season of intercessory prayer (v. 6).

Yahweh must have struck Jeroboam's arm and his altar almost simultaneously. 'The altar was torn and the ashes were poured out from the altar' (v. 5a). Here was a *clear* mercy. Jeroboam probably didn't see the mercy but couldn't miss the clarity. The man of God from Judah had announced this sign or wonder in verse 3. His prophecy in verse 2 predicted something in the future (at the time who knew how long in the future?). How could anyone know if such a prediction would come true? So he announced a more immediate matter: the altar will be torn and the ashes spilt (v. 3). When that happened before their very eyes (v. 5) most thinkers could catch the argument: as this predicted wonder has occurred (vv. 3, 5), so that predicted word (v. 2) will as certainly occur. 'The God who can ensure that prophecy comes to pass in

For an excellent literary study of chapter 13 in its relation to 12:25-33, see D. W. Van Winkle, '1 Kings XII 25 – XIII 34: Jeroboam's Cultic Innovations and the Man of God from Judah,' *Vetus Testamentum* 46 (1996): 101-114.

the short term can surely do so over the longer term.'[3]

Who knows if Jeroboam saw more? The man of God spoke of the altar being 'torn' (vv. 3, 5). The verb (*qāra'*) is significant. Yahweh uses this verb (11:11, 12, 13) when he tells Solomon he is going to 'tear' the kingdom from him. The verb occurs in 11:30 when Ahijah the prophet 'tore' his new cloak into twelve 'torn pieces' (cognate noun) and explained it meant that Yahweh 'was tearing' the kingdom from Solomon (11:31). Would Jeroboam remember Ahijah and get the point? A torn cloak had meant a torn kingdom, a kingdom under judgment. Now, at Bethel, a torn altar signified torn religion, a religion under judgment.

Let me digress momentarily to emphasize *how clearly* Yahweh spoke to Jeroboam that day, what evidence he gave him that Yahweh himself was speaking and acting. One could say Yahweh gave Jeroboam a barrage of signs. He gave a sign of *power*, the paralyzed hand (v. 4), as if to say, 'This is my servant; I sent him; and if you try to harm him, you're toast!' He gave a sign of *truth*, the torn altar (vv. 3, 5), which, as already explained, gave present proof of future fulfillment (v. 2). No one could dispute that an unseen hand had assaulted the altar before their very eyes. And yet he granted a sign of *grace*, for when the man of God interceded, Yahweh restored the king's hand (v. 6). Was that not the immense kindness of Yahweh? Was it not a token of what Yahweh would delight to do for Jeroboam? Was it an invitation to return and enjoy his goodness? Manipulation, however, was not the way back (v. 7) and Jeroboam's smooth tactic meets a direct rebuff, a sign of *repudiation* (vv. 8-9). Leaving lunchless was a form of acted excommunication – the true man of God was to have no dealings, enjoy no fellowship, carry on no relations with the apostate regime. Jeroboam & Co. were cut off from the true people of God. The acted sermon was as clear as the spoken.

Our main contention is that verses 1-10 have mercy written all over them. Granted, the prophet's intrusion was socially obnoxious, a violation of every canon of proper religious decorum. The king became the public target of Yahweh's brute power and

---

[3] Iain W. Provan, *1 and 2 Kings*, New International Biblical Commentary (Peabody, MA: Hendrickson, 1995), 113.

was abruptly repudiated by his prophetic visitor. Jeroboam was not pleased. But this was mercy. Whenever someone, like Jeroboam, commits himself to the path of perverted worship and God intrudes to stop him in his tracks, is that not mercy?

When Charles Spurgeon was a small lad his grandfather was pastor at a chapel in Stambourne. Young Charles noticed his grandfather was especially grieved over one of the church members named Roads, who enjoyed the public house and smoking his pipe and guzzling his beer therein. One day little Charles announced his decision: 'I'll kill old Roads, that I will!' After receiving admonitions that he should not talk that way, the child assured his grandfather, 'I shall not do anything bad; but I'll kill him though, that I will.' Not very long afterwards Charles traipsed in and declared: 'I've killed old Roads; he'll never grieve my dear grandpa any more.' His grandfather was aghast, but the lad assured him he'd done nothing wrong but had only been 'about the Lord's work'.

It wasn't long before Thomas Roads came seeking his pastor with obvious sorrow. And the story came out. Roads was sitting in the pub with his pipe and mug. Little Charles comes striding in, points at him with his finger, and says: 'What doest thou here, Elijah? sitting with the ungodly; and you a member of a church, and breaking your pastor's heart. I'm ashamed of you! I wouldn't break my pastor's heart, I'm sure.' Then the lad walked away. Roads confessed he did feel angry – and yet knew it was true. So he abandoned pipe and beer, went to a lonely spot to seek the Lord, then to the manse to seek forgiveness from his pastor.[4] 'I've killed old Roads.' But it was mercy-killing in the proper sense. He was angry at the audacious rebuke, angry at the embarrassment in front of others, angry at a mere slip of a kid having the gall to quote 1 Kings 19 at him. It was both disturbing and merciful.

Yahweh hasn't changed and he does not hesitate to come barging after you right into the middle of your idolatries. He'll throw roadblocks in your path and sometimes send reasonably obnoxious servants to you as well. But it's good news that he'll

---

[4] *C. H. Spurgeon Autobiography*, vol. 1, *The Early Years* (Edinburgh: Banner of Truth, 1962), 11-12.

do most anything to pry you loose from your golden calves. His mercy makes waves before his judgment arrives.

What about Jeroboam? He simply repaired the altar and went on worshiping there (vv. 33-34). The word of God was his mercy – and he despised it.

The man of God from Judah: the word of God was his safety – and he abandoned it (vv. 11-24)

The man of God from Judah is a mystery. Clearly, he knew Yahweh's 'abstinence orders', for he twice quotes them immediately and decisively (vv. 8-9, 16-17). Yet when the old prophet identifies himself as a colleague in the cloth (v. 18a) and claims he has received a divine revelation countering that given to the man of God (v. 18b), the latter follows him like a sheep to the slaughter (v. 19). No protest, no debate, no questions, no suspicion that we can see.

The writer, as we have noted, has no inclination to satisfy our whys and what ifs. One wonders, however, if he was tempted to add a marginal note at verse 19: 'Can you believe he did that?' At the very least the man of God should have registered suspicion, since the old prophet if only by his residence was associated with the apostatizing northern kingdom.[5] He *swallowed a counter revelation-claim in opposition to the clear word already received.* That is the essential problem. And that is a recipe for disaster.

During the 1915 baseball season the St. Louis Cardinals were playing Brooklyn in St. Louis. Miller Huggins, the St. Louis manager, was directing his team from the third base coach's box. It was the seventh inning, with two outs, the score tied, and one of Huggins' Cardinals on third base, ninety feet away from a score. Huggins hollered at the Brooklyn pitcher Ed Appleton: 'Hey, bub, let me see that ball!' Appleton was a 23-year-old rookie; with all due respect he tossed the ball to Huggins. But the St. Louis manager had not called time out. So he simply stepped aside, let the ball

---

[5] Johannes Fichtner holds that as a man of God he had to know that God does not revoke his orders, not even through the word of another prophet (*Das erste Buch von den Königen*, Die Botschaft des Alten Testaments, 2nd ed. [Stuttgart: Calwer, 1979], 208).

roll past, and watched his Cardinal runner trot over home plate with (what proved to be) the winning run.[6] Maybe it was the tone of managerial authority in Huggins' demand. In any case, Appleton complied. And lost.

Baseball doesn't matter but faithfulness does. But the problem both in the game and in the text is the same – knuckling under to the tone of authority without examining the word it speaks. One can almost hear John screaming: 'Test the spirits!' (1 John 4:1). Could there be a more contemporary word than verse 18 of our text? Are we not in allegedly Christian circles awash in folks blabbering, 'The Lord said to me,' and with teacher-types claiming to have held interviews with Jesus and quoting his 'words'? Are we to swallow these claims or cling only to the sure and written word of the prophets and the apostles (cf. 2 Pet. 3:2 in light of 2 Pet. 2)? Surely, 1 Kings 13 teaches that the given word of God is adequate for his servants and that it is not safe to receive anything beyond or beside that word.

But the man of God from Judah did. The old prophet who was a liar spoke the truth about him: he had 'rebelled against the mouth of Yahweh' (vv. 21, 26). There is some terror in this text for those in the teaching ministry, isn't there? The text warns us that the ministry of proclaiming the word does not exempt us from the duty of obeying that word.[7] That lifeless form in the road from Bethel (v. 24), like Uzzah's (2 Sam. 6:6-8), bears silent witness that it is never safe to venture outside the shelter of Yahweh's explicit word.

---

[6] Daniel Okrent and Steve Wulf, *Baseball Anecdotes* (New York: Oxford, 1989), 72.

[7] Cf. H. L. Ellison, *The Prophets of Israel* (Grand Rapids: Eerdmans, 1969), 24: 'It is a common failing of ministers of the Word that though they believe it they do not take it seriously. This seems to have been the case with our prophet. He had demonstrated the impurity of Israel in the clearest possible way, but as soon as he had placed a hill between him and Bethel, instead of hurrying as fast as possible towards the frontier, he sat down under a terebinth to rest and think, and maybe to regret the festival meal and the reward he had had to forego. If any think this a harsh judgment, let them bear in mind that it was only about six miles from Bethel to the frontier of Judah.'

One additional note. Did you notice how steadfast and rock-solid the man of God was in his encounter with King Jeroboam (vv. 1-10)? He neither succumbed to the king's intimidation nor to his blandishments. Yet he fell when faced with the poppycock of a religious deceiver. This pattern is instructive: sometimes we have courage to face major crises but lack sense for subtle dilemmas. We can muster defiance for the danger of the hour but cannot find discernment for the ploy of the moment. Ministry must be grounded in both the power of God *and* the wisdom of God.

The old prophet: the word of God was his profession – and he abused it (vv. 18-32)

> I too am a prophet like you, and an angel has spoken to me by the word of Yahweh, saying, 'Bring him back with you to your house, and let him eat bread and drink water' (v. 18).

Such was the come-on of the Bethel prophet. The writer's appended note at the end of verse 18 is more abrupt than most translations have it: 'He lied to him.' No conjunctions, no 'but' or 'however'. Only two words in Hebrew.

A little later the old prophet rides to the scene of the disaster. No paramedics feverishly working. No red and blue lights flashing from emergency vehicles. Something far more arresting than such tame tokens: the donkey and lion standing beside the slain man of God. The lion was apathetic; it neither attacked the donkey nor ravaged the corpse. All sorts of people witnessed the scene (vv. 24-25). The strange lion was the signature of God. Inexplicable. Had the lion mauled and feasted on the corpse and at least traumatized the donkey, folks, on seeing the evidence, could say it was 'one of those things.'[8] That's what happens when lions get involved. But here was a lion that, after the lethal assault, seemed to be on Yahweh's leash. The eccentric lion was testimony to the

---

[8] Note Ellison (*The Prophets of Israel*, 25) again: 'We need find no difficulty in the miraculous. In the Bible it is almost invariably found in moments of crisis, when the fate of the nation was at stake. Such a moment was Jeroboam's remodelling of religion to suit his purposes. The lion and

presence of God. This was no normal lion attack: *God* was at work here in judgment. His disobedient servant lay slain, that and nothing more. The event had 'supernatural' written all over it.

So the old prophet handled the funeral. But what are we to make of this fellow? We'll never know why he lied to the man of God. The writer is too stingy to reveal the old prophet's motive. It doesn't matter anyway. For whatever reason, he lied. And though Yahweh gave this rascal a true word of judgment to speak against the man of God (vv. 20-22), that doesn't excuse his previous lie, his deception. True, the man of God should have discerned and rejected the old prophet's invitation. Yet the fact remains: here was a prophet who by his lie destroyed a servant of Yahweh.[9] Because the man of God from Judah was foolish does not mean the old prophet was guiltless.

The old prophet sports an alarming combination: he speaks the truth of God (vv. 20-22) and destroys the servant of God (v. 18). We could 'principlize' that: he has orthodoxy without sanctification. Jesus told us there would be folks like this (Matt. 7:21-23). In fact, he said that *many* (Matt. 7:22) will commend to him their ministries of pulpit and power at the last day, ones whom he will address as 'those working lawlessness' (v. 23). You should be terrified if you have the truth and yet that truth does not grip, control, and transform you. For the old prophet the truth seemed to be more of a game than a love. 'I too am a prophet.' The word of God was his profession – and he abused it.

---

donkey standing watch over the dead man were needed lest any should say with a shrug of his shoulders, "How dangerous the roads have become since Solomon's death," and dismiss the whole matter as an accident.'

[9] The double-edged situation here reminds me of Mark 14:21, where Jesus says: 'For the Son of man goes as it is written of him, but woe to that man by whom the Son of man is betrayed! It would have been better for that man if he had not been born' (RSV). One may be an instrument in accomplishing God's sovereign purpose/intention and yet be blameworthy in doing so. It may be a head-scratcher, but it's in the text.

Chapter 15

The Beginning Has Been
the Beginning of the End

1 Kings 14:1-20

There was trouble in Tirzah. Jeroboam's son was ill; seriously ill, it seems. That was a double difficulty, for the hopes of a dynasty (cf. 11:38) could rest on a male heir, and yet parental compassion must have played its part. Even calf worshipers care about their kids. What to do? The king did what many still do: seek out a clergyman they've met at some time in their lives. For Jeroboam that means Ahijah the prophet (11:29-40) and another episode that centers on the word of Yahweh. Here slick Jerry meets the word of God, the word that exposes men and governs history. The teaching of the text centers upon ...

The Freedom of the Word that Exposes Trickery (vv. 1-6)
Abijah is sick (v. 1) and Jeroboam wants to know whether he will recover. Why does he hide behind his wife? Why does he not go to Ahijah the prophet himself? And why must his wife disguise herself so that no one knows she is Mrs. Jeroboam (v. 2)? The text does not answer these queries directly but, presuming we have been reading the Jeroboam story since chapter 11, it allows us to divine the king's scheme. Ahijah had admonished Jeroboam to function according to the David-standard (11:37-38), but he had not done so; Jeroboam had determined that neo-bovinism would do more for royal stability than covenant orthodoxy. Hence his bull cult (12:25-33). He likely knew Ahijah would hold a 'jaundiced' view of his religious innovations. He therefore dare not approach Ahijah directly, nor must his wife in any recognizable form.[1] That would be sure to bring a bad word from the prophet.

---

[1] Who knows whether Ahijah actually knew Jeroboam's wife on sight? There were at that time no widely-circulated news magazines nor tabloids

But if the royal wife appeared simply as an anxious Israelite mother seeking a word from God regarding her stricken son, why, the prophet might well be prone to give her a 'good' word. Certainly a gift (fee for services?, v. 3) wouldn't hurt. In fact, the situation was better than Jeroboam dared hope, for Ahijah could scarcely see a thing anymore (v. 4b)! It may be Jeroboam did not know of Ahijah's cataracts, for he may have had precious little contact with the prophet in recent years. He still remembered Ahijah's address (v. 2); he may not have been current on Ahijah's condition (v. 4).

Here is the king, then, with his magical view of the word of Yahweh. If he can only weasel a positive pronouncement out of the prophet, his son will surely recover. Even a manipulated word will be a certain word.

Ahijah, however, did not need his eyes because the Lord had his ear:

> but Yahweh had told him, 'Jeroboam's wife is now on her way to ask you for a prophecy about her son, as he is sick. You will tell her such and such. When she comes, she will pretend to be some other woman' (v. 5, NJB).

There it is: who, why, what, and how – everything! So when he heard the crunch of feet, Ahijah began his punch-line: 'Come in, wife of Jeroboam; why do you pretend to be another? For I am charged with heavy tidings for you' (v. 6, RSV).

Jeroboam's tactic reminds me of one of Charles Schulz' *Peanuts* cartoon strips. Lucy and Linus appear before Charlie Brown, holding hands and smiling. Lucy announces, 'We're brother and sister and we love each other.' Charlie Brown is incensed, recognizing such blatant hypocrisy on sight and accusing them of such. He asks the premier question: 'Do you really think you can fool Santa Claus this way?' Lucy's hardened retort is: 'Why not? We're a couple of sharp kids, and he's just an old man!' That was Jeroboam's foible. He thought he was a sharp

---

loaded with photographs. The point is that Jeroboam could not risk her sporting any décor that might suggest her true status.

king simply dealing with an old man (Ahijah). He forgot that every time one deals with the word of God one is dealing with the God whose word it is. The word of God is not some extraneous object out there for us to squeeze to our liking; rather it is always warm with the breath of God's own mouth. Yahweh is never detached from his word; Jeroboam and other superstitious folks learn that to their dismay. That word is not mine to capture but is free, and it exposes me right down to my hidden motives.

Interestingly, this very text has been known to unmask people. Charles Spurgeon knew of at least two instances. One of them occurred at the Metropolitan Tabernacle on Sunday evening, July 31, 1864. A man living in Newington had been converted under Spurgeon's preaching and became a regular worshiper at the Tabernacle over his wife's strong objections, for she was a staunch adherent of the Established Church. One Lord's Day evening, however, after her husband had left for the service, insatiable curiosity overcame her. She determined to go hear Spurgeon. However, she did not wish to be recognized and so tried to disguise herself by putting on a thick veil and a heavy shawl, and, to minimize visibility, by going up to the upper gallery. She was, of course, late reaching the building and so just as she entered she heard the preacher announcing his text: 'Come in, thou wife of Jeroboam; why feignest thou thyself to be another? for I am sent to thee with heavy tidings' (v. 6, KJV). She averred that Spurgeon pointed directly at her when he announced those words! His sermon was apparently suited to her case, indicating, as he did, that God's gospel will 'search you out, and unmask your true character, disguise yourself as you may'.[2]

We do not need such dramatic exposure, however, for the Spirit can use Jeroboam himself in this text as a mirror. When is it that the king seeks the word of Yahweh? When he's in trouble. Nothing wrong with that in itself (see Ps. 50:15). Jeroboam, however, turned a deaf ear to the word of God in chapter 13; yet now when the

---

[2] The woman's first response was to accuse her husband of somehow tipping Spurgeon off about her presence! He assured her he was innocent of the charge. For this anecdote, see C. H. Spurgeon, *Autobiography,* vol. 2, *The Full Harvest* (Edinburgh: Banner of Truth, 1973), 59-60.

dark days come he seeks what he had despised. Jeroboam wants the help of the word in the emergencies of life but not the rule of the word over the course of life. He desires only the occasional word of God. He wants the word of God for his crisis but not for his routine or practice. He craves light in his trouble but not on his path. He doesn't want to live with the word but only visit it – like one does a whore. Is that your portrait? It *is* unnerving to stand before a Lord who sees our thoughts and intentions: 'You seek me ... because you ate of the loaves and were filled' (John 6:26).

The Severity of the Word that Attacks Idolatry (vv. 7-11)

Ahijah was right: he was sent to Mrs. Jeroboam with a harsh message. He announces that message in verses 7-11. Note how he expresses it:

Messenger formula, 7a
('Here's what Yahweh ... says')

Accusation, 7b-9
('Because...')

    Rehearsal of grace, 7b-8a
    ('I ... I ... I ... I ...')

    Rehearsal of guilt, 8b-9
    ('but you ... you ... you ... you ...')

Announcement of judgment, 10-11a
('Therefore ...')

Confirmation clause, 11b
('... for Yahweh has spoken')

Ahijah clearly categorizes the king's offense as a sin against grace. Yahweh had been so good to Jeroboam: 'I raised you up ..., and I placed you as leader ..., and I tore the kingdom from the house of David, and I gave it to you' (vv. 7b-8a). But Jeroboam had not responded in kind: 'But you have not been like my servant David ... so that you acted wickedly ..., and you made for yourself other gods ..., but me you have thrown behind your back' (vv. 8b-

9). Jeroboam had received grace and despised it. That's why his dynasty would be annihilated (vv. 10-11).[3]

The heart of Ahijah's – and Yahweh's – accusation is in verse 9: 'You made for yourself other gods, molten things, to provoke me, but *me* [emphatic] you have thrown behind your back.' As noted before, this doesn't sound like Yahweh viewed the royal bull images as relatively harmless liturgical aids. They are 'other gods' – and they provoke Yahweh. The verb usually translated 'provoke' is *kā'as*. It appears in 1 Samuel 1:6-7, describing what mouthy, fertile Peninnah did to poor, childless Hannah whenever Elkanah's family went to Shiloh to worship. Peninnah made it a point to ridicule and belittle Hannah, to irritate, aggravate, and exasperate her. That is *kā'as*.[4] Peninnah wanted so to gall Hannah as to push her over the edge or, as we say, drive her up a wall.

But why should Jeroboam's 'other gods' push Yahweh beyond the brink of his patience? Why do they so rankle Yahweh? Partly, because of what they signify; Yahweh states the corollary of 'other gods' in the last line of verse 9: 'But *me* you have thrown behind your back.' Still, why should Yahweh be so irate? None of the other gods or goddesses of the ancient Near East demanded or expected *exclusive* worship from their devotees. Is Yahweh a dysfunctional deity who needs therapy in order to deal with his irrational rage and bring him into line with what folks expect of

---

[3] Most modern translations sanitize Ahijah's 'toilet prophecy' in verse 10, which more literally reads: 'Therefore, Look! I am going to bring disaster to the house of Jeroboam, and I shall cut off to Jeroboam one urinating against the wall, bound or free [this may = everyone involved, no matter what his condition in life, though see John Gray, *I & II Kings*, 337-38] in Israel, and I shall burn after the house of Jeroboam as one burns dung until it's consumed.' Granted, 'every male' has a refinement that 'one urinating against the wall' does not, but such bleached renderings miss the bite of Ahijah's language (so back to KJV here). Iain Provan is right: 'The [translators'] desire for discretion obscures the obvious connection between the urine and the dung or excrement that God uses as fuel for the fire of destruction. Jeroboam's house smells; radical action is needed to deal with the sanitation problem' (*1 and 2 Kings*, New International Biblical Commentary [Peabody, MA: Hendrickson, 1995], 119).

[4] See Jerome F. D. Creach, NIDOTTE, 2:684-86, and Gerard Van Groningen, TWOT, 1:451.

'normal' deities? No, the fact that there was no other deity like Yahweh in this respect should clue you that in him you are not dealing with any run-of-the-mill 'deity'. Yahweh has done what no other god had done – entered into a covenant with his people, a marriage-like relation, which demands exclusive devotion. Even so we can hardly grasp it. But when there is a marriage relation and one of the spouses commits infidelity, the other spouse will be devastated, crushed, and – hopefully – furious. Why? Because it is the proper character of love within an exclusive relationship to be jealous, to be rightfully possessive of the one who has promised to be totally his/hers. If such an aggrieved spouse reacted with apathy or indifference we would question if any love were present. Yahweh is the unusual God who has entered into covenant with a people and 'no other gods' is his premier demand (Exod. 20:3). To violate that is to invite his fury.

Naturally the world does not get this. I read a recent interview with a famous agnostic who said, 'I don't have a lot of respect for the view of God as some authority figure who wants you to come and kneel before him every week.' I suspect there's some baggage behind the comment, but her point seems to be that even if God is real, worship should be optional. But covenant people have no choice: either seek his face or face his fury. Yahweh is unique precisely because he is intolerant. And you can't escape this by running to the New Testament. Don't you remember the holy egotism of Jesus in Luke 14:26? And he said those words with a straight face.

The Curse of the Word that Hangs over History (vv. 12-18)
Ahijah still had not addressed the king's wife's concern for her ill son Abijah (v. 1). Was he to be exterminated in the prophesied annihilation of Jeroboam's dynasty (vv. 10-11)? No. Ahijah is not finished; he turns to Jeroboam's wife with a supplemental prophecy (vv. 12-16). Here he outlines in more detail the judgment on, and because of, Jeroboam:

Death of the son, vv. 12-13
Overthrow of the dynasty, v. 14
Exile from the land, vv. 15-16

Mrs. Jeroboam must, therefore, trudge back home. Her son's death will coincide with the moment she enters town (v. 12). Perhaps this lad had displayed some marks of genuine piety (cf. v. 13b); in any case, he will have the privilege of a normal burial rather than a violent end as decreed for the rest of Jeroboam's seed. The move to overthrow Jeroboam's dynasty will be afoot soon (v. 14).[5] Worse than that, the whole nation is doomed – Yahweh will destabilize (15a), uproot (15b), scatter (15c), and give up (16a) Israel, because Israel has made their Asherahs (15d) and 'on account of the sins of Jeroboam which he sinned and which he caused Israel to sin' (v. 16b). All three threats are fulfilled:

Vv. 17-18	Death of son
15:25-30	Destruction of dynasty
2 Kings 17:21-23	Removal from land

Jeroboam's wife never talks in the story. She simply turns to go home and, upon her arrival, her son dies – just as Ahijah had said (vv. 17-18). These verses and this episode are important, for they assure the reader that just as the first 'leg' of Ahijah's prophecy has occurred, so the rest of it will surely come to pass. The death of the son is both a sign and a preview of the death of the dynasty and nation.

Now step back from your Bible page and note that Ahijah has been talking from verses 6-16. His prophecy dominates the chapter. And once you see that his word of judgment embraces son, dynasty, and nation, and climaxes in 2 Kings 17, you realize that Ahijah's 1 Kings 14 prophecy is a programmatic piece that controls the whole history of the northern kingdom. That's what the writer(s) of 1-2 Kings intended. And in case you were a bit dull when you read 1 Kings 14, the writer makes sure you don't forget Ahijah's prophecy, for he takes its tailpiece, makes it his refrain, and – like a jingle on a radio commercial – drums it into your head again and again. There is no escape; over and over you hear 'the sins of Jeroboam, which he sinned, and which he caused Israel to sin'

---

[5] This seems to be the general sense of the terse expressions in verse 14b, lit., 'This today! And what? – Even now!'

(14:16 + 1 Kings 15:26, 30, 34; 16:19, 26; 22:52; 2 Kings 10:31; 13:6, 11; 14:24; 15:18, 24, 28; 17:21-23). The first king of the ten tribes finished them. The beginning was the beginning of the end. Jeroboam went bullish and damned a whole people. The curse of Ahijah's word hangs over the next 180 years.

That can easily happen: a single policy can pack a huge punch for years. Absolutist king Louis XIV was determined that all his people be Roman Catholics and so increased the pressure on the French Huguenots until he revoked the Edict of Nantes in 1685, stripping them of their rights and protections. Thousands emigrated. Eighty thousand ended up in England, Ireland, and America. The Elector in Prussia gave 20,000 Huguenots free land near Berlin. Tallies for the total exodus run from 200,000 to 500,000 or more. And who were they? Oh, they were teachers, philosophers, craftsmen, artists, weavers, farmers, stoneworkers, merchants, gunsmiths, iron workers, sculptors, writers, architects – in short, 'intellectuals and the industrious middle class.'[6] Their departure spelled economic disaster for France. Louis XIV asserted his authority and gutted his kingdom.

One needn't be a king, however, to propagate such ruin. Our times are impatient with orthodoxy and with the intolerant God of the Bible who won't negotiate on the first commandment. Our narcissistic contemporaries assure us we can do as we want and needn't stay obligated to such Bible-bound worship. And, of course, they're right. You can choose your calf and damn your descendants for generations.

The Focus of the Word that Emphasizes Priorities (vv. 19-20)
We will get used to these little concluding summaries as we read 1–2 Kings. They frequently include a bibliographical note like verse 19, indicating that those who want more data on, e.g., Jeroboam's reign, may find it in the annals or chronicles of the kings of Israel. That's for the 'rest of the acts of Jeroboam' (19a),

---

[6] See Janet Glenn Gray, *The French Huguenots: Anatomy of Courage* (Grand Rapids: Baker, 1981), 244. See also S. M. Houghton, *Sketches from Church History* (Edinburgh: Banner of Truth, 1980), 134-37, and Barbara W. Tuchman, *The March of Folly* (New York: Knopf, 1984), 19-23.

that is, what the writer has *not* told you here. And what would that material deal with? Oh, 'how he fought and how he reigned', i.e., military and political affairs. Maybe his relationship with the media and that sort of thing. But the writer is clear that that has not been his interest. He has not focused on those concerns. He has been deliberately selective. He has centered on how Jeroboam *worshiped*.

What then is the implication of these observations? Why, that the word (as opposed to the world) is unimpressed with Jeroboam's achievements. The writer has little interest in Jeroboam's military and political successes but has spilled all his ink on how the king responded to the basic covenant demand. Accomplishments don't matter; fidelity does. Verse 19 is frightening: all the energy and exertion you have poured into making your mark in your calling may prove one huge irrelevance. The only thing that matters is whether you worshiped Yahweh alone. Were you contented with the real God? We think verse 19 is only a throw-away bibliographical note. Actually, it's a disturbing world view.

One of Gary Larson's 'Far Side' cartoons shows a fellow sinking in a pit of quicksand. A dog is standing on firm ground beside the quicksand. The man cries, 'Lassie, Go get help! Get help, Lassie!' The dog bolts away, running past trees, leaping over logs, riding in an airplane (!), and dashing down a street. Suddenly, the canine stops and thinks: '*My* name's not "Lassie".' Of course, the cartoon is strange (it was meant to be), but the dog's objection is irrelevant. Why quibble over one's name when there's a fellow disappearing in quicksand? And that is the writer's point in our text. Why be so entranced with military and political prowess when covenant disaster looms so large?

Apply it to yourself. If it's your obituary, does it really matter that you built a successful business from scratch, or retired from your company after thirty years of stellar service, or belonged to the Rotary Club, or loved science fiction movies, or played Bridge every Monday night with your social clique? Does anything matter if you don't worship the God and Father of our Lord Jesus Christ?

167

Chapter 16

A Lamp in Jerusalem

1 Kings 14:21–15:24

When television networks cover sporting events, they try to cover games that hold at least a modicum of interest for viewers. Currently it is February and college basketball seizes its share of 'tube' time in the USA. Sometimes, however, a highly-touted game turns out to be a bore because one team is having an 'off' night: the score is lop-sided, and the hapless team is suffering disgrace as well as a loss. On such occasions I have noticed TV networks sometimes abandon the scheduled programming and switch to another game in progress, one which has not become an athletic disaster. One has an initial impression of the same phenomenon at 1 Kings 14:21-15:24. The writer has just shown us that the northern kingdom will be plummeting to ruin (14:15-16) and now he switches to the southern kingdom, depicting about sixty years of life in Judah (931-870 BC, the reigns of Rehoboam, Abijam, and Asa). Maybe matters will prove more hopeful here.

The writer tints each of the three reigns with a distinct theological emphasis; underscoring these emphases is the best way to get at the teaching of the text.

The judgment that must come (Rehoboam, 14:21-31)
There may be a different game in Judah but not necessarily a better one. The writer no sooner introduces Rehoboam and mentions Jerusalem than he expands on the latter as 'the city where Yahweh chose to put his name out of all the tribes of Israel' (v. 21). Here at least is the center of orthodoxy – perhaps he intends a contrast to the bullish mess at Bethel and Dan (12:25-14:20). But any optimism begins to fade with the next clause: 'the name of his [Rehoboam's] mother was Naamah the Ammonitess.' In fact, the

169

writer wraps this Rehoboam segment by references to the king's Ammonite mother (vv. 21, 31).[1] Such framing of the Rehoboam report should give the reader a case of creeping dread. What good can come from such pagan influence behind the throne (cf. 11:1-2)?

But our writer does not depend on artistic hints; he also inflicts brutal broadsides like verses 22-24:

22. Then Judah did what was evil in Yahweh's eyes, and they stung him to jealous anger, more than all their fathers had done by their sins which they sinned.
23. So they also built for themselves high places and pillars and Asherah poles on every high hill and under every leafy tree.
24. And even male prostitutes were in the land – they acted in line with all the abominations of the nations which Yahweh had dispossessed before the sons of Israel.

We need not bother much about the cultic furniture: the 'high places' (v. 23; which needn't be on a hill, Jer. 7:31) were alternative shrines; the stone 'pillars' symbolized the male deity in Canaanite fertility worship; the wooden Asherah poles or posts likely represented the female mother goddess, the consort of El or Baal; the male prostitutes (v. 24; the masculine form may intend to include both males and females) refer to the sexual staff who serviced the worshipers at the fertility shrines. (Hosea took his camcorder one day and captured the whole lurid scene at one of the northern shrines [Hos. 4:14]). We do need to note that the writer depicts here what *Judah* was doing, how *they* stirred Yahweh to jealousy, built high places, and so on. The writer is not castigating Rehoboam in particular but Judah in general. And the threat of verse 24 is hardly veiled: since the people of Judah delight

---

[1] James Montgomery thought the reference to Naamah in verse 31 is 'erroneously repeated' from verse 21; he follows LXX, which omits the reference in verse 31 (*A Critical and Exegetical Commentary on the Books of Kings*, International Critical Commentary [New York: Scribners, 1951], 267-68). However, he's wrong. I don't think he considered the two references as the writer's deliberate literary device, casting a pall over Rehoboam's reign.

to ape Canaanite religion they will suffer a Canaanite fate – relieved of their place in the land.

I think the focus on Judah collectively rather than on Rehoboam individually is deliberate. Verses 22-24 are not meant only for Rehoboam's reign. The writer wants to give a summary of the *whole trend* of Judah's kingdom, which began with Rehoboam, and of the dark end that kingdom will meet. Verses 22-24 constitute a programmatic text. As 14:15-16 depicts the tragic end of the northern kingdom, beginning with Jeroboam, its first king, so 14:22-24 relates the fatal errors of the southern kingdom, beginning with its initial king, Rehoboam.[2] In both cases, the seeds of demise are there at the beginning. This then is not going to be a happy history that we read. The divided kingdom is a depressing story from the very first.

Immediately after these three depressing verses (i.e., vv. 22-24) we hear of the invasion of Shishak (or Shoshenk I, 945-924 BC, founder of the 22nd dynasty), the king of Egypt, in the fifth year of Rehoboam. He marched against Jerusalem

> and carried off the treasures of the House of the LORD and the treasures of the royal palace. He carried off everything; he even carried off all the golden shields that Solomon had made (v. 26, NJPS).

Clearly, we are meant to understand Shishak's plundering expedition as an initial blow of Yahweh's judgment upon Judah's infidelity – and as a sign that there would be more of the same at the end (see v. 24b). It may be that Shishak did not actually assault Jerusalem – Rehoboam may have bought him off with all the loot.[3] In any case, it hurts – seeing all the glitter and glory of the previous era being carted off to Egypt. So you can shun Yahweh if you like, but you must remember that he has Egyptian Pharaohs – and a whole raft of other subordinates – at his beck and call.

---

[2] For a similar view, see Iain W. Provan, *1 and 2 Kings*, New International Biblical Commentary (Peabody, MA: Hendrickson, 1995), 121.

[3] For a lucid discussion of Shishak/Shoshenk and his biblical connections, see John D. Currid, *Ancient Egypt and the Old Testament* (Grand Rapids: Baker, 1997), 172-89. Shoshenk's Palestinian exploits are recorded on his war stela from Karnak.

Our passage also contains a symbolic representation of Judah's demise. After Shishak hauled off, among other spoil, the ceremonial gold shields Solomon had made (v. 26b), we read that 'King Rehoboam made bronze shields to replace them' (v. 27a). These shields were carried by the royal guard whenever they escorted the king to the temple. Gold shields replaced by bronze. The splendor is fading. But the pomp and ceremony must continue. And if we cannot have shields of department store quality, we shall have ones of discount store variety. The show must go on. We may willingly sacrifice the pure worship of God (vv. 22-24), but we must not give up our sorry attempts to imitate the old glory with our trinkets and tinsel.

In 1973 a church in North Hollywood, California, became concerned about, shall we say, church continuity. This church had 2,000 members and a property then valued at $1.5 million. This church held what is called the 'pre-tribulation rapture' view of Christ's second coming, that is, that the first installment of the second coming consists of Christ's taking his people out of this world. (This is not the place to debate the cogency of this view). Now the leadership assumed that most of the leaders and officers would be taken but apparently did not entertain such high hopes for others. They worried about how the remaining members could keep the property going should the 'rapture' occur. Solution: they changed the church bylaws to allow those left behind to elect a temporary chairman, who could then call a church council to elect new corporate officers.[4] I know: it's bizarre. It's also absurd. Keep a church going without any Christians? Maintain an empty semblance when there would be (on their suppositions) no substantial reality? It's something like a kingdom where you still strut around with bronze shields but have dumped faithful worship. Rehoboam's reign then foreshadows the judgment that must come.

The grace that still remains (Abijam, 15:1-8)
Nothing good is said about Abijam. In fact, hardly anything is said about Abijam, aside from the usual stylized formulas.[5]

---

[4] I didn't make this up. Skeptics may see *The Presbyterian Journal* (April 11, 1973), p. 5.

However, verses 3-5 take up a distinct chunk of the Abijam section and are obviously significant as theological commentary on his reign.[6]

Here we note the concern for heart condition: 'his [Abijam's] heart was not wholly devoted to the LORD his God, like the heart of his father David' (v. 3b, NASB). Actually, 3b seems to explain 3a, which tells us Abijam 'walked in all the sins of his father [=Rehoboam] which he had done before him.' Obviously, the condition of the heart (3b) determines the walk of the feet (3a). One could say Abijam had two fathers, for both Rehoboam (3a) and David (3b) are called his 'father.' Here in one verse one meets two normal connotations of that term: immediate progenitor and more remote ancestor. These respective fathers also constituted two models; sadly, Abijam chose Rehoboam as his pattern rather than David.

This calls for an explanation. If Abijam holds to the half-heartedness of Solomon (v. 3b, and see 11:4) and maintains the perversions that came under Rehoboam, why is there still a kingdom in Judah? Why doesn't Yahweh write 'Finis!' over David's fief? Verses 4-5 supply an answer:

4. But on account of David Yahweh his God gave him [David] a lamp in Jerusalem by raising up his son after him and by making Jerusalem secure;

---

[5] The Chronicler gives Abijam/Abijah far more press, a whole chapter (=2 Chron. 13:1-22) actually, and makes him appear in a distinctly different light. But the writers of Chronicles and Kings are making two different points. Chronicles implies Abijah was reasonably orthodox when compared with Jeroboam; Kings says he is covenantally defective when compared to David (vv. 3-5).

[6] Some commentators are sure such theological explanations cannot be original; hence vv. 3b-5 come from a 'later deuteronomistic redactor' (G. H. Jones, who also thinks it took three different writers to produce vv. 3-5). The upshot of this judgment is that such material may be disregarded, since, as anyone can imagine, a later deuteronomistic editor has his own theological fish to fry and can hardly be depended upon for an accurate assessment. What the critic asserts is that the clear judgments of the word of God may be safely set aside as biased opinions of man.

5. because David had done what was right in Yahweh's eyes, and he did not turn aside from all that he commanded all the days of his life, except in the affair of Uriah the Hittite.

One wonders whether 'on account of David' (v. 4a; or, 'for the sake of David') means 'on account of David's fidelity' (as v. 5 may suggest) or whether it means 'on account of Yahweh's promise to David' (=2 Sam. 7:12-16). I think 2 Kings 8:19 (cf. also 1 Kings 11:13, 32, 34) favors the latter option. Hence there may be a double rationale for the kingdom's continued existence: Yahweh's covenant commitment (v. 4) and David's covenant consistency (v. 5). The latter was not perfect (note the 'except'-clause) but typical. If Jeroboam was poison and death to his kingdom (14:15-16), David was blessing and life to his.[7] Iain Provan sums it up well:

> Because of the special place held by David and Jerusalem in God's affections, however (11:11-13, 31-39; 14:21), the idolatry of Solomon and Rehoboam had not brought upon them the judgment of God that had been expected. It is no different with Abijam.... This dynasty, unlike Jeroboam's, is secure; sin cannot affect *its* fortunes in any ultimate sense.[8]

So why is there still a kingdom in Judah? Because of David. Because of his faithfulness (v. 5). But more than that – because of Yahweh's faithfulness (v. 4). He had made a promise, and in that very promise he seemed to recognize that David's descendants might well be scoundrels (2 Sam. 7:14b). But the kingdom remains – not because man obeys but because God has decided. Why don't the kingdom and people of God vanish into the mists of history? Because God will not permit it. He has decided that his kingdom *will* come. Grace is not only greater but more stubborn than our sins.

---

[7] The glory of David's Descendant is that *his* righteous obedience is impeccable (Rom. 5:18-19), and thankfully so, for our destiny rests on it.

[8] Provan, *1 and 2 Kings*, 124 (emphasis his).

The hope that may appear (Asa, 15:9-24)

This section displays two pictures of the new king: (1) Asa the reformer (vv. 11-15) and (2) Asa the politician (vv. 16-22). I want to look at each of these in turn and then to draw some inferences from them.

The air seemed to turn fresh when Asa began to reign (ca. 910 BC). For the first time we read of a king who 'did what was right in the eyes of Yahweh as David his father [had done]' (v. 11). So Asa's righteousness was distinctive. And also destructive: he sent the fertility functionaries packing (v. 12a), removed the idols his predecessors had made (v. 12b), and hacked down and burnt up some sort of 'horrid object' the queen mother had apparently originated for use in worship of the goddess Asherah (v. 13). This last demonstrates how consistent Asa's righteousness was – his purge extended even to the royal household. No pampered exceptions. He even deposed Maacah from her position as 'big lady' (*gĕbîrâ*) in the realm.[9] Granted, there were limitations to his reform (v. 14a), but there was no doubt about the sincerity of Asa's heart-orientation (v. 14b – in contrast to his father in v. 3). Now let us leave religion for a while and dive into politics.

It goes without saying that there were unceasing hostilities between Asa and Baasha king of Israel (v. 16). Don't be disturbed because you, the reader, have not yet been formally introduced to Baasha. The writer of Kings cannot do several things at once. He will do the formal honors at 15:27, but, for right now, take his word for it that Baasha is king of Israel.

And Baasha stirred up a political crisis. He came down to Ramah of Benjamin and fortified it (lit., 'built it,' v. 17a). Ramah was strategic: it was only five-plus miles north of Asa's Jerusalem, sat astride the north-south trunk road, and controlled Judah's best western access to the coastal plain via Beth-horon. Baasha's design was no secret; it smells like an economic blockade (v. 17b).

What to do? Asa empties the exchequer ('all of the silver and

---

[9] Maacah was likely Asa's grandmother since she is designated as Abijam's mother as well in verse 2. For discussion of the 'great lady,' see Roland de Vaux, *Ancient Israel*, 2 vols. (New York: McGraw-Hill, 1965), 1:117-18.

gold,' v. 18 – note the same among his dedicated items in v. 15) and sends both commissioners and cash to Ben-hadad of Damascus requesting a treaty (v. 19a).[10] The most essential treaty provision was its flip-side: 'Go, break your treaty with Baasha king of Israel, that he may go up from me' (v. 19b). Ben-hadad, believing that the hand that fills the coffers should get the help, sent military detachments into northern Israel, attacking Ijon, Dan, and Abel-beth-maacah, indeed causing havoc all over the territory of Naphtali (both west and north of the [New Testament] Sea of Galilee; v. 20). He was only too delighted to do so; controlling these sites gave Damascus dominance of the east-west caravan route to the Mediterranean.[11] Economics has a secure place in every nation's pantheon.

Baasha could hardly play construction supervisor at Ramah when the other extremity of his realm was under attack; so he left (v. 21), just as Asa had designed. Asa then activated the draft for a patriotic public works project, and his people carted off Baasha's construction materials, using the pilfered stuff to fortify Geba and Mizpah as Judah's defensive outposts (v. 22).

It was a slick move, textbook diplomacy; even amusing – the way Asa outflanked Baasha. How often does one enjoy such unqualified success? But how does the writer of Kings view Asa's ploy? I raise this question because in the Chronicles account Hanani the seer rakes Asa over the coals for his faith in Aram rather than in Yahweh (2 Chron. 16:7-10). But none of that appears here in Kings. The Kings account seems more objective, more non-committal about Asa's liaison with Aram. No overt criticism here. Does this mean Kings approves of Asa's scheme? I think not. The criticism is more muted than in Chronicles but is nevertheless present. Note, for example, how the writer simply passes on Asa's own crass political message to Ben-hadad: 'See! I have sent to you a bribe, silver and gold' (v. 19). The noun *šōḥad*

---

[10] This would have been Ben-hadad I (ca. 900-860 BC). For the various Ben-hadads, see K. A. Kitchen, NBD, 3rd ed., 129.

[11] See Carl G. Rasmussen, *Zondervan NIV Atlas of the Bible* (Grand Rapids: Zondervan, 1989), 127, and John Gray, *I & II Kings*, Old Testament Library, 2nd ed. (Philadelphia: Westminster, 1970), 354.

appears twenty-three times in the Old Testament and almost always in an odious sense. Why versions launder Asa's money for him, calling it a 'gift' (NIV) or 'present' (NASB) here (and in 2 Kings 16:8), is a bit baffling. It is a bribe. Moreover, Asa wants Benhadad to break (*pārar*) his treaty or covenant with Baasha (v. 19b). The Bible does not smile on broken covenants. Even a covenant oath to a pagan king should be kept; Zedekiah of Judah was scored for proving false to his covenant with the king of Babylon (Ezek. 17:11-21). And God will judge pagan Egypt for not keeping its word to Israel (Ezek. 29:6-9), even though the latter was both wrong and stupid to seek help from Egypt. In light of this biblical mentality I doubt that Kings regards Asa's pitch to Ben-hadad as simply a bit of neutral politics.

Time for inferences. What does this Asa account press upon us? First, *the unfaithfulness of success* (vv. 16-22). As just noted, the Kings writer does not overtly denounce Asa's bit of foreign policy but allows Asa's own words (v. 19) to leak a negative color over the enterprise. Asa was a smooth politician – and his stratagem worked. As pragmatists we admire that. And that is why we find the Bible so disturbing, for it tells us that success is no authentication of fidelity. Circumstantial success and covenantal failure can exist side-by-side.[12]

There is, however, a second and more positive point the text wants to raise: *the possibility of faithfulness* (vv. 11-15). The picture of Asa in 1 Kings 15 is not so bleak and critical as that of 2 Chronicles 16. Does the writer of Kings then want us to see more the positive than the negative side of Asa's rule? Remember verse 11. Asa is the first king after the division of the kingdom of whom such words were written. It *is* possible to walk David-like. Purity of worship *can* be protected and preserved. Times of hope and reform can appear within a history plummeting to disaster.

One finds this pattern repeatedly in the history of revivals. Before the 1859 revival in Wales, Principal T. C. Edwards of Bala said that 'the churches were withering away in our country; a wave of spiritual apathy and practical infidelity had spread over Wales.'

---

[12] See also my *1 Samuel: Looking on the Heart* (Ross-shire: Christian Focus, 2000), 118-19.

However, in the year after the revival, the number of criminal cases before the Welsh courts had dropped from 1,809 to 1,228, and the revival solidly affected one hundred thousand people (a tenth of the population), most of these standing the test of time.[13] I suppose Asa's work was primarily a reform rather than a revival, but the point remains. We can sometimes wonder if the church has not been consigned to corporate victimhood, so bleak are its prospects, so unclear its witness, so alarming its apostasies, so trivial its concerns. And then the Lord in his mercy brings something resembling an Asa era.

Asa's reign, therefore, was one of Yahweh's mercies; he raised up one who – despite his faults – nevertheless slowed the slide to infidelity. Here is an argument against a fatalism that despairs over the alarming and increasingly unfaithful condition of the church. There are times, says our text, when Yahweh intervenes to reform, renew, and restore. What else would we expect from One who has decreed always to keep a lamp in Jerusalem?

---

[13] J. Edwin Orr, *The Light of the Nations* (Grand Rapids: Eerdmans, 1965), 141. Cf. also Earle E. Cairns, *An Endless Line of Splendor* (Wheaton, IL: Tyndale House, 1986), 53-55, on conditions in Britain prior to the 18th century revival.

Chapter 17

Evil Men in the Hand of a Good God

1 Kings 15:25 –16:7

On an autumn evening several years ago my wife and I attended a local high school football game. It was raining – umbrellas and rain parkas were in vogue. Our neighbors, Gary and Peggy, were there. For good reason. Their daughter belonged to the home-team entertainment troupe that was performing at half-time. Others were there for similar reasons – their sons or grandsons played on the football team. I'm sure some, who may have recognized us, were mystified about our presence. We had no children in either high school. Why would we be sitting in drenching rain watching two teams in which we had no personal stake? Because my wife enjoys football, and where there's a game Barbara will often be near if she can. She's simply that sort of woman.

Our passage is something like that. The writer turns his attention to the northern kingdom again and picks up the story right after ¬Jeroboam's death as Nadab his son begins to rule (ca. 909 BC), only to be liquidated by Baasha who reigns in his place. The passage deals with the reigns of two evil kings, and yet three statements (15:29-30; 16:1-4; 16:7) dominate the account, indicating what God is about in the midst of it all. What is a holy God doing amidst all this evil? He is not there because he relishes it – obviously he abominates it. But he is there because he is simply that sort of God. He is sovereign, and no moment in history, however given to evil, will find him in absentia. Hence here we meet evil men in the hand of a good God.

The Usefulness of Evil (15:29-30, 34)
Nadab, Jeroboam's son, assumed Israel's throne and reigned at least part of two years (v. 25). He was Jeroboam, Jr., as far as his

religious policy went (v. 26), which is all that mattered. Nadab and Israel were conducting a siege of Gibbethon (three miles west of Gezer), originally allotted to Dan (Josh. 19:44) but now under Philistine control (v. 27). Baasha conspired against Nadab, assassinated him, and took the throne (vv. 27-28). Not that Baasha was a reformer. 'He did evil in the eyes of Yahweh' (v. 34a). He took over Jeroboam's throne and kept practicing Jeroboam's religion (v. 34b). One evil king knocked off another evil king.

Where is Yahweh in all of this? In verses 29-30. How is he there? By his word. Baasha not only eliminated Nadab but annihilated all of Jeroboam's descendants. All this bloodshed took place 'according to the word of Yahweh which he spoke by the hand of his servant Ahijah the Shilonite' (v. 29). The reference, of course, is to Ahijah's prophecy of 14:10-11, 14. Baasha the butcher was simply a servant of Yahweh's word. This is basic biblical theology: Yahweh uses evil men to punish other evil men and later judges the evil instruments he used for their own evil (see Isa. 10:5-19; Jer. 27:1-7).

In April 1945 Berlin was near its last gasp. One evening General Erich Dethleffsen, Hitler's Assistant Chief of Staff, was driving toward Berlin to attend the Führer's night conference. He was heartened to notice a flight of Luftwaffe planes above him heading south. At the night briefing Dethleffsen heard a Luftwaffe officer tell Hitler about a successful air attack upon Soviet tanks. That remark was wide of the mark. The 'Soviet tanks' had actually been the buses and trucks of a German army convoy heading south.[1] The Germans had blown up their own kind.

So here. A Baasha eliminates a Nadab. An evil aspirant massacres an evil dynasty. Yahweh uses evil men to annihilate their own kind. Evil Baasha is simply a servant carrying out Yahweh's good word. This text makes a profound point: here you see how subservient evil really is – it is only a slave of Yahweh. What a cut-down for evil and what a bracing encouragement (if she has eyes to see it) for the church.

---

[1] Cornelius Ryan, *The Last Battle* (New York: Simon and Schuster, 1966), 413.

The Tedium of Evil (15:33-34)

I hope you did not pin your hopes on Baasha. Patterson and Austel pointedly sum up Baasha's takeover: 'Political change did not signal a change in spiritual outlook.'[2] Baasha's reign was simply more of the same. Verse 34 says it all: 'He did what was evil in Yahweh's eyes, and he walked in the way of Jeroboam and in his sin which he made Israel sin.' No change: Baasha was 'like the house of Jeroboam' (16:7).

Just step back for a moment and take in Baasha's whole reign (15:33-16:7). Here is a 24-year reign, yet there is nothing here about 'his might' (16:5), only minimal factual data (15:33), a negative assessment (15:34), a sermon against him (16:1-4), a mention about what doesn't matter (16:5), an obituary notice (16:6), and the reason he was denounced (16:7). Out of nine verses, six are prophetic critique, three contain minimal necessary detail. When all the ink is spilt what do you learn about Baasha? He was like Jeroboam. More of the same.

Have you ever wondered why parts of the Bible are boring? Like this text? They're boring because they are the records of sinful men who simply repeat the sins and evil of those before them. Sin is never creative but merely imitative and repetitious. Maybe you can sin with a flair but you can't sin with freshness. You can only ape what's already been done. Goodness has an originality inherent in it which evil hasn't got. Evil can distort and ruin and corrupt and do re-runs, but it can't be original, nor even scintillating. Evil carries a built-in yawn. 'And he walked in the way of Jeroboam and in his sin' (v. 34a). What tedious stuff! If the Bible is boring, blame Baasha. It's his fault.

Albert Speer recalled the days at Obersalzberg as a part of Hitler's entourage. Every day, Speer avers, was the same. Hitler

---

[2] Richard D. Patterson and Hermann J. Austel, '1, 2 Kings,' *Expositor's Bible Commentary*, 12 vols. (Grand Rapids: Zondervan, 1988), 4:132. Their point should not be lost on the church today. How often Christians fall for the 'if-only' heresy. If only we can get another regime into power, another administration elected, another party in control, then.... Then what? Then there will likely be more of the same. We are slow to get the point that our help is in the name of the Lord, not in the next election. The church repeatedly practices the idolatry of change.

would appear about eleven in the morning. After he heard reports the routine began with a prolonged afternoon dinner. After dinner, a half-hour walk to the teahouse, situated at a most picturesque overlook. The group always marveled at the scenery in the same phrases. Hitler always agreed in kind. So it was dessert and drinks and listening to the Fuhrer's monologues. After two hours, teatime was over. Two hours later, about eight, was dinner. And a similar routine. With dinner digesting, the same group ambled into the salon, facing either a movie with trivial discussion or selections from Wagner's operas. Perhaps about 2:00 a.m. his mistress and, a bit later, Hitler himself would bid the party goodnight. The liberated ones who remained might ply themselves on champagne and cognac. Speer wrote: 'In the early hours of the morning we went home dead tired, exhausted from doing nothing.' He himself 'felt exhausted and vacant from the constant waste of time'.[3]

This text implies that such monotony is a trademark of evil. One doesn't have to wait till Ecclesiastes to learn that life apart from the living God is futile. Baasha can teach us, right here in 1 Kings, that godlessness is dull.

The Opportunity of Evil (16:1-4)

We don't have much of a resume on Jehu the son of Hanani (cf. 2 Chron. 19:2; 20:34), but his prophecy is all that keeps Baasha's inauguration (15:33-34) from running into his obituary (16:5-6). Yahweh gave Jehu a word to speak against Baasha (16:1):

> (2) Because I raised you up from the dust, and I set you as leader over my people Israel – then you walked in the way of Jeroboam and made my people Israel sin to outrage me with their sins, (3) See! I am going to burn after Baasha and after his house, and I shall appoint your house to be like the house of Jeroboam son of Nebat: (4) The one belonging to Baasha who dies in the town, the dogs will eat up, and the one belonging to him who dies in the open country the birds of the sky will eat (16:2-4).[4]

---

[3] Albert Speer, *Inside the Third Reich* (New York: Avon Books, 1971), 133-37 (quotations from p. 137).

[4] I have taken *bāʻar* in verse 3 as 'burn'; others posit a parallel root

Hardly a prophetic pleasantry – unless you're a dog or a bird. Jehu could not be clearer: you walk in the way of Jeroboam (v. 2) and you meet the end of Jeroboam (vv. 3-4). And yet is not Baasha a privileged man? Between his introduction (15:33-34) and his conclusion (16:5-6) stands the word of God (16:1-4). One could do worse. What can one say, distinctively, about Baasha's reign? That Jehu son of Hanani spoke the word of Yahweh to him. Was this not, for all its severity, Baasha's opportunity? Had he realized it, he teetered on the abyss of blessing.

A bit later we shall hear Elijah announce Yahweh's scathing judgment upon antichrist Ahab (1 Kings 21:21-24). Yet when Ahab showed signs of visible remorse – he was at least emotionally moved (21:27), Yahweh moderated his judgment though he did not cancel it (21:28-29). Does this not, however, show how eager Yahweh is to extend mercy when there is the merest response to his threats? Hence Baasha, had he only realized it, stood next to the scourging kindness of Yahweh, who takes no pleasure in the death of the wicked but finds it when they turn from their ways and live (Ezek. 18:23).

The Responsibility for Evil (16:7)

The *New Jerusalem Bible* provides a translation of verse 7 that is generally accurate and certainly clear:

> Furthermore, the word of Yahweh was delivered through the prophet Jehu son of Hanani against Baasha and his House, first because of the many ways in which he had displeased Yahweh, provoking him to anger by his actions and becoming like the House of Jeroboam; secondly because he had destroyed that House.

The last clause reads, literally, 'And also because he had struck it down,' the 'it' referring to the house/dynasty of Jeroboam. It is one thing for Yahweh's word to come against Baasha for his own evil deeds and for aping Jeroboam, but some wonder why Yahweh should censure him for destroying Jeroboam's house when Yahweh himself had previously authorized that (cf. 15:29).[5] But the text is

---

meaning 'purge, remove.' Cf. DCH, 2:242-43. The verb is used in 14:10 in reference to the house of Jeroboam.

clear. The word of Yahweh condemned Baasha because he had eliminated Jeroboam's household. God judges him because he did what the word of God had predicted someone would do. Baasha was to blame. Where's the problem in that?

Let us trace the development of this matter in the text:

(1) 14:10-11
Yahweh's word through Ahijah: he will totally eliminate the house of Jeroboam
(2) 15:27, 29
Baasha carries out what Yahweh's word had predicted
(3) 16:7
Baasha is judged for having done so

Yahweh had declared he would annihilate Jeroboam's house (14:10-11) and Baasha wickedly (16:7) carried out (15:27, 29) what Yahweh had determined. So Baasha reveals that Yahweh's word is totally true and that he himself is a murderous power grubber. Is this a mystery? I suppose so. Is this a problem? I don't think so.

This conundrum is simply basic biblical theology. Listen to Jesus' solemn and sad lament in Mark 14:21: 'For the Son of man goes as it is written of him, but woe to that man by whom the Son of man is betrayed! It would have been better for that man if he had not been born' (RSV). Jesus' death is a matter of God's sovereign plan ('as it is written') assisted by man's wicked deed ('betrayed'), and this is terrifying ('It would have been better...').

---

[5] Some commentators (i.e., Montgomery and Gray) hold that the preposition and particle in this last clause may be taken concessively: '*even though* he had struck it down.' Hence Baasha receives a quasi-justification. But the previous use in this verse of the same preposition ('*al*) in a causal sense makes one expect its second occurrence to carry the same sense. Others (e.g., G. H. Jones) allege that verse 7 is a later addition from the agile pen of some shadowy but omnipresent deuteronomistic editor, who viewed Baasha's deed as sinful rather than as God's will per 15:29b, 30. Apparently the deuteronomistic theological mind was not supple enough to think both could be true.

Cranfield nicely explains when he writes that

> the delivering up of Jesus is not simply an act of Judas, but part of a bigger purpose than his – he is in fact being used for the fulfilment of God's purpose. Nevertheless, it is his act, and he is responsible.... The fact that God turns the wrath of man to his praise does not excuse the wrath of man.[6]

Or consider Yahweh's accusation of Babylon in Isaiah 47:6 (NIV):

> I was angry with my people
> and desecrated my inheritance;
> I gave them into your hand,
> and you showed them no mercy.
> Even on the aged
>   you laid a very heavy yoke.

Hence it will be curtains for Babylon (47:8-9). Yahweh, in judging his people, delivered them over to Babylon, who, by treating them with heartlessness and cruelty, placed herself under Yahweh's judgment. Yahweh brings judgment on the instruments who carry out his judgment; he will judge nations or individuals for the unjust manner in which they carry out his just judgment. You may inflict God's judgment and in so doing incur God's judgment. There is no automatic exemption.

We do not always think that way. William Sangster once passed on an amazing story from the first world war. It was 1918. A small Hull steamer named *The Flixton* was making its way up the English Channel. The look-out man spied a white line darting toward the ship. He knew it: a torpedo from a German submarine which, at that very moment, was surfacing to relish the disaster its missile would bring. The look-out gave a shout. Everyone ran to that side of the ship, but it was hopeless. It was too late to turn the vessel; in a matter of seconds they would be blown to bits. Then a strange thing happened. Within yards of its target,

---

[6] C. E. B. Cranfield, *The Gospel according to St. Mark*, Cambridge Greek Testament Commentary (Cambridge: CUP, 1966), 424. Ponder also Acts 2:23 on this matter.

something went wrong with the torpedo mechanism. It reared its nose above the water, abruptly turned in its course, and shot straight back on the path it had traversed. The hapless British seamen saw the torpedo slam the German sub and blow it to Davy Jones' locker.[7] I doubt the German crew had any idea that the havoc they had unleashed would ravage them.

That is the primary testimony of 1 Kings 16:7 – the instruments of Yahweh's judgment are subject to his judgment. We are probably more fascinated with the theological riddle: how is it that God uses evil men as his servants and yet judges these men for the evil they commit in fulfilling his designs? We do better, however, to tremble before the sobering clarity, for from Baasha and 1 Kings 16:7 it is but a step to Matthew 7:21-23, where the same principle is enunciated yet both more broadly and more pointedly. Jesus speaks of his judgment on his instruments. He says that those who have been used as his servants may find themselves shut out at the last. Like Baasha, you may knock off Jeroboam's house and be judged for it; or, like others, you could cast out demons in Jesus' name and end up spending eternity with them. A solemn matter.[8]

---

[7] In Robert J. Smithson, ed., *My Way of Preaching* (London: Pickering & Inglis, n.d.), 137-38.

[8] Our passage (15:25-16:7) is hardly the most buoyant and joyous of texts. Yet neither is it depressing or hopeless, because 15:29, 16:1, and 16:7 make it clear that the word of Yahweh controls and directs history. So it is not as though chaos reigns. Here is history falling out according to Yahweh's word, which always trumps evil.

Chapter 18

We Three Kings

1 Kings 16:8-28

This text has it all: carousing and conspiracy, assassination and civil strife – everything that gives the evening news its reason for existence. The northern kingdom appears to be careening down the waterslide of history, bashing along to its own self-destruction when, suddenly, it levels out on the hill of Samaria and enjoys a bit of stability under Omri's reign. Kings have their own interests. One prefers to drink himself silly (v. 9); another practices treachery and commits spectacular suicide (vv. 10, 18); another struggles for dominance and builds himself a new capital (vv. 22, 24). Yet they have something in common: each of these politicians stands under divine judgment.

The map of the passage falls into four segments:

Elah's reign, vv. 8-14
Zimri's reign, vv. 15-20
Political limbo, vv. 21-22
Omri's reign, vv. 23-28[1]

We couch our exposition in terms of what the word of God would say to these kings – and to us.

How Stupid Your Diversions Are (Elah, vv. 8-14)
Elah's two years (v. 8) may have been no more than a few months (parts of years being counted as wholes). Baasha's dynasty bit the dust in Elah's assassination:

---

[1] Should you want approximate dates for these kings: Elah, 886-885 BC; Zimri, 885 BC; and Omri, 885-874 BC. Omri reigned twelve years (vv. 15-16, 29) but he took three or four of those to put down Tibni (v. 23).

Zimri, one of his officers, captain of half his chariotry, plotted against him. While he was in Tirzah, drinking himself senseless in the house of Arza who was master of the palace in Tirzah, Zimri came in, struck him down and killed him... (vv. 9-10a, NJB).

The text doesn't answer all our questions. Was Zimri on duty nearer Tirzah rather than with the army down at Gibbethon (vv. 15-16)? Apparently. Was Arza in on the plot? Who knows? But, clearly, Elah has one passion – turning himself into a besotted fruitcake. Now the text is not a temperance tract; it is not suggesting that Elah should've been a teetotaler. But doesn't the text sigh with disappointment? Is this what leadership in the kingdom ought to be about? Isn't it a disgrace when the king's preoccupation consists of drinking himself under the table? Is this the legacy a ruler should leave? 'Elah? Oh sure, I remember him – he could really party!' I think in verse 9 the writer wants you to see King Elah in all his asininity.

Charles XII was king of Sweden, absolute monarch. He was cold, arrogant, and violent, an avid participant in all physical exercises and activities that were both demanding and dangerous. In 1698, when Charles was about sixteen, his cousin Frederick IV, Duke of Holstein-Gottorp, arrived in Stockholm to marry Charles' older sister. For five months the Duke and Charles with their lackeys went on a binge of wild behavior. They raced their horses until the beasts, foaming, collapsed to the ground; they smashed palace windows with pistol balls and hurled tables and chairs down into the palace courtyard; during dinner, they threw cherry pits in the faces of the king's ministers and knocked dishes out of the servants' hands; they would gallop through the streets, waving swords and jerking hats and wigs from the heads of those they could reach. Once, the king led his marauders on horseback into a room where his grandmother was playing cards – she promptly collapsed from fright. So one Sunday during this melee three Stockholm clergy all preached sermons on the same text, 'Woe to you, O land, when your king is a child' (Ecc. 10:16)! This criticism deeply affected Charles and apparently worked a decided change in his demeanor.[2]

Elah could have used that whole Stockholm text:

Woe to you, O land, when your king is a child,
and your princes feast in the morning!
Happy are you, O land, when your king
   is the son of free men,
and your princes feast at the proper time,
   for strength and not for drunkenness
     (Ecc. 10:16-17, RSV).

Whether a king gets crocked like Elah or plays juvenile delinquent like Charles, it is in any case a perversion of his calling as a magistrate under God. The potential damage is greater when a ruler turns diversions into occupations, but, sadly, it is not merely a royal malady. The epitaph has already been earned, for example, by any number of professing Christian men who populate our evangelical churches. How would one of their lives be summed up? 'He really loved his football! Why, he wouldn't leave that tube for anything while....' We have men in our churches who can name all the linebackers on the New York Jets but have never taught the catechism to their children. How stupid our diversions are! How easily we corrupt our calling. Better not get too self-righteous when you see Elah slobbering in his wine.

How Fleeting Your Success Is (Zimri, vv. 15-20)

Zimri was ruthless and efficient. When he cut down tipsy Elah (vv. 9-10), he wasted no time in obliterating Baasha's whole household, whether relatives or friends (v. 11).[3] Zimri reigned from Tirzah, six miles northeast of Shechem (v. 15), while the army was assaulting Gibbethon (v. 15b; see 15:27), a good way to the southwest in the Philistine sphere of influence. Zimri was a military man (v. 9) but was not with the army at Camp Gibbethon. The field army there was pro-Omri. Zimri learned to his chagrin that one dare not carry out a coup without the army's support. When news of Zimri's deed reached Gibbethon the army felt that

---

   [2] See, for this account, Robert K. Massie, *Peter the Great: His Life and World* (New York: Ballantine Books, 1981), 326-29.

   [3] The language of verse 11 parallels that of 14:10, on which see chapter 15, fn. 3. Zimri's lineage ('son of...') is not given; hence he may have been a commoner.

one coup deserved another and so proclaimed Omri king (v. 16). They then marched on Zimri and Tirzah and took the outer city (vv. 17-18a). Zimri went into the inner bastion of the king's house and burnt it and himself in one blaze of despair (v. 18b).

There are two arresting statements in this Zimri section. The first is in verse 15b: 'Zimri reigned seven days in Tirzah.' What temporary tenure! The second is in verse 19, which supplies the reason for Zimri's demise: 'because of his sins which he sinned, to do what was evil in Yahweh's eyes, to walk in the way of Jeroboam and in his sin....' He reigned seven days and made no change of policy. We, of course, would lighten up. What's seven days more of Jeroboamism? But Yahweh seems to regard this perversion as so culpable that he judges a man for not making a change within a seven days' reign! Seven days is a brief time; seven days is a responsible time.[4] It's long enough to show your colors.

'Zimri reigned seven days in Tirzah' (v. 15b). What a haunting line! He scarcely had time to wash Elah's blood off his hands before he himself became toast. Is Zimri not a paradigm of how vacuous our highest successes can be?

General Ritter von Greim had been summoned to the Chancellery in Berlin. It was April 28, 1945. When von Greim

---

[4] Some commentators can't believe the import of verse 19. G. H. Jones, for example, objects that 'the statement that he walked in the way of Jeroboam ... is hardly appropriate for such a short reign, and must be taken as a later addition' (*1 and 2 Kings*, New Century Bible Commentary, 2 vols. [Grand Rapids: Eerdmans, 1984], 1:294). Jones' comment seems a kind way of saying that no writer in his right mind would have said what verse 19 says of Zimri; hence the verse must come from a later editor who was not as discerning as we are. But what if the writer was aware of the apparent anomaly? What if he deliberately placed verse 19 in order to make us think? If in Israel a king regularly issued a *mešārum*-edict upon his accession indicating what form of tradition he would maintain, Zimri may have indicated that he intended to continue the time-honored religious policy of Jeroboam. On the *mešārum*-edict, see D. J. Wiseman, 'Books in the Ancient World,' *The Cambridge History of the Bible*, 3 vols. (Cambridge: CUP, 1970), 1:43-44, and his article, 'Law and Order in the Old Testament,' *Vox Evangelica* 8 (1973): 11-12; cf. also Hannes Olivier, NIDOTTE, 2:563-64. However, we cannot be sure of this specific suggestion.

arrived Hitler immediately made him a field marshall; he would replace the 'traitorous' Hermann Goering as head of the Luftwaffe.[5] Of course, the Luftwaffe no longer existed and in two days Hitler would put a pistol in his own mouth and pull the trigger. There's a kind of absurdity about holding advanced rank in a non-government. At least von Greim knew it at the time. It took Zimri seven days to discover his status was worthless. And we are sometimes slower to learn how flimsy our monuments are (cf. Ps. 39:6). Zimri's ashes assure us that our finest hours are momentary. Zimri, the 'week' king.

How Trivial Your Pursuits Are (Omri, vv. 21-28)

Zimri's cremation did not clear up Israel's political dilemma. The people were divided, some devoted to Omri and some to Tibni son of Ginath (v. 21). Tibni may have had more social clout than Omri (note his patronym, 'son of Ginath'), but the truth is we simply know next to nothing about them. Political limbo went on for about four years (compare vv. 15 and 23) with Omri's partisans gathering strength (v. 22a); then we read that marvelously laconic statement, 'So Tibni died and Omri became king' (v. 22b, NIV). Was Tibni knocked off? Or did pneumonia or a ruptured appendix get him? We have no certainty either way – only that Tibni has his funeral and Omri his coronation.

Now the official entry about Omri consists of six verses (vv. 23-28). He reigned for twelve years (v. 23). Omri is no hapless boozer like Elah and no flash in the week like Zimri; he establishes a bona fide kingdom and instigates a stable regime. However, our writer gives Omri only six verses of 'press' and *almost all of that consists of the usual formulas* used in such entries. Only one verse highlights anything distinctive about Omri: verse 24 reports his purchase, building, and naming of Samaria, his new capital. Omri built Samaria and did evil. Any questions? Are you beginning to get the picture?

Actually, Omri left his mark on the history of the day. As verse 24 says, he bought Shemer's hill, built and fortified it, and handed

---

[5] Cornelius Ryan, *The Last Battle* (New York: Simon and Schuster, 1966), 482-83.

Israel a new capital. Located twelve miles west of Tirzah and seven northwest of Shechem, Samaria sat on a hill three hundred feet high with a sweeping view of the plain below, invulnerable except to siege. So Omri probably did it for defense; and for economics, since Samaria commanded the trade routes through the Plain of Esdraelon; and for propaganda – he may have wanted Israel to break with the past few years and get a fresh start with a regime that was going somewhere. We also know from King Mesha's admission on the Moabite Stone that Omri threw his military weight around in northern Moab (he 'humbled Moab many years'). Diplomatically, Omri probably engineered an alliance with the Phoenicians, by marrying his son Ahab to Jezebel daughter of Ethbaal (see 16:31). Omri knew Phoenicia spelled commerce and that meant a bull market in Israel. Politically, Omri left a legacy – for the next hundred years the Assyrians would refer to Israel as the 'house of Omri'.[6] Omri was a king on the make. He was an achiever. He made things happen. Omri was something of a military, cultural, commercial, and political powerhouse.

You can imagine, therefore, how the events of verse 24 would have been handled. The camera crew from 'Good Morning, Israel' would have caught up with Omri on his preliminary inspection tour and the anchor man from the network studio inquires just what it was that inspired the king to make this brilliant move in changing capitals. After a passing comment on military preparedness Omri makes extended remarks about the need to break with the past, of how the city will serve as a symbol of a new era, of how Israel must free herself from the tyranny of nostalgia and press on into hope. Of course, a premier female reporter sits with Shemer on the roof-deck of his home, asking him how he felt about selling the hill to Omri. A fawning press would provide Omri with a proper media event.

But that is not the emphasis of the Bible. Our writer is not overly impressed with the great Omri. Omri bought the hill and

---

[6] For lucid summaries on these matters see Walter C. Kaiser, Jr., *A History of Israel from the Bronze Age through the Jewish Wars* (Nashville: Broadman & Holman, 1998), 323-26; and Merrill F. Unger, *Israel and the Aramaeans of Damascus* (1957; reprint ed., Grand Rapids: Baker, 1980), 62-64.

Omri did evil. Here is a king who packs significant historical weight and the Bible assumes practically the whole story can be told in the usual formulas. He reigned, he did evil, he was buried. You want to know more? Go to the local library and punch in 'royalchronicles.com' (v. 27). The Bible's account is as scintillating as an obituary. And with good reason: Omri did evil; he was more evil than all who preceded him; he walked in the way of Jeroboam. You've heard it all before. The writer is not saying he is ignorant of Omri's achievements – he is saying they don't matter. The Bible does not call Omri's pursuits stupid, like Elah and his orgy; nor are they fleeting, like Zimri's rise, for Omri institutes a substantial regime; but they are inconsequential. When the first two commandments (=Exod. 20:3-6) are despised nothing else counts.

Isn't this a sobering text? Isn't this what Jesus is teaching us, but in a different mode, in Matthew 13:44-46? Are there, among the preoccupations of your life, any that are not ultimately trivial? Do the passions that drive your living and doing only elicit a yawn from heaven?

How Solemn Your Responsibility Is (vv. 12-13, 19, 25-26)
One almost surmises from reading this whole passage that Israel has determined to self-destruct. From verses 8-22 we meet nothing but chaos, conspiracy, and disorder. Even after Zimri has turned to ashes there is no resolution. Tibni and Omri vie for leadership and civil schizophrenia must have plagued the land. No one seems to be in control. But 1-2 Kings knows better. This is where its doctrine of the word of God is so crucial. Contrary to the rag-tag appearance of history the word of God rules. History even in this apostasy-ridden domain is not merely one disaster after another. No, the word of God controls history. How do you explain Zimri's ghastly blood bath, not only his assassinating Elah (vv. 9-10) but exterminating Baasha's whole male line (vv. 11-12a)? Zimri deluged Tirzah with blood and gore. Yes, it was 'in line with the word of Yahweh which he spoke against Baasha by the hand of Jehu the prophet, because of all the sins of Baasha and the sins of Elah his son...' (vv. 12b-13). The Lord had spoken through Jehu

(16:1-4); now he fulfilled that word through Zimri. Mystery indeed (see our discussions in the previous chapter), but clarity too: Yahweh's decree not Zimri's glands directs history.

But the word of God not only rules and controls history but also defines sin and condemns those who persist in it. This is so obvious that we easily miss it. What was the sin of Zimri? 'To walk in the way of Jeroboam and in his sin' (v. 19). Omri reached new depths of evil (v. 25b) but remained in the same genre: 'He walked in all the way of Jeroboam son of Nebat and in his sins which he caused Israel to sin, to exasperate Yahweh, the God of Israel, with their worthless idols' (v. 26; this last clause also in v. 13). The sins of Baasha and Elah, of Zimri and Omri seem to be their goose-stepping to Jeroboam's faith with its 'worthless idols'. As noted previously, these were violations of the first and second commandments (Exod. 20:3-6) and by practicing them it was as if Israel was trying to exasperate Yahweh (vv. 13, 26).

The word I have here translated 'exasperate' is *kā'as*, often rendered 'provoke' in standard translations.[7] It is the verb used in 1 Samuel 1:6-7 where it depicts Peninnah's needling, goading, and irritating of Hannah because of Hannah's inability to have children. She was trying to exasperate Hannah, to push her over the edge. That's what we do, our writer implies, when we defy the first and second commandments – we will exasperate and infuriate Yahweh, so that he will pour out his wrath upon us. We push him beyond the edge of his patience.

Now why should our writer repeat this matter unless he was trying to get the attention of his own generation, the Israelites who had been battered by Babylon and were languishing in exile (see 2 Kings 24, 25) because by repeated idolatry they had thumbed their noses at Yahweh's commandments? Could Israel in 560 BC not see where false worship had led her? Could she not see her responsibility to repent, i.e., to worship only Yahweh and to do so in the way Yahweh prescribes, if she were to be restored? Is not the rehearsal of Elah, Zimri, and Omri's reigns a solemn call for Israel to repudiate the bastard religion to which these kings clung?

---

[7] This discussion parallels my similar remarks in chapter 15 above, on 14:1-20.

Yet it can be most difficult for us to take this text seriously. It is, after all, so foreign to our western culture. Our culture seems to view politics as the main scene and religion, though nice, as tangential and, in any case, governed by the pluralistic expectations of democratic society. Our culture, for the life of it, cannot understand how a deity could be upset over varied religious preferences. How could there be a God who could possibly get exasperated over anything, let alone idolatry? Why should any god care that much? We may not buy our culture's judgment, but we may have imbibed enough of its attitude, so that we find it hard to hear this text in all its frightfulness.

And sometimes advanced levels of Bible study can suck the seriousness out of a text like this. Commentaries frequently dub theologically evaluative texts in Kings (i.e., texts that speak of doing evil, walking in the way of Jeroboam, and exasperating Yahweh) as 'deuteronomistic.' That is, such texts are the work or insertion of one of this conjectured group of editors who were always tinkering with the text of Deuteronomy through 2 Kings. You see what happens then? You label verses 13 and 26 'deuteronomistic' and you immediately tame it. You are saying, in effect, that these sentiments are something dear to the heart of these editors and this is their position that is reflected here. The text then is a *human opinion*. The idea is that these deuteronomistic editors had their special concerns, their pet biases, and you cannot blame them for inserting them throughout. But, of course, we are wise to how they thought about things and so when we see their editorializing we can label it as such and need never consider it as a word from God. In the text Yahweh is warning you that your idolatry is pushing him beyond the limits of his patience; but you can read it and say, 'You can't fool me; that's a deuteronomistic idea; I may or may not agree with it.'[8]

I recently read of a murder trial in Jefferson County (Louisville), Kentucky, circuit court. The defendant, 28, was accused of killing

---

[8] Critics would accuse me of being too simplistic here; they would say their position does not necessarily demote the text as the word of God. Perhaps not necessarily, but certainly predominantly. I know. I've read their commentaries.

his girlfriend the previous May. The jury of five men and seven women deliberated for nine hours over two days but was unable to decide on a verdict. What to do? They flipped a coin to decide. The defendant lost. They found him guilty. When the judge heard how the jury had reached its verdict he declared a mistrial. I don't know – maybe the fellow was guilty. But the jury not only used the wrong procedure but had the wrong attitude: 'It's not that serious; it doesn't really matter; let's flip for it.' So don't trivialize the warning of the text. If you are goading Yahweh beyond the limits of his patience you may discover that weeping and gnashing of teeth is not a metaphor.

Chapter 19

Antichrist Casts His Shadow

1 Kings 16:29–17:1

They didn't expect to be shocked out of their boots that morning of September 5, 1698. They'd heard the Tsar had returned. Peter the Great had been on an eighteen month excursion to western Europe to learn how to build ships and to sample other technological achievements. Word went round Moscow that Peter was back and so boyars and cronies came flocking to welcome him. After a barrage of embraces Peter suddenly brandished a long, sharp barber's razor and himself proceeded to hack off the beards of the gathered groupies. (One didn't usually resist Peter's imposing six-foot, seven-inch bulk). One after the other was required to submit until the whole company was beardless with chins and jaws naked and bare of their masses of hair for the first time since puberty. It constituted a social earthquake – some held shaving to be a mortal sin. But Peter had been to the west. He'd become convinced that such tradition and mores were holding Russia back and making her the object of ridicule. So Peter decided to make a statement, as we say. The close shave was a clear sign: with Peter Russia was entering a whole new era.[1]

That is how the Bible regards Ahab's reign (ca. 874-852 BC) over Israel. It was a new departure, a definite turn in the road. One suspects Ahab's importance from the fact that in a very selective narrative he receives six chapters of press (from here to nearly the end of 1 Kings). Ahab's regime had its own distinctive flavor; it was unique. But not in a good way – it looked like Antichrist had arrived ahead of time.

This brief passage should, I think, be considered by itself, so

---

[1] Robert K. Massie, *Peter the Great: His Life and World* (New York: Ballantine Books, 1980), 243-45.

we can grasp what a singular danger Ahab's tenure posed for Israel. The message of the text may be summarized in two propositions.

The Days Are Evil (16:29-34)

They didn't seem so evil – not if you were a politician or economic advisor. Ahab did, after all, reign 'over Israel in Samaria for twenty-two years' (v. 29). That spells stability – no coups, no wild Zimri-types sharpening their assassination skills (cf. 16:9-10). And then there was this marriage alliance: Ahab had married the Phoenician princess Jezebel (v. 31). Perhaps Omri had engineered this masterstroke. No matter. Israelite goods now had access to world ports via Phoenician seamanship. The alliance profited both countries. The economy was booming. Who can argue with prosperity? What could be very wrong when every merchant seemed to have a laptop computer in his bag and a cell phone clipped to his belt?

But the text holds a prophetic rather than a political view. It avers that Ahab was uniquely evil: 'Ahab son of Omri did what was evil in Yahweh's eyes more than all who were before him' (v. 30). Omri, Ahab's father, had just been rated the acme of evil to date (v. 25), but suddenly the award is wrenched from him and handed to Ahab, who apparently excelled his father in that category. The writer emphatically repeats his estimate in verse 33b: 'So Ahab did more to exasperate Yahweh God of Israel than all the kings of Israel who had been before him.' What did Ahab do to merit this distinction?

> Now it happened – was his walking in the sins of Jeroboam son of Nebat a trivial matter? – that he took as wife Jezebel, daughter of Ethbaal, king of the Sidonians, and he went and served Baal and worshiped him. And he erected an altar for Baal [in] the temple of Baal which he built in Samaria; and Ahab made an Asherah [image] (vv. 31-33a).

Baal worship – that's what engraved Ahab's name in first place on the monument of apostasy. The text fairly bounces on Baal. We meet the term first in the name of Jezebel's father,

Ethbaal,[2] and then, staccato-like, we are told of Ahab's worship of Baal, altar to Baal, and house of Baal. The text clearly assesses Ahab's Baalism as more deplorable than Jeroboam's bull worship. By comparison, Jeroboam's was a pastel evil, Ahab's a darker, deeper hue. Jeroboam's state cult is like drinking polluted water; Ahab's imported paganism is like sucking raw sewage. Neither is good, but one is worse than the other. Some debate whether this Baal is to be identified with the Tyrian deity Melqart or is the same presupposed in the rest of the Old Testament.[3] Does it matter? Either way we'll be right back at Judges 2:11-13 with Israel worshiping hormones.

Baal worship is lethal on any account but all the more so when it comes packaged with its own passionate in-house evangelist. Jezebel was not content to practice her foreign superstition privately within the confines of her palace chapel. No, she practiced 'world-view Baalism'. She came to Israel with her own horde of Baal enthusiasts, skilled in fertility theology and enjoying the free board at the royal cafeteria (18:19). Jezebel wore the pants in the kingdom (21:25) and that meant butchering Yahweh's prophets (18:4, 13) and squashing Yahweh loyalists under a scam of justice (21:7-15). It may have been Jezebel's orders – perhaps via the zeal of some fawning Israelite converts – that mandated the smashing of kosher Yahweh worship centers (18:30; 19:10, 14). Not that Ahab was totally passive; he himself hated prophetic criticism and was not above oppressing Yahweh's prophets (22:8, 26-27). But Jezebel was the driving force, the avid propagandist, determined to establish a bridgehead for the faith of her fathers in Israel. She hadn't an ecumenical bone in her body. She made Baalism doubly deadly.

So far, of course, our writer has given us a summary of Ahab's reign and the excessive evil that marked it. But before he leaves

---

[2] According to the later Jewish historian Josephus, Ethbaal was a priest of Astarte and gained the throne by assassinating the previous king (cf. *Antiquities* 8.13.2; *Against Apion* 1.18); Pauline A. Viviano, 'Ethbaal,' ABD, 2:645.

[3] Though many suggest the Melqart connection, note the arguments of John Day, 'Baal (Deity),' ABD, 1:548.

his general 'Ahab introduction' he appends in verse 34 a sample
of how things were during Ahab's time:

> In his days Hiel the Bethelite (re)built Jericho; at the cost of Abiram
> his firstborn he laid the foundation, and at the cost of Segub his
> youngest he set up its doors, in line with the word of Yahweh which
> he spoke by the hand of Joshua son of Nun.[4]

This is not a piece of unrelated trivia about construction work.
The writer includes it as what was characteristic of Ahab's reign.
The opening phrase, 'in his [Ahab's] days,' implies that Hiel did
not undertake this project on his private initiative but under Ahab's
direction.[5] To 'build' (*bānāh*) here means to 'rebuild' or 'fortify'
as in 15:17. After the destruction of Jericho Joshua had pronounced
a curse upon anyone who would rebuild Jericho (Josh. 6:26), the
curse to which our writer refers in the last half of this verse. The
curse did not prohibit folks from living on the site, for there seem
to have been post-conquest settlements there (cf. Josh. 18:21; Judg.
3:13; 2 Sam. 10:5). The curse was on anyone who dared to rebuild
Jericho as a fortress.

After the division of the kingdom (931 BC) Jericho apparently
came under the aegis of the northern kingdom. It was a strategic
site, standing at the southeast corner of that part of Israel's territory
that lay west of the Jordan. Ahab may have wanted it fortified
both as a defensive measure and as an outpost for keeping Moab
under control. But what regime would ever want to defy Joshua's
curse? Ahab's. He told the Defense Department to give the contract
to Hiel of Bethel. Hiel repaired the foundation; his firstborn Abiram
died. He finished off the project, installing the doors of the gates;
then he made arrangements for the funeral of Segub, his youngest.[6]

---

[4] My 'at the cost of' phrases take the preposition *bĕ* as indicating price
or exchange; see Ronald J. Williams, *Hebrew Syntax: An Outline*, 2nd ed.
(Toronto: University of Toronto, 1976), sect. 246.

[5] Cf. Johannes Fichtner, *Das erste Buch von den Königen*, Die Botschaft
des Alten Testaments, 2nd ed. (Stuttgart: Calwer, 1979), 247.

[6] I do not think these deaths were foundation sacrifices of infants (as do
Simon De Vries and Paul House); they were deaths of sons, however old,
inflicted by Yahweh as acts of judgment.

The text is telling you that *open defiance of Yahweh's word* typified Ahab's regime. Our writer makes this clear in that he does not merely say Hiel's sons died in accord with Joshua's curse; rather, he explicitly says it was 'in line with the word of Yahweh which he spoke by the hand of Joshua.' Was Jericho fortified? Oh yes – a monument to Ahab's defense strategy. But there were other monuments. Walk outside Bethel to Hiel's family burial plot and see the graves of Abiram and Segub, monuments to Yahweh's certain judgment. But that was the reign of Ahab – folks thought nothing of flying in the teeth of Yahweh's word.[7]

In verse 34 then the writer says, 'There, that is symptomatic of Ahab's time; that typifies the mood, gives you the flavor of that era.' J. Barton Payne ran into one of these 'symptomatic' events when he began his seminary training in 1942. He had enrolled in a seminary on the US west coast. In his first Old Testament class he was shocked when the professor led the class out to the parking lot, tossed his Bible down on the pavement, put his car jack on top of the Bible, and then jacked up his car on top of it![8] It was a symbolic episode, intended to dramatize for nascent theologs that the Bible should receive no more reverence than any other book. In fact, it likely typified the attitude taken to the Bible by that seminary. In the same way verse 34 says, 'This is the age of Ahab – when the word of God doesn't count.'

Now what good is all this evil? What possible benefit can there be in letting the Bible (or its commentator) pound into us how Ahab took the prize for excessive evil and gross godlessness? For one thing, this text *sobers us with its realism.* How often God's people assess their times, find they are facing cultural decadence, vanishing standards, godless governments, and spiritual compromise, and deduce that things can't get any worse. And our text says (helpfully, I think), 'Oh yes, they can!' Evil is capable of exponential 'progress.' You may have been scrapping against a

---

[7] For a very helpful theological exposition of 16:34, see M. B. Van't Veer, *My God Is Yahweh* (St. Catharines, Ont.: Paideia, 1980), 9-26.

[8] Philip Barton Payne, 'J. Barton Payne,' *Bible Interpreters of the Twentieth Century*, ed. Walter A. Elwell and J. D. Weaver (Grand Rapids: Baker, 1999), 345.

Jeroboam level of godlessness and then find yourself warring against an Ahab level. There may be times when you think Antichrist has moved on to your front porch. Again, this passage *sustains us with its hope.* How is there hope here? Because here is Yahweh's word describing the excruciating times through which Yahweh's people must live, which simply means that Yahweh always knows the peculiar circumstances his people are facing. He knows when the heat is turned up. Is this not the testimony of Revelation 2:13? Surely waves of comfort must have washed over the believers at Pergamum when they heard Jesus' words: 'I know where you dwell – where Satan's throne is.'[9] The days are evil, the Lord says. And because he says this we know that he knows exactly what we are facing. 'I know where you dwell.'

The Defense Is Ready (17:1)

Sometimes when we have dinner guests in our home, my wife, exercising – I admit – her prerogative as hostess, will inquire at the conclusion of the main course whether our guests would prefer to have dessert immediately or adjourn to visit and come back for dessert later. This pleasantry always disturbs me, and I always cast my vote for plunging right into dessert and seek to persuade the guests, who feign their expected neutrality, to declare themselves my allies. What abysmal nonsense it is to enjoy a perfectly fine meal and then declare a truce when you're getting to the best part! This scenario applies to the ways we frequently read our Bibles. We come to the end of a chapter and assume there must be a break, forgetting that on more than a few occasions chapter divisions obscure rather than assist interpretation. Hence, as with dessert, we must school ourselves to plunge right on into the next chapter lest we find ourselves missing an important connection. The end of 1 Kings 16 is a case in point. You must deny that yawning gulf of several blank centimeters between chapters and rush right into 1 Kings 17:1, for it belongs with 16:29-34.

---

[9] Pergamum was the premier center for emperor worship in Asia and also sported an altar to Zeus (40 feet high) on its acropolis. 'Satan's throne' may allude to either of these; cf. ISBE, 3:768.

If we do this, 17:1 is striking. We are impressed with *the suddenness of Elijah's appearance.* Everything seemed to be capitulating to Baal (16:31-33a) when suddenly we are staring at a prophet whose confession of faith is his name: 'My God is Yahweh' (=Elijah). We are not used to this. Even in the Bible we expect a bit of a warm-up, a far more deliberate approach. In KJV or RSV style we would expect to read, 'Now, behold, there was a man who lived in Gilead, a prophet, Elijah the Tishbite by name, the son of so-and-so, and it came about when Ahab had begun worshiping Baal that the word of the Lord came to him, saying, "Arise, go to Samaria and say to Ahab...."' And so on for several more lines. Instead we have 17:1 ...

> Then Elijah the Tishbite from the sojourners in Gilead said to Ahab, 'By the life of Yahweh the God of Israel before whom I stand, there will not be dew nor rain these years except by my word.'[10]

Awfully abrupt. No introduction. Hardly a snatch from his *curriculum vitae.* We've never heard of him before and now he is just – there. We know nothing about him. Where did he go to seminary? Does he have a wife and children? Is he a sports fan? What hobbies does he enjoy? Does he like being a prophet? All the inane queries North Americans at least are dying to know. We don't even know where Elijah met Ahab.[11] As so often in the Bible, details are suppressed because the message is supremely important.

We will return to Elijah's sudden appearance momentarily, but we need to give some attention to *the significance of Elijah's message.* The message is simple: 'There will not be dew nor rain these years except by my word' – uttered within a solemn oath formula.

Elijah is saying that Yahweh is going to inflict the covenant curses upon Israel for her covenant-breaking. Moses had warned

---

[10] Some translate 'the Tishbite from Tishbi in Gilead.' The text is tough. Note that Elijah swears by 'Yahweh the God of Israel'; the writer used the same terminology in 16:33; hence the very same God Ahab provoked is now announcing judgment on him and his land.

[11] Fichtner, *Das erste Buch von den Königen*, 252.

that if Israel worshiped other gods, Yahweh would, among other things, 'shut up the heavens so that there will be no rain and the ground will not yield its fruit' (Deut. 11:16, 17, NASB; see also Deut. 28:23-24). Moreover, Elijah announces the curfew on dew and rain ahead of time. Such a 'predictive prophecy' cuts the ground from under excuse-makers and other secularists. The ongoing absence of moisture couldn't be interpreted as a 'bad break' or an impenetrable mystery because Elijah had already announced it as Yahweh's deed to Ahab.[12] No doubt then about the hermeneutics of dearth.[13]

The rain delay will also strike a blow at the alleged prowess of Baal. However one cuts it Baal was a fertility god, a storm god, who, among other life-giving activities, sent rain to fructify the earth. In Canaanite mythology Lady Asherah thanked El for permitting Baal to have his own palace since

Now Baal will begin the rainy season,
the season of wadis in flood;
and he will sound his voice in the clouds,
flash his lightning to the earth.[14]

Such meteorological displays were signs of Baal's vitality. Elijah's 'no dew or rain' then constitutes a challenge to Baal. Ahab and Israel will now be able to see what sort of fertility god Baal is. If he cannot produce in the area of his expertise, in his specialty, his reputation will suffer a shattering blow. Baal's deity will shrivel as the cracks in the fields get wider. Elijah so much as says that Yahweh has decided to shut Baal's faucet off. Yahweh has decreed that Baal will pale.

Now I want to come back to the point about Elijah's sudden appearance, for it is there that we grasp *the encouragement in*

---

[12] See M. B. Van't Veer, *My God Is Yahweh*, 51.

[13] On dew and rain, see Mark D. Futato, NIDOTTE, 1:900-902 (on *gešem*) and 2:363-64 (on *ṭal*). See also Frank S. Frick, 'Palestine, Climate of,' ABD, 5:122-25. Dew (*ṭal*) encompasses what we call dew as well as light rain or drizzle. During the dry season (May-September) the heavy dews are vital.

[14] Michael David Coogan, ed./trans., *Stories from Ancient Canaan* (Philadelphia: Westminster, 1978), 101.

Elijah's intervention. Let me come at this point via the back door.

In 1865, near the end of the War between the States, the Federal and Confederate lines were strung out for some miles south and southwest of Petersburg, Virginia. George Pickett had moved against troops on the Federal left, his men inflicting 1,800 casualties. Pickett had then withdrawn to a location called Five Forks, apparently to General Robert E. Lee's chagrin. He was told to hold Five Forks at all hazards (since it protected Confederate railroad transport). General Pickett was confident that his attack the previous day had shocked Union troops sufficiently to make them delay any attack upon his position. He did, however, place his men in proper defensive position and had no doubt he could maintain his place even if Phil Sheridan did attack. He received an invitation to dinner from one of his colleagues who had been lucky catching shad in the Nottoway River. So Pickett, along with cavalry commander Fitzhugh Lee, eagerly accepted and went behind lines. They didn't tell anyone where they were going – why divide delicious fish too many ways? So when Sheridan attacked – and attack he did – no one knew where to find either Pickett or Fitzhugh Lee. They were absent three hours at a shad bake. When Pickett returned to his division half its members had been shot or captured.[15]

Now I think that is the scenario we often subconsciously envision as kingdom servants. A fresh crisis erupts somewhere for the people of God and we are decimated because proper vigilance was lacking. We were left to fend for ourselves. But that is not the picture 1 Kings 17:1 gives in context. One can hardly improve on the way Ronald Wallace puts it:

> For to see him [Elijah] appear thus [i.e., so suddenly] reminds us that we need not despair when we see great movements of evil achieving spectacular success on this earth, for we may be sure that God, in unexpected places, has already secretly prepared His counter-movement. God has always His ways of working underground to undermine the stability of evil. God can raise men for His service

---

[15] Shelby Foote, *The Civil War: A Narrative,* vol. 3, *Red River to Appomattox* (New York: Vintage Books, 1986), 870.

from nowhere.... Therefore the situation is never hopeless where God is concerned. Whenever evil flourishes, it is always a superficial flourish, for at the height of the triumph of evil God will be there, ready with His man and His movement and His plans to ensure that His own cause will never fail.[16]

I think Wallace has his finger on the pulse of this text in its context. The government is pumping raw paganism into Israel and it looks like Baalism will win the day and extinguish Yahweh's remnant. 'Then Elijah ... said to Ahab....' Yes, 'we may be sure that God ... has already secretly prepared His counter-movement.' Satan's throne has been installed in Samaria, but 'at the height of the triumph of evil God will be there, ready with His man.' Doesn't it put iron in your bones and steel in your guts to see that, whatever threat arises, with Yahweh the defense is always ready?[17]

---

[16] *Elijah and Elisha* (Grand Rapids: Eerdmans, 1957), 3.

[17] I call attention to Alexander Maclaren's encouraging exposition of 'As Yahweh ... lives before whom I stand'; one may find it in his *Expositions of Holy Scripture*, vol. 2 of the Baker reprint edition, part 2, pp. 240-44.

Chapter 20

The Beginning of a God War

1 Kings 17:2-16

Late in 1863, during the War between the States, two children were sitting on the rug in front of the fire in the White House. One was showing photographs to the other for the evening's entertainment. Tad Lincoln proudly held up a picture of his father for his little cousin Katherine Helm and declared, 'This is the President.' Katherine shook her head in trenchant denial: 'No, that is not the President, Mr. Davis is President.' Tad, in something of an outrage, shouted, 'Hurrah for Abe Lincoln,' to which his cousin retorted, 'Hurrah for Jeff Davis.'[1] Katherine was from Kentucky; she knew Abe Lincoln was her uncle but was just as sure he was *not* her President! And that is pretty much the situation in Israel in 1 Kings 17. Avant-garde evangelists were crying 'Baal is god,' while the orthodox kept insisting 'Yahweh is God.' We have the beginning of a God war.

I will not center this exposition upon any single theme; rather I intend to discuss the primary teaching points of the passage.

The Absence of Yahweh's Word (vv. 2-3)
Not that there isn't a main theme in this chapter. That theme is the word of Yahweh. Elijah hints at this in verse 1, when he warns of 'no dew nor rain except at my word.' But since he 'stands before' Yahweh, Elijah's word will surely be nothing other than Yahweh's word. The 'word of Yahweh' (v. 2) directs Elijah's itinerary (vv. 2-4), while Elijah himself obediently conforms to this word (v. 5). Under changed circumstances the word of Yahweh (v. 7) orders Elijah's next move (vv. 8-9) and also provides the reassurance (v. 14) to encourage a hopeless widow to gamble her whole livelihood

---

[1] Ruth Painter Randall, *Mary Lincoln: Biography of a Marriage* (Boston: Little, Brown and Co., 1953), 300.

(v. 13), so that she daily discovers Yahweh's word is as good as Elijah's prediction (v. 16). Yahweh's word (v. 24) even proves reliable in the face of gut-wrenching loss (vv. 17ff.). The word of Yahweh is the theme that pervades and binds the chapter together. Let us allow that fact to lie in state momentarily.

Yahweh's word was clear to Elijah if not to us:

> Go from here, and you shall turn yourself eastward, and you shall hide yourself by the wadi Cherith, which is near the Jordan (v. 3).[2]

Why, however, was Elijah to hide himself? Most expositors assume the answer is obvious. If the queen was butchering Yahweh's prophets (18:4) and if Ahab had a quasi-international search warrant out on Elijah (18:10), why even raise the question? Clearly, this was Yahweh's witness protection programme designed to secure Elijah from Ahab's malice. That may be the partial truth but not necessarily the premier truth.

When John F. Kennedy's *While England Slept* came off the press it vaulted onto the best-seller lists. How does one account for that? How does a book by a twenty-three-year-old get to be a best-seller? Why, naturally, because so many copies were purchased. True, but there's more to it. His father, Joseph Kennedy, bought between 30,000 and 40,000 copies of the volume, thus greasing the road to literary success.[3] The obvious explanation is too simple.

I suggest that is the case with Elijah's disappearance – safety from royal rage does not explain it all.[4] How then should we look at it? Van't Veer is helpful here. It is crucial, he says, that we

---

[2] Wadi Cherith's location is elusive. It was in the vicinity of the Jordan, not necessarily east of it as NASB, NIV, and others have it. The Hebrew preposition (*'al pĕnê*) is not that exact; see Joel Drinkard, "*'al pĕnê* as "East of"," *Journal of Biblical Literature* 98 (1979): 285-86.

[3] Marvin Olasky, *The American Leadership Tradition* (Wheaton, IL: Crossway, 2000), 233-34.

[4] When the prophet shows himself to Ahab again (18:1-2) the text betrays no anxiety that Elijah's life was in danger. This leads Simon De Vries to conclude that the hiding in chapter 17 'has a symbolic intent' (*1 Kings*, Word Biblical Commentary [Waco: Word, 1985], 218).

view Elijah properly. We must not look upon him as representing the believer in general. Rather, 'Elijah's role in this story is that of an office-bearer.' Elijah functions in his capacity as the bearer of Yahweh's word. When he vacates the premises at God's direction, it is not as though just any Tom, Dick, Harry, or Azariah is disappearing. Instead, 'the bringer and bearer of the Lord's Word is withdrawing from the people of the Lord.'[5] The disappearance of Elijah spells the absence of the word of God from the life of Israel. Israel's judgment is the drought of the land and the silence of the Lord.

Scripture always treats the withdrawal of God's word and the silence of his voice as an agonizing judgment (see 1 Sam. 28:6, 15; Ps. 74:9; Amos 8:11-12). The church in the west may not feel this way. After all, we are not dependent on a restricted number of copies of the Scriptures or on the presence of an actual prophet. We are the post-Gutenberg church that has the Scriptures at our fingertips – how could the word of God ever be absent from us?

Walter Kaiser relates an incident from the days he was attending an east coast university. A well-known Ivy League professor was conducting a special seminar on the Origins of Christianity. One day devious souls sidetracked the professor into discussing his understanding of Romans 1-5. He held forth for some time, carefully and eloquently explaining the text, underscoring the miserable sinfulness of everyone in the seminar, the necessity of believing in the Son of God sacrificed for sins in order that they might receive God's verdict of acquittal, and so on. Kaiser says he has rarely heard such a bold and fair treatment of that text. The seeming tirade began to unravel students' nerves (the ash trays were apparently running over). When, however, one of the Jewish students demanded to know if 'the professor of this class believes this stuff,' the prof scoffed: 'Who said anything about believing it? I am just arguing that this is what Paul said.'[6] He had Romans,

---

[5] *My God Is Yahweh* (St. Catharines, Ont.: Paideia, 1980), 65. See, along the same lines, S. G. De Graaf, *Promise and Deliverance*, 4 vols. (St. Catharines: Paideia, 1978), 2:246-47.

[6] Walter C. Kaiser, Jr., and Moises Silva, *An Introduction to Biblical Hermeneutics* (Grand Rapids: Zondervan, 1994), 167-68.

he understood Romans, he explained Romans, and he disdained Romans. The point? You can have the Bible in your hand and suffer the absence of God's word. You may own a dozen translations and use several of the fifty-eight 'study Bibles' marketed for multiple evangelical cliques and yet find that, for all its availability, the word of the Lord has withdrawn from you. It's a scary affair – more so if you're not even aware of it.

The Strangeness of Yahweh's Habits (vv. 4-9)
'Every day and every night it was the same story: "The heavens are telling the anger of God, and the firmament proclaims the heat of His wrath."'[7] It was drought with a vengeance in Israel. But Elijah received special care. Yahweh told him he had commanded the ravens to sustain him at Cherith (v. 4b) and Elijah found Yahweh as good as his word: 'The ravens kept bringing him bread and meat [lit., flesh] in the morning and bread and meat in the evening' (v. 6). The birds are consistent but the brook plays out (v. 7). Not to worry – Yahweh's word is adequate for this new development (v. 8): Elijah is ordered to Zarephath where Yahweh has commanded a widow woman to sustain the prophet (v. 9). Here is a graphic picture of Yahweh's marvelous provision for Elijah in desperate circumstances. Here our problem arises: we look at this picture and infer it intends assurance for us. Oh, not in the same way, we are quick to add. Yahweh, hopefully, will not use literal ravens dropping at our feet road-kill high in cholesterol. However, what could be more consoling in our unemployment or financial straits or fears of the future? And off we go to Matthew 6:25-34 or Luke 12:22-34, looking for a proof text.

But does this passage contain such a 'promise'? Why do we think so? Because we 'principlize' the text – a perfectly legitimate procedure, by the way – as we interpret and apply Scripture. Our trouble comes when we, easily yet perhaps subtly, identify ourselves with Elijah. Elijah was a believer; I'm a believer; what God did for him I can expect him to do for me in similar circumstances. Or, Elijah was the Lord's servant; I am the Lord's servant; therefore, he will marvelously provide for me as well.[8]

---

[7] Van't Veer, *My God Is Yahweh*, 84.

But why do I identify with Elijah? Why don't I identify with that believing remnant (19:18) within Israel, those folks who were clinging to Yahweh in spite of government policy, who suffered under the drought with the rest of Israel, and who never met a raven bearing food or a widow offering hospitality? What gives me the right to identify with Yahweh's special agent rather than with the common people of God? God's prophet receives particular care, but God's people suffer the ravages and deprivation of Yahweh's temporal judgment just as every Baal-kissing apostate did.[9] This passage then offers me no prophylactic from starvation or other disasters. I am called to go on worshiping Yahweh though I never meet ravens bearing gifts.

Does Yahweh's provision for Elijah contain no comfort for Joe Schmoe or Jane Doe believer? Not exactly. I think Van't Veer has 'principlized' properly:

> Elijah's life had to be preserved, for his task had not yet been completed. Until his work was done, God would see to it that he was preserved. That's the comfort of the Word of the Lord.

This characterizes God's pattern with all his servants: so long as the work God calls us to do is not complete, he will see to it that we are sustained. (George Whitefield would say that he was immortal until his work was finished). Hence:

> When our task in this life is completed, the Lord takes us away by His chosen means – by sickness or accident or pestilence or starvation. How death comes does not matter to those who recognize death as the Lord's way, for they listen to their Savior when he tells them not to worry about food and drink.[10]

---

[8] Note that I am *not* arguing that the Lord does *not* marvelously provide for his people, but only questioning whether *this text* gives us grounds for inferring that he will infallibly do so.

[9] I have found M. B. Van't Veer (*My God Is Yahweh*, 73-79) to be of immense help in the interpretation and application of this section. While I question a detail or two, I find the bulk of his discussion both cogent and convincing.

[10] Van't Veer, *My God Is Yahweh*, 79.

While my calling is incomplete I will be preserved. Some may wish for more, but, if you think about it, that's not bad.

However, having spilled all this ink, I think there is a more excellent hermeneutical way in this text, one that looks to Yahweh's manner rather than to our needs, and which is, therefore, more likely to lead to praise. Isn't there something typically creative in the means Yahweh uses to provide for his prophet?

'The ravens I have commanded to sustain you there' (v. 4). An Israelite might cringe a bit at this statement. Ravens themselves were unclean (Lev. 11:15; Deut. 14:14), i.e., off limits so far as Israel's menu was concerned. Yet these scavengers of the sky kept bringing bread (food) and meat to Elijah twice daily. What kind of meat would ravens bring? Don't ask. Simply cook it very well and eat up. And when the wadi dries up, Yahweh's word has fresh direction for changed circumstances: Elijah must get himself to Zarephath where 'I have commanded a widow woman there to sustain you' (v. 9). 'Widow' and 'sustain' in the same breath sound oxymoronic. 'Widow' almost certainly connoted poverty and abject need.[11] A widow in Iron Age Israel didn't attend night school, gain computer skills, and nail down a position on the office staff of the local medical clinic. She didn't open up her own Kiddie Kare in her home to care for the children of mothers in the work force. Widowhood was usually a dead end street, an existence of dirt under the fingernails, of scratching out the barest of livings. If one could choose, ravens sounded more dependable than widows.

Is this not vintage Yahweh? Who else would ever design to use the *unclean* (ravens) and the *unlikely* (widow) as sustainers of his servant? Who am I to object if Yahweh delights to use dirty birds and hopeless women? We should, however, adore the scintillating creativity of a God who brings help to his people through channels they would never suspect.

I recently saw a news clip in our local paper about Judge Donald McDonough in Fairfax County, Virginia. On any given Friday McDonough apparently runs at assembly-line efficiency, handling one hundred and fifty landlord-tenant disputes one after the other.

---

[11] See ISBE, 4:1060-61; or C. van Leeuwen in NIDOTTE, 1:413-415.

But at 10 a.m. on a recent Friday something made him pause. There was a middle-aged deaf couple before him, facing eviction for falling $250 behind in their rent. The landlord was insisting on a judgment against the couple. Judge McDonough abruptly left the courtroom, returning momentarily with two crisp $100 bills and a $50 bill in his hands. 'Consider it paid,' he said, as he leaned over the bench and handed his own money to the landlord's shocked attorney. Who could have guessed that help would have come from, of all people, the judge? But careful Bible readers are not so surprised, for we have seen that what is exceptional for the judge seems to be typical for Yahweh, who is not above trucking in widows and ravens and other unlikely agents in order to sustain his people.

The Circle of Yahweh's Goodness (vv. 8-12)

Let us look more closely at this widow. What really fascinates us is her mailing address: 'Rise, go to Zarephath which belongs to Sidon' (v. 9). Zarephath stood about eight miles south of Sidon and thirteen miles north of Tyre (and about 80 miles north of Samaria), in the domain of Jezebel's daddy Ethbaal (16:31). So Elijah is headed for Baalsville in Gentileland. Here one of Baal's subjects[12] will trust in Yahweh's word (vv. 14, 15) and will find that Yahweh daily sustains her (v. 16), though Baal had left her in the pit of hopelessness and on the verge of death (v. 12). Yahweh will press her into his service for the benefit of his prophet and yet in the process give her far more than he demands of her. Here is a gentile widow awash in the wideness of God's mercy; here is grace that moves beyond the boundaries of the covenant people and embraces one of Baal's most hopeless pawns. We know her address but not her name, and yet this nameless widow joins the likes of Melchizedek (Gen. 14), Jethro (Exod. 18), Rahab (Josh. 2, 6), Ruth, Naaman (2 Kings 5), and Ebedmelech (Jer. 38) as one of those standing within the circle of Yahweh's grace long before

---

[12] I do not think, as some do (e.g., Keil), that the widow was already a worshiper of Yahweh when Elijah encountered her. Admittedly, her oath in verse 12 is sworn in Yahweh's name, but it is 'in the name of Yahweh *your* [i.e., Elijah's] God.'

the glad day when Peter preached Jesus in Cornelius' house and the Holy Spirit fell upon all the riff-raff (Acts 10-11).[13] What happens in the street and house in Zarephath in 1 Kings 17 is but a foregleam of that day when God would grant 'even to the gentiles repentance that leads to life' (Acts 11:18).

Zarephath, however, is not entirely good news. Jesus got himself into nearly mortal trouble by bringing it up in the Nazareth synagogue one Sabbath day:

> There were many widows in Israel, I can assure you, in Elijah's day, when heaven remained shut for three years and six months and a great famine raged throughout the land, but Elijah was not sent to any one of these: he was sent to a widow at Zarephath, a town in Sidonia (Luke 4:25-26, NJB).

Why did a mere Old Testament allusion throw the hometown folks into such a rage (Luke 4:28)? Because they understood Jesus' point. There were plenty of widows in Israel qualifying as valid home missions projects during Elijah's time, but Yahweh directed Elijah to none of them; instead he sent him to relieve that desperate widow in Heathensburgh. In doing so Yahweh was *bypassing Israel*; in conferring his favor on this gentile he was removing it from Israel. Elijah's journey to Zarephath, therefore, was an *act of judgment* upon Israel. The folks at Nazareth had quick minds to follow Jesus' logic and sensitive nerves to catch his innuendo.[14]

The principle involved here is easy enough to grasp. Two sons of John Brown of Haddington had prepared for the ministry, and the elder one, also John Brown, was serving in a congregation in London in 1776 or shortly afterwards. Young John let it be known

---

[13] Being a gentile myself I have the right to use such derogatory terms of my own kind.

[14] Fichtner (*Das erste Buch von den Königen*, 255) holds that Elijah could not have been sent to any Israelite widow because he would not have been secure from Ahab's pursuit within Israel. But that doesn't wash. There were doubtless enough widows in obscure places in Israel where Elijah would have been secure enough. There is no need to doubt that Jesus' inference from the text is the correct one.

that a young lady of noted personal beauty but of humble social position had captivated him. She was from the borders of Scotland, staying with an aunt in the city, and working as a dressmaker. The older John Brown, apparently dubious of her suitability as a help mate for his older ministerial son, sent his younger ministerial son, Ebenezer, to meet and assess the spouse-elect. When Ebenezer returned his father eagerly inquired if he had met the young girl. Ebenezer, himself captivated, nearly threatened, 'Father, if John does not marry her, I am going to marry her myself.'[15] That sounds like: If he is such a fool as to let such a gem slip through his fingers, then his stupidity will turn to my benefit. In short, a privilege rejected is a privilege extended – elsewhere (cf. Rom. 11:11).

This is a solemn matter. Yahweh's grace is being extended through Elijah beyond Israel because that grace has been ignored within Israel. It is a sobering personal word as well. If you go on despising his word, God may withdraw his light and allow you to walk in the darkness you seem to prefer.

The Challenge of Yahweh's Demand (vv. 10b-16)

To have a stranger ask a bit of water is one thing (v. 10b), to hear him claim first crack at your last meal is quite another (v. 11). Hence the widow goes on oath (she seems to know he's an Israelite and swears by his God) to assure Elijah she has no food and only scant materials for baking her last meal (v. 12). Her hopelessness could not be more dismal: 'See, I am gathering a couple pieces of wood, and I shall go and make it for myself and my son, and we shall eat it and die' (v. 12b). She is at the end of her resources. A handful of meal, a skiff of oil, and, literally, the last supper. Almost cruelly Elijah intensifies her trouble; he asks for the first helping of the last supper (v. 13). 'But first make me a little cake of it' (NRSV).

Let us leave Elijah's heartless request for a moment simply to sketch the development of the text:

---

[15] Robert Mackenzie, *John Brown of Haddington* (London: Hodder and Stoughton, 1918), 235-36. The younger John was no fool; Isabella Cranstoun became his wife.

Assurance and demand, v. 13
Explanation and promise, v. 14
Obedience and fulfillment, vv. 15-16

Elijah's demand is not so harsh as it seems; he softens it with
Yahweh's favorite preface, which is both customary and fresh:
'Don't be afraid' (v. 13a). Now note how he continues; the causal
particle in verse 14a is 'huge,' as they say.

For here's what Yahweh, God of Israel, says: the jar of meal will
never come to an end and the jug of oil will never be empty until the
day Yahweh gives rain upon the face of the land.

'Don't be afraid ... for....' 'First make me a little cake ... for....'
Here is the *basis* for the obedience Elijah calls for; here is the
reason why the woman needn't be afraid to take a major risk;
here is the *encouragement* to gamble everything.[16] 'So she went
and did according to the word of Elijah' (v. 15). Can there be a
clearer picture of what faith essentially is? Faith is staking
everything upon Yahweh's sheer word, wagering all upon the
veracity of God.

And don't forget that there was something continuous about
this miracle (vv. 15b-16).[17] It's not as though there were suddenly
several twenty-five pound bags of meal slouching against the wall
of the widow's kitchen. Instead it was a quiet daily drama of the
jar and the jug. When she went to the cupboard on Monday there
was enough meal in the jar and still some oil in the jug for that
day. And so it went on through the weeks. Every morning was a

---

[16] Van't Veer seems to say it is as if God says, 'Give me everything you
have [v. 13], for I will give you everything you need [v. 14].' It is Yahweh's
paradox of demand and gift. See *My God Is Yahweh*, 99-103.

[17] I make no apologies for dubbing this 'miracle.' John Gray suggests
that the 'factual basis may be that the generosity of the widow touched the
conscience of her better-provided neighbors' (*I & II Kings*, Old Testament
Library, 2nd ed. [Philadelphia: Westminster, 1970], 381). Presumably, Gray
thinks the widow's unselfishness shamed those better-off into opening their
pantries and providing for the widow and her guest. This is called rationalism.
And it's pretty pitiful.

fresh episode of the faithfulness of Yahweh to his promise. He had not said 'the jar of meal will overflow' but only that it 'will never come to an end.' The word of Yahweh that brings drought (v. 1) can at the same time sustain whom he wills. Pancakes never tasted so good.

Most of us believers can never get more sophisticated than this Phoenician widow. Some of us may know more apologetics or philosophy or theology than she ever did, but at the end of the day we find that faith consists in leaning all our weight upon the mere word of God. For all the additional light we may have, we still step over the edge of life onto the brink of eternity with nothing to support us except some word like 'the one who comes to Me I will certainly not cast out' (John 6:37b, NASB). We can do no better than old Robert Bruce at his last breakfast when he divined his Master was calling him and asked his younger daughter to 'cast me up the eighth of Romans.' His eyes failed but his memory held as he repeated the latter part of the chapter. When he had recited verses 38-39, he ordered his daughter to 'set my finger on these words.' 'I die,' he said, 'believing in these words.'[18] Dying or facing our last meal, has faith anything else than the word of Yahweh, God of Israel?[19]

---

[18] See Marcus L. Loane, *The Hope of Glory* (Waco: Word, 1968), 160.

[19] The Syrophoenician woman in the Gospels (Matt. 15:21-28; Mark 7:24-30) is a New Testament counterpart of the widow of Zarephath. Note how her faith stands in sharp contrast to the density of the Pharisees and scribes in the preceding context, much as the faith of the gentile widow in 1 Kings is a rebuke to Israel's unbelief.

Chapter 21

Dare We Trust God?

1 Kings 17:17-24

Every morning she would go to the pantry shelf and find there was enough meal and a little oil for the daily miracle of life, signaling that Yahweh wills that she and hers live for another day. Perhaps some days she quietly sang 'morning by morning, new mercies I see' as she ambled over to the jug and jar. This morning was no exception – and yet it was. The meal and oil were there but her son had also become sick. He worsened and died.[1] The tokens of life sat on her shelf while the fact of death lay in her arms.

I want to move right into the exposition of this text and treat literary matters at appropriate points along the way.

The Perplexity Yahweh Causes: A Primer for New Converts (vv. 17-18)

Bible readers feel the edge of verses 17-18 (or indeed of vv. 17-24) because they take them in connection with verses 2-16. As they should. Ah, but some scholars say verses 17-24 had nothing to do with verses 2-16, that they constitute an 'independent' narrative. But you will say that verse 17 begins with 'Now it came about *after these things*', which links verses 17-24 to verses 2-16. Ah, but that clause is a bit of later editing and that's what leads you to think that the woman of verse 17 is the same as the widow of verses 9-16. But, you counter, Elijah in his prayer in verse 20 refers to 'the widow with whom I am staying,' which seems to

---

[1] I think the lad actually died. The words of both the widow and Elijah (vv. 18, 20) make that the more natural assumption. Some think a severe coma more likely. The conservative K. C. W. F. Bähr argues the latter case (*The Books of Kings*, Lange's Commentary on the Holy Scriptures, in vol. 3, *Samuel-Kings* [1868; reprint ed., Grand Rapids: Zondervan, 1960], 195).

identify her with the woman of verses 9-16. Ah, but another scholar asserts that verse 21 is Elijah's original (=real) prayer and contains no such identification and that verse 20 is 'secondary' (=added later; likely unreliable).[2] I am convinced, however, that the 'naïve' view is correct, for the literary pattern of the whole chapter argues that verses 17ff. are structurally united to verses 2-16. Note the following overview:

Pattern of 1 Kings 17

Yahweh's word: direction, 2-3, and explanation, 4
    Prophetic obedience, 5
        Fulfillment, 6
            Inadequacy/change, 7

Yahweh's word: direction, 8-9a, and explanation, 9b
    Prophetic obedience, 10a
        Fulfillment, 10b
            Inadequacy, 10c-12

Yahweh's word: direction, 13, and explanation, 14
    Widow's obedience, 15a
        Fulfillment, 15b-16
            Inadequacy/change, 17ff.

One can see in this layout the symmetrical development of the text/story. Yahweh is at work preserving life and yet in every segment some frustration, some obstacle arises, that threatens to prevent his work: the wadi dries up (v. 7); or the channel of supply is herself destitute (vv. 10b-12); or death attacks one of their lives that has been preserved to date (vv. 17-18). Rip verses 17-24 from the rest of the chapter and you wreck what seems to be a deliberate, cohesive literary pattern. In verses 17-18 death itself seems to assault Yahweh's reputation as life-giver and this climactic difficulty must be resolved (vv. 19-22) as the previous hindrances

---

[2] One can see this kind of analysis in all its contorted, arid splendor in G. H. Jones, *1 and 2 Kings*, New Century Bible Commentary, 2 vols. (Grand Rapids: Eerdmans, 1984), 2:307, and in Simon J. De Vries, *1 Kings*, Word Biblical Commentary (Waco: Word, 1985), 221-22.

(vv. 7, 10b-12) were. Verses 17-24 are simply interlocked with verses 2-16 and must not be separated from them.

I usually don't spill ink on 'critical' matters in an expository treatment like this. But it is tragic when biblical criticism in its seeming sophistication chops up a united text and thereby destroys its theological profundity. Any alert believer reading 1 Kings 17 reels at the contrast between the steady provision of verses 15-16 and the sudden loss of verses 17-18. He or she will properly ponder how believers often meet such severe jolts of providence. The pastor observing this textual sequence will immediately think of two households in his parish who have plunged from the light of God's goodness into the muck of trouble. But one would never see this paradox/dilemma if one followed critics who allege that verses 17-24 constitute an 'independent' narrative and had no original connection with verses 2-16. Such critics not only ignore the literary character of the text but obscure the disturbing and experiential theology of that text – and thereby rob God's people of his strangely comforting word, 'comforting' because they sense this word *understands* them and their circumstances.

Back to the text as we have it. Here is a widow who had acted on Yahweh's bare word and had found he was as good as his word (vv. 15-16). What a delight to enjoy the quiet miracle of Yahweh's provision day after day. Then her boy died. Yahweh both provides and perplexes. He seems to be both faithful and fitful. He sustains life and then takes it away. What is one to make of him?

In one sense there is no problem. Yahweh gives and Yahweh takes away (Job 1:21). He has a perfect right to take what he has given. If all we have is only of grace, what possible complaint can we lodge should Yahweh take away part or all of it? But there's more of a difficulty in this text, for Yahweh's promise (v. 14) and provision (vv. 15-16) indicated his intention to sustain the widow and company. Hence the death of her son seemed to contradict Yahweh's declared purpose. Why does Yahweh act this way? Why does he follow an everlasting jar of meal with the devastating death of a son? Does he do good only to make distress more galling? Does he supply the means to sustain life only to take the life he sustains?

No wonder the woman is at the end of her tether (v. 18). She suspects Elijah has come to expose her iniquity and that her son's death constitutes punishment for such. Many Christians know her mind. On a sunny day they may remember John 9:3, but let God's hand strike and in their despair they dredge up all sorts of guilt that God must be punishing.

We may think we would have been kinder than God. Here is a widow having just escaped from Baal worship, who had only begun to taste and see that Yahweh is good. And he crushed her. Why didn't he wait until she was more mature in her faith? Why shatter a new convert with the dark mysteries of his ways? We cannot answer such queries. We can only say this woman discovered early on that Yahweh both sustains and bewilders, both delights and devastates. And as you watch and hear her in the text you know that you have been there: just as perplexed, as much in a maze, in just as much darkness before God, in knots about what sin God was punishing. 'Why,' you have lamented, 'did he light my way with tokens of his favor and then crush me with such a grievous distress?' And yet there is a sort of backhanded comfort in the rugged honesty of the Bible. It hides nothing but warns clearly that Yahweh both blesses and baffles his servants.

The Servant Yahweh Hears: A Review for Veteran Disciples (vv. 19-22)

Now it will be helpful to look at the structure of verses 17-24:

Setting, v. 17

Widow's accusation, v. 18
    Elijah takes her son away from her dead, v. 19
        Elijah's prayer, v. 20 [Accusation]
            Elijah's action, v. 21a
        Elijah's prayer, v. 21b [Petition]
            Yahweh's answer, v. 22
    Elijah takes her son back to her alive, v. 23
Widow's confession, v. 24

Note the two references to Elijah's prayer in the middle of the episode, each introduced with the same formula: 'Then he cried out to Yahweh, and he said, "O Yahweh, my God...."' (vv. 20a, 21b). The two pleas, however, are not identical (cf. our structural layout). The former is an accusation in which Elijah expresses the very anguish of the widow: 'Even against this widow with whom I am sojourning have you brought disaster by putting her son to death?' (v. 20b). Note how he picks up the widow's distress from verse 18, turns it into prayer, and pleads from her point of view. Do we ever pray like that? Do we place ourselves in the position of other people and plead their anguish before God for them? In such situations we may think we need to formulate a response, to hazard an explanation to the person in distress. No, you don't have to have an answer; you have a throne to approach.

Elijah next engages in what seems a strange prophetic action (v. 21a) before uttering his explicit prophetic petition (for Yahweh to restore the lad's life, v. 21b).[3] Then we read the miracle words on which the whole story depends: 'Yahweh listened to the voice of Elijah' (v. 22). And the lad lives.

The double references to Elijah's 'crying out to Yahweh' are very significant. Elijah, great prophet that he is (or will become), does not work some holy abracadabra. He doesn't have some easy, convenient gift by which he gets out of this jam. He is not a religious magician, who struts into the widow's distress brandishing some instant razzle-dazzle that is always at his disposal. He is no candidate for super-prophet. He is rather a servant, who can do nothing but plead with Yahweh over the affliction of this recent convert. Yahweh reduced his servant to weakness.

This seems to be one of Yahweh's repeatable patterns. When John Stott was preaching at the University Mission in Sydney in

---

[3] De Vries has, I think, got it right about Elijah's action in verse 21a: 'Elijah stretches himself three times "out over" or "upon" the lad; it is not magic, but a typical symbolic act familiar to the prophetic movement in Israel. It is an "acted out" way of saying, "Let his lifeless body be as my lively body," and the prayer [v. 21b] that accompanies it fortifies this symbol' (*1 Kings*, 222).

1958 he began having voice trouble near the end of the mission. Before the final Sunday evening service with a thousand people attending, Stott whispered his request to the mission committee chairman that he read the 'thorn in the flesh' passage from 2 Corinthians 12. After the reading, the chairman prayed for Stott. When time came for his address Stott 'croaked the gospel through the microphone in a monotone'. He could not modulate his voice or vary his manner. At the end Stott gave clear, basic instruction on how to come to Christ and there was a reasonably large response. Whenever Stott has returned to Australia someone always comes up to him and says, 'Do you remember that final service of the 1958 mission in the University Great Hall, when you lost your voice? I came to Christ that night.'[4]

Yahweh's way with Elijah is similar: he shuts Elijah up to the helplessness of prayer. Hence Elijah simply *pleads with Yahweh in prayer*. Prayer is God's appointed means of grace for our difficulties (James 5:13),[5] the way we must take through the maze. God's veteran servants find they must learn this again and again.

The Life Yahweh Restores: A Prophecy for Mortal Believers (vv. 23-24)

Elijah had carried a breathless form up to his room (v. 19); now he brings down a living child (v. 23); he had taken him from his mother's lap; now he returns him doubtless to the same mother's embrace; his abrupt 'Give me your son' (v. 19) now gives way to an equally concise 'See! Your son lives' (v. 23b). We are back to the theme of 1 Kings 17: the word of Yahweh gives life. Yahweh lives (vv. 1, 12), and so does this lad (vv. 22, 23).

The widow's confession brings the chapter to its climax: 'Now I know that you are a man of God and that the word of Yahweh in your mouth is reliable' (v. 24).[6] What is she saying? Is she not

---

[4] Timothy Dudley-Smith, *John Stott: The Making of a Leader* (Downers Grove: InterVarsity, 1999), 404-405.

[5] See Calvin's perceptive remarks on James 5:13 in his commentaries.

[6] I am taking '*ĕmet* (lit., 'truth') adjectivally (='reliable'), which more clearly fits the concern of the story.

referring to the insight she has gained through her agonizing experience? Wasn't it the reliability of Yahweh that seemed up for grabs? He had indicated by his previous promise (v. 14) and by his daily provision (vv. 15b-16) that he intended to preserve her and her household. Her son's death (v. 17) seemed to blow a huge hole in Yahweh's word. Was Yahweh, after all, like pagan gods – spasmodic, capricious, unpredictable? Making promises but unable or uninterested in keeping them? But now, as it turned out, she sees that Yahweh's word that Elijah speaks *is* reliable. At the end of her trial Yahweh has proven himself faithful.

Is this revelation valid only for Phoenician widows? Doesn't this bit of Zarephath theology carry a heartening word to God's people at large? It simply testifies that in the face of Yahweh's perplexing, seemingly absurd and contradictory ways, he will show himself faithful to his people at the end of their trial. This is the God Moses commended to Israel: 'Who fed you in the wilderness with manna ... that he might humble you and test you, *to do you good in the end'* (Deut. 8:16, RSV; emphasis mine). Sometimes this testimony is all that keeps us sane.

But the mission of this passage goes far beyond trials in general and tackles the one great trial in particular. Its focus is the d-word. When the widow's boy dies a whole new challenge arises to Yahweh's adequacy and authority. Iain Provan puts it well:

> It is one thing to rescue people from the jaws of death, but can he do anything when death has clamped tight its jaws and swallowed the victim up? He can act across the border from Israel in Sidon, but is there a 'border' that he ultimately *cannot* cross, a kingdom in which he has no power? When faced by 'Mot,' [Death, the god of the underworld in Canaanite mythology] must the LORD, like Baal, bow the knee?[7]

And 1 Kings 17 trumpets its answer: Yahweh is not only victor over dearth (vv. 1-16) but over death (vv. 17-24). No scourge can

---

[7] Iain W. Provan, *1 and 2 Kings*, New International Biblical Commentary (Peabody, MA: Hendrickson, 1995), 134.

handcuff Yahweh's supremacy, least of all death. No one in death's turf is beyond the pull of Yahweh's irresistible power. That is the testimony of this text.

I should think the implication of this story would have been of immense comfort to perceptive Israelite believers. Admittedly, 1 Kings 17 is not telling us of an empty tomb like Mark 16, or of a supper at Emmaus like Luke 24, or of breakfast at Galilee like John 21. This text is not in the same category as the resurrection narratives. It is rather a 'sign' passage, somewhat like Mark 5:21-24, 35-43 (Jairus' daughter), Luke 7:11-17 (the only son of the widow of Nain), and John 11 (Lazarus) – all of which reveal that Jesus' power extends over and into the realm of death, where he can plunder its prey at will! Sign passages like 1 Kings 17:17-24 should not be despised, for signs are, after all, significant, and for that reason more subtle, and, perhaps, more telling.

In 1841 the Church of Scotland sent four men to Pesth (Budapest), Hungary, to carry on what was really missionary work. They began holding services for English workmen in the city. In time a few Jews began to attend these services, one Israel Saphir among them. One of the Scottish clerics was Dr. John Duncan, known as Rabbi Duncan for his proficiency in all things Hebrew. Israel Saphir attended at first out of desire to improve his English, but in continued conversations with the missionaries, and with Rabbi Duncan in particular, Saphir's interest deepened. He was not a token Jew. He was a Hebrew scholar and educator. He had studied Judaism for forty years and was regarded as the most learned Jew in Hungary. Yet Rabbi Duncan ably showed him the harmony between the Hebrew Scriptures and the New Testament faith and the light began to draw him. Saphir, however, never came alone but always brought along his young son Adolph. They made quite a picture: the sixty-three-year-old Israel sitting in a chair with his frail but intent boy of eleven standing between his knees. One day at home Adolph begged that he might offer thanks before their meal. He did so – and concluded his prayer by offering it in the name of Jesus. It was a shot heard round the land. Israel lost his close friendship with the chief rabbi, had to resign from the synagogue, and so on. His new faith – and that of his son –

was out in the open.[8] Yet it was only a prayer. Merely a grace at mealtime. But the 'in the name of Jesus' formula was no formality. One might allege it was only a sign, but it was a sign that revealed all, disclosed all, confessed all. So this story of restoring the widow's son to life is only a sign, a hint. But true Israelites latch hold of it as a prophecy of things to come, for in it they rightly hear Yahweh saying, 'I am the living one, and I have the keys of death and hades' (cf. Rev. 1:18), and therefore know that not even death can place them beyond the grip of his hand, the sound of his voice, and the touch of his power.[9]

---

[8] Faith Cook, *Singing in the Fire* (Edinburgh: Banner of Truth, 1995), 166-69.

[9] Note how 1 Kings 16 closes with the word of God despised by Israel, while 1 Kings 17 closes with the word of God embraced by a gentile.

Chapter 22

Will the Real God Please Stand Up?

1 Kings 18:1-40

William Grimshaw was not convinced. A married couple in the village of Haworth had made high claims to holiness but their pastor harbored doubts about the genuineness of their professions, especially since rumors reached him of the couple's tight-fistedness and hard-heartedness. Grimshaw (ca. 1740) borrowed a beat-up weaver's jacket and cap and, disguised as a destitute beggar, arrived at his parishioners' house pleading for a night's lodging. The man refused. The 'beggar' pressed his case, citing his need and destitution. The man was unyielding – no help would be extended. With that Grimshaw whipped off his disguise and lectured the fellow about covetousness and callousness.[1] Why such extreme pastoral measures? Because sometimes only extreme measures can flush out the whole truth.

That is the situation in 1 Kings 18. There had been some three years of no dew, no rain. Bad press for Baal and his alleged fertility. Now, however, Yahweh, the real and only fertility God, has determined to send rain again (18:1). Ah, but he dare not do it just yet. Not without getting 'extreme'. For three years now people realized that Baal had a massive case of impotence, but had Yahweh simply given rain again, they would have blabbered about how Baal had 'recovered', that Baal had been rejuvenated. So, before it is safe for Yahweh to send rain, Baal must be discredited – clearly, publicly, obviously, decisively, in living color, and on national prime time. Hence the extreme measures. After Baal is exposed as a non-god, no one with a clear head should think the rain comes from him. Hence, there will be a God contest in Israel.

---

[1] Faith Cook, *William Grimshaw of Haworth* (Edinburgh: Banner of Truth, 1997), 106.

A literary 'map' may be useful before wading into our exposition. Verses 1-2 strike the keynote of the chapter: Yahweh will send rain – which he does in verses 41-46. But most of the chapter rehearses the prelude to that blessedly wet epilogue.

Movement of 1 Kings 18:3-40

Preparation (vv. 3-19):

> Ahab and Obadiah, 3-6
> Obadiah and Elijah, 7-15
> Ahab and Elijah, 16-19

Confrontation (vv. 20-29):

Elijah's speeches and responses:

> Challenge, 21a
> > Silence, 21b
>
> Proposal, 22-24a
> > Acceptance, 24b (but only 2 words in Heb.)
>
> Direction, 25
> > Yelling and silence, 26
>
> Mockery, 27
> > Yelling, gashing, & silence, 28-29

Resolution (vv. 30-40):

> Altar and water, 30-35
> Prayer and answer, 36-38
> Confession and destruction, 39-40

'Who is the real God?' is the question that dominates the text (note vv. 21, 24, 36, 37, 39). Yahweh discloses himself as the real God and because of his disclosure we make certain discoveries about the real God. I will allow these discoveries to structure the following exposition.

The service of the real God is so diverse (vv. 3-15)
Obadiah wins a good bit of the writer's attention; he figures in
two scenes, one with Ahab (vv. 3-6), the other with Elijah (vv. 7-
15). In the first section the writer both identifies Obadiah (3a; he
is the head domestic administrator) and includes a revealing
parenthesis about his character and activities:

> Now Obadiah feared Yahweh very much. So when Jezebel cut off
> the prophets of Yahweh, Obadiah took a hundred prophets and hid
> them, fifty to a cave, and sustained them with bread and water (vv.
> 3b-4).

Here (vv. 3-6) is an interesting contrast between Ahab and
Obadiah. Obadiah saves prophets.[2] Ahab wants to save mules and
horses (v. 5).[3] That is typical of kings and governments: the
economy is everything. As for Obadiah, note that no sooner does
the writer inform us of his 'fearing' Yahweh (v. 3b) than he shows
in verse 4 that this fear was not simply some private feeling or
insulated piety. His activity (v. 4) is the fruit of his fear (v. 3b).
He hides prophets of Yahweh at great risk. If discovered, he would
lose far more than his spot at the top of the civil service sector.
This brief parenthesis packs some virile theology, for it shows
that *Obadiah's work is a quiet monument to Jezebel's failure.* His
courage stymies the full success of her Yahwist liquidation policy.
Sometimes Yahweh attacks evil with the in-your-face style of an
Elijah (17:1), and sometimes he frustrates it by the simple
subversion of an unobtrusive agent. You find faithful servants of
God even where Satan's throne is (cf. Rev. 2:13 again). If you

---

[2] Obadiah duplicates the sustaining work of the ravens (17:4) and of the
widow (17:9), for the same verb (*kûl*) is used of Obadiah's work (18:4, 13).

[3] The writer suggests a neat contrast with his two uses of the verb *kārat*
(to cut, cut off): Jezebel cuts off Yahweh's prophets (v. 4), while Ahab is
concerned that the livestock not be cut off (v. 5). Ahab cares little when
Yahweh's servants die under Jezebel's purge, but he rues having to lose a
good mule. See Robert L. Cohn, 'The Literary Logic of 1 Kings 17-19,'
Journal of Biblical Literature 101 (1982): 338. In a similar vein Matthew
Henry quips that Ahab 'took a deal of pains to seek grass, but none to seek
the favor of God.'

have a kingdom view of things this textual parenthesis fairly explodes with hope.

Obadiah stands in contrast not only to Ahab but also to Elijah, for verses 7-15 suggest a clear distinction between the civil servant and the prophet. Elijah seems bold, confrontational, intrusive, while Obadiah appears hesitant, cautious, and fearful. Because of this, some interpreters in my opinion misjudge Obadiah. Some see Obadiah as essentially a compromiser (like Israel in v. 21), a boss-serving, career-protecting, life-preserving fence straddler.[4] Now, clearly, Obadiah is afraid Ahab will execute him should he herald Elijah's return; he alludes to such a fate three times (vv. 9, 12, 14). Imagine that: a servant of the Lord who prefers not to die. Is that so strange? Yet Obadiah's fear does not arise from a reluctance to say (literally), 'Behold, Elijah!' (vv. 8, 11, 14)[5] to Ahab but from his supposition about what will happen after he announces Elijah's return. He spells this out in verses 11-12: Obadiah will announce Elijah, Ahab will go to meet him, but the Spirit of Yahweh will 'spirit' Elijah away (as a protective measure against Ahab's designs?), and so Obadiah will be executed for the prophetic no-show (cf. 2 Kings 2:16).[6] That was Obadiah's suspicion, whether justified or not.

When all is said, it seems to me that the text views Obadiah positively. To be sure, Obadiah cites his life-long commitment to Yahweh (v. 12b) and his secret rescue of Yahweh's prophets (v. 13) as arguments against his death-inviting mission to Ahab.

---

[4] E.g., Choon-Leong Seow, 'The First and Second Books of Kings,' *New Interpreter's Bible*, 12 vols. (Nashville: Abingdon, 1999), 3:133, 138. For the argumentation behind such a view of Obadiah, see Jerome T. Walsh, *1 Kings*, Berit Olam (Collegeville, MN: Liturgical, 1996), 239-42, 259-60.

[5] Since Elijah's name means 'My God is Yahweh,' some interpreters hold that when Elijah told Obadiah to declare 'Behold, Elijah!,' he was ordering Obadiah to confess openly his faith to Ahab, as though he were saying, 'Behold, my God is Yahweh.' I think this is overly-subtle; Obadiah's statement in verses 11-12 explains his reluctance.

[6] Obadiah's scenario reminds me of the signs around airport security areas, warning that wisecracks about bombs or guns are taken with utmost seriousness. So if Obadiah's 'Elijah's here!' proved empty, he would court disaster. Like airport security, Ahab had no tolerance for 'Elijah jokes.'

(Elijah might place an enemy under such a threat, but surely not a compatriot!) These items from Obadiah's resumé, however, do not represent his own inflated view of himself. The narrator himself has already informed us of these very facts in his 'parenthesis' (vv. 3b-4). That is the writer's view of Obadiah and we should stick with it. It took guts to do what Obadiah did (vv. 4, 13). He didn't have to be told what would happen to him if his prophet preservation programme was uncovered. Yet just because he had guts did not mean he was fearless (vv. 9ff.). We shouldn't sit in our comfortable study chairs and berate Obadiah because he is not Elijah, Jr.[7]

We may draw a legitimate application based on this discussion. Obadiah is obviously very different from Elijah. Elijah's ministry is more public and confrontational; Obadiah works quietly in behind-the-scenes fashion and yet is faithful in the sphere where God placed him. The Bible never tells us that there is only one kind of faithful servant (1 Cor. 12:4-6); it never demands that you must be an Elijah clone. Models are helpful but slavish imitation of them is foolish. In the War between the States the Army of the Cumberland surprised Confederate defenders (and their own officers!) by scrambling up Missionary Ridge (Chattanooga) and overrunning the enemy's strong position. When Major General Phil Sheridan arrived at the top he leaped on to one of the just-captured Confederate cannons, twirled his cap, and 'rode' the gun like a horse. One of Sheridan's brigadier generals, Charles Harker, noted Sheridan's antics and decided he could horse around too. Harker leaped astride another cannon and felt instant regret. Apparently his cannon had been fired more frequently and recently than Sheridan's and it burned Harker's backside so badly he couldn't sit in the saddle of his horse for two weeks.[8]

How helpful then that Elijah is not Yahweh's only faithful servant. Faithfulness is not so dull that it comes only in one flavor. Moreover, your own pride requires the correction this narrative

---

[7] In this particular, A. W. Pink, *The Life of Elijah* (London: Banner of Truth, 1963), 99-100, is right on target.

[8] Clint Johnson, *Civil War Blunders* (Winston-Salem, NC: John F. Blair, 1997), 202-203.

can give: you are not called to great works but to good works, not to flamboyant ministry but to faithful ministry, not to be a dashing but only a devoted servant. Elijah and Obadiah – two faithful and different servants. The service of the real God is so diverse.

The demand of the real God is so disturbing (vv. 20-21)

Now we are atop Mt. Carmel (on which more below) and hear Elijah speak the first words: 'How long will you go on limping upon two opinions? If Yahweh is God, go after him; but if Baal, go after him' (v. 21).[9] Elijah's challenge may leave us a bit cold. We are not likely tempted to Baal worship in any strict sense. Happily – and hopefully – we know more about Yahweh than Baal. And therefore we may not fully appreciate the lure and attraction of Baal worship upon Joe or Jane Israelite. Hence a brief digression: why might Baal worship prove appealing to ninth-century Israel?

Let us try to trace then the 'case for Baal worship'. First, it carried the appeal of royal sanction. Queen Jezebel was an avid devotee of Baal and Asherah and a zealous evangelist for their cause. Ahab may have lacked Jezebel's fanaticism but obviously supported her faith (16:31-33). Power tends to be persuasive. Israelites who wanted to 'get on' were well-advised to align themselves with the religious preferences of the power elite. There was, secondly, the appeal of tradition, of history. Years before when Israel had crossed the Jordan, Baal worship was alive and well and waiting to lure Israelite converts (Judg. 2:11-13). Baalism was no untried innovation, no recent fad; its cult and practices went back hundreds of years. And yet, third, Baal worship offered an appeal of relevance, an ability to touch felt needs. What, after all, did Baal theology claim about its premier deity? Baal was the

---

[9] The difficulties of the text do not diminish its clarity. 'Go limping' translates the verb *pāsaḥ*, a form which occurs in verse 26 when the Baal prophets 'limp' around the altar in their cultic ritual. 'Opinions' is a possible rendering of *sĕ'ippîm*; the term may also refer to branches (of a tree) or, by extension, to crutches. For the options, see G. H. Jones, *1 and 2 Kings*, New Century Bible Commentary, 2 vols. (Grand Rapids: Eerdmans, 1984), 2:317-18.

storm and fertility god, who bestowed upon man and soil the blessings of fruitfulness. He sent forth lightning, fire, and rain. He gave grain, oil, and wine. He could revive the dead, heal the sick, and grant the blessings of progeny.[10] What could be more relevant to the life of any Canaanite farmer anxious over his wheat crop and cattle shed? When Baal was in top form, the world was pregnant with life. Here was a faith that suitably scratched where folks existentially itched. Finally, Baalism packed an appeal to sensuality. Sexual rites were built into the liturgy. Baal allowed you to serve him with all your glands. What did it matter if one's marriage was rotten, one's wife uninteresting, one's life generally dull? There was always a 'holy' whore to be had at the Baal shrine.[11] Perhaps such considerations can help us appreciate how Baalism could fascinate and charm.

But it doesn't matter if Canaanite apologetics can make a case for Baal. What matters is whether he – or Yahweh – is the real God. As noted earlier, this burning question ignites the whole episode, and Elijah first presses it upon Israel in verse 21. Note carefully how Elijah couches Yahweh's demand: 'If Yahweh is God, follow [lit., go after] him, or if Baal, follow him.' This is no mere academic question. Elijah's formulation assumes that *theology leads to discipleship.* Commitments have consequences. Elijah will not allow you to attend a 'God contest' simply so that you can conclude, 'Well, now we know that Yahweh is the real God. What movie do you want to see?' Elijah, the Bible, Yahweh himself, will not allow you the comfort of such detachment. 'If Yahweh is God, *follow him.*' The existence of the real God is not a detached but a demanding matter. (Atheists may be smarter than we think – they smell the implications?) The God of the Bible refuses to be the topic of your rap session. He is not an idea you

---

[10] Leah Bronner, *The Stories of Elijah and Elisha as Polemics against Baal Worship,* Pretoria Oriental Studies (Leiden: Brill, 1968), 54. For an even-handed discussion of Baal and Baal worship, see DeMoor and Mulder's article in TDOT, 2:181-200.

[11] Some downplay or reject cultic/sacred prostitution as a part of Canaanite religion; e.g., Karel van der Toorn, ABD, 5:510-13. I am not convinced, but the matter lies beyond the scope of this book.

play with but a King to whom you submit. You'd better understand up front all that is involved.

Warren G. Harding was the Republican candidate for president of the United States in 1920. He ran a front-porch campaign from his home in Marion, Ohio. Occasionally, however, his managers sent him out on the stump with some ghost-written speeches. Once in the middle of one of these packaged pieces he stumbled over a passage, paused, and then candidly told the audience: 'Well, I never saw this before. I didn't write this speech and don't believe what I just read.'[12] One finds such candor both endearing and stupid, the latter because anyone who is going to use a ghost-written speech should at least go over the document beforehand to see if one agrees with the ghost – lest the ghostly become the ghastly. More was involved than Harding, too late, realized.

Yahweh, however, is very straight-forward. If I am God, he says, follow me. Here is no tame God; he – we might say – keeps slopping over into my life, claiming it, invading it, refusing to allow me to put him in his religion box. We may prefer a god we have domesticated – we show him his deity litter and keep him in his place. But that is not the real God. You hear him in 1 Kings 18:21, and, if you transpose that text into New Testament theology, you will realize it does not permit nonsense like having-Jesus-as-your-Savior-but-not-as-your-Lord. He doesn't give you that option.

The nature of the real God is so different (vv. 19-39)
The whole Carmel contest highlights the differences between Yahweh and Baal. I want to outline these differences and then dwell on one of them in some detail. Perhaps the best way to summarize these is to couch them as affirmations about Yahweh.

Yahweh is the God with whom geography is no hindrance (vv. 19, 20). Elijah may have specified Mt. Carmel for a reason. Carmel juts out into the Mediterranean near modern Haifa and, as a range of limestone hills, extends southeast for some eleven miles. In Egyptian records from the second millennium BC. Mt. Carmel is called 'Holy Head,' suggesting it was a sanctuary. In the annals

---

[12] Paul F. Boller, Jr., *Presidential Campaigns* (New York: Oxford, 1985), 213.

of Assyrian king Shalmaneser III (841 BC) Mount Carmel appears as 'the mountain of Baal of the promontory.'[13] One might simply say, 'Baal's Bluff.' Carmel may well have been ground sacred to Baal, and Elijah may have chosen it for that very reason. If Carmel was Baal's turf (note that Yahweh's altar there had been pulled down, 18:30), then he had what in contemporary athletics we call 'home court advantage'. Teams playing at 'home' enjoy thorough familiarity with the court or field and can count on the psychological boost of their partisan fans. If Yahweh whips Baal on the latter's own turf, it will only highlight the supremacy of Yahweh and magnify the impotence of Baal.

Yahweh is the God for whom numbers are of no consequence (vv. 22, 25). Baal's prophets tally 450 versus Elijah as Yahweh's sole representative. In the deity dispute Elijah orders them to go first, 'for you are many' (v. 25). If today's poll-peddling press were reporting, it would recite Yahweh's plummeting 'approval ratings'. But Yahweh's power has never depended on how many cheerleaders he has. And Carmel Day showed that popularity does not determine reality.

Yahweh is the God for whom activity is no inducement (vv. 26-29, 36-38). We will discuss this in more detail below. Here let's simply say that the antics of Baal's prophets measure very high on the scale of religious fervor. But all that is absent in Elijah. Not that he is not earnest; but he is not frantic. Because he does not need to be.

Yahweh is the God for whom handicaps are no obstacle (vv. 32-35). I am tempted to say that Elijah was a far more formidable opponent of Yahweh than Baal or his prophets were. A half-pagan brain might think Elijah had just ruined Yahweh's chances of success. He orders four jars full of water poured over the sacrifice; in fact, he has it done three times.[14] He then prays that Yahweh

---

[13] M. C. Astour, 'Carmel, Mount,' IDBS, 141; see also Henry O. Thompson, ABD, 1:874-75.

[14] Some are perplexed at the lavish use of water on Carmel when drought was so severe. There were some springs on Mt. Carmel, and (should someone want to be difficult) the Mediterranean Sea was not far away. The latter has never dried up in a famine. On this matter, cf. H. H. Rowley, *Men of God* (London: Thomas Nelson & Sons, 1963), 55.

will consume his sopping mess (vv. 36-37). Israelites were not witless. They knew wet stuff doesn't burn. Elijah had stacked the deck against Yahweh, so that when his fire came there could be no other explanation except that it was an 'act of God.' Some Israelites may have walked away muttering Genesis 18:14 to themselves.

Now I would like to return to the third assertion: Yahweh is the God for whom activity is no inducement (vv. 26-29, 36-38). But it was not so with Baal – at least his prophets did not think so. Let us discuss the text before moving to application.

All morning long the Baal prophets carried on their liturgical hoopla, crying for Baal's intervention (v. 26).[15] At noon Elijah mixes sarcasm with their screams, urging them to increase the decibels:

> Call out with a loud voice, for he is a god;
> either he is occupied or gone aside,
> or is on a journey,
> or perhaps he is asleep and needs to be awakened (v. 27, NASB).

Elijah's reasoning ('for he is a god') may sound strange to us but wouldn't to a pagan. In paganism gods and goddesses engaged in the whole gamut of activities we call human. Elijah adopts this perspective in order to ridicule it. He suggests Baal may be 'occupied,' perhaps preoccupied, either because he is thinking or speaking.[16] Others prefer to take 'occupied' (*śîaḥ*) very closely with 'gone aside' (*śîg*). Why would Baal have gone aside? To, as

---

[15] The writer is brusque in reporting the result: 'But there is no voice, and there is no one answering' (v. 26). Jerome T. Walsh (*1 Kings*, Berit Olam [Collegeville, MN: Liturgical, 1996], 248) points out: 'First, the narrator does not say, "Baal did not answer," as if Baal exists and can answer but for some reason remains silent. By phrasing the sentence in terms of absence ("There is no") rather than presence, the narrator hints at Baal's nonentity.' Walsh goes on to say that 'the sequence "no voice, no answerer"…implies a causal relationship: there is no voice *because* there is no one to answer when Baal is invoked.'

[16] Cf. BDB, 967 (first entry).

we say, use the facilities. Elijah suggests Baal may be defecating.[17] Or he may be out of town, on a journey. In the Ugaritic materials Baal's sister Anat comes to his house looking for him, only to be told that Baal had gone hunting.[18] Alas! Baal has no beeper. Or maybe Baal is asleep and needs a wake-up call. When, as in paganism, god is made in the image of man, nothing is more natural than regular divine sleep.[19]

The Baalists took Elijah's counsel to heart, working themselves up into a feverish pitch in a cacophony of noise and a trail of blood. This bedlam prevailed until at least mid-afternoon. Both tragedy and relief come in verse 29b: 'And there is no voice, and there is no one answering, and there is no attention.' In contrast to their hyper-kinetic frenzy, Elijah's approach is simplicity itself. He prays (vv. 36-37). Fire falls (v. 38).

Don't think Elijah was casual while the prophets of Baal were intense. Elijah was intense and earnest (note the repetition in v. 37a). But he knew Yahweh's nature; he didn't have to badger, coerce, manipulate – didn't need to blabber on and bleed half the day to secure a hearing. A scorched, smoking spot on the ground testifies to that.

Christians are apt to feel detached from this text. We will protest that we don't carry on with all that pagan hullaballu; we don't gash ourselves; we aren't pagan blockheads. I will grant that we may be more refined. Please note, however, the assumption on which the Baal prophets operate: God will begin to do things if only we get a flurry of passionate religious activity going. Do we not then have our own 'evangelical Baalism'? Christians and churches in the west seem to believe that God will surely work if only we ... spend longer in personal devotions and more time in private prayer; belong to a home Bible study group or form a peer accountability group; get more people involved in our visitation

---

[17] See Gary A. Rendsburg, 'The Mock of Baal in 1 Kings 18:27,' *Catholic Biblical Quarterly* 50 (1988): 414-17.

[18] George E. Saint-Laurent, 'Light from Ras Shamra on Elijah's Ordeal upon Mount Carmel,' *Scripture in Context: Essays on the Comparative Method* (Pittsburgh: Pickwick, 1980), 133.

[19] See 'Prayer to the Gods of the Night,' ANET, 390-91. Afterwards read Psalm 121.

evangelism program; attend week-end marriage enrichment seminars or hold a singles' retreat; start neighborhood clubs for kids or early morning men's prayer breakfasts or provide mothers' morning out; hold more missions conferences and increase 'faith promise' giving; or add a spring Bible conference; solicit someone to direct the 5th and 6th grades choir; become involved in a parachurch ministry on a local college campus or go on a short term mission trip to Jamaica or take the youth on a ski trip to Colorado; get a church bus ministry off the ground and spearhead the start of a Christian school; and be able to dim the lights in the sanctuary to create ambiance, while spending quality time with spouses and families. All this Christian busyness is as exhausting as Baal worship, even minus the gashes. Most of these are not illegitimate activities (I am not opposing, e.g., more time spent in Bible study or missions trips), but might an illegitimate rationale drive them? Are these means of grace or gimmicks designed to manipulate, impress, or stir up God? You may not be a prophet of Baal, but you may think like one. If only we ..., then God will....

Jesus makes the same point in Matthew 6:7-9. Pagans pray a certain way because pagans think a certain way (v. 7), but if you know the real God, your Father who knows what you need before you ask him (v. 8), then (v. 9) your praying is different.[20] Then you can pray briefly, simply, comprehensively, as in verses 9b-13.

Theology, not psychology, explains Elijah's simplicity (vv. 36-37) on Mt. Carmel. Because he knew the real God he had no need to ape the antics and hype of Baal's prophets. Do you see the *relief* that enters your life and ministry when you serve the real God?

The provision of the real God is so gracious (vv. 30-38)
There is, on the whole, a severe tone about 1 Kings 18. It makes sense: Israel is in frightful shape if Yahweh must stoop to raw miracle to penetrate her density and extract an orthodox, first-

---

[20] It is important to mark the 'therefore' or logical 'then' (Greek: *oun*) in Matthew 6:9, for it indicates that the-Lord's-prayer-kind-of-praying flows out of the theology of verse 8b.

commandment level confession from her. Yet, for all that, there is a hint of mercy and a glimmer of hope in the text. If Elijah is Yahweh's prosecutor, he is also his evangelist. If Carmel is Israel's rebuke, it is also her invitation. I want to retrace part of the text to explain and justify this point.

When Elijah's turn came, he repaired (lit., 'healed') 'the altar of Yahweh that was torn down' (v. 30). Significantly, he used twelve stones for his repair. The writer explicitly says they stand for the twelve tribes of Israel (v. 31; see also Exod. 24:4 and Josh. 4:1-10) and so are 'an implicit condemnation of the existence of the northern kingdom.'[21] All Israel is one and belongs together; whatever the *ten* tribes are, they are not Israel in the proper sense of the word. Equally significant, Elijah builds the altar 'in the name of Yahweh' (v. 32), i.e., under his authority and with his authorization.[22] He fixes the wood, hacks up the bull, and places the pieces on the wood (v. 33) – almost ready for fire.

When Elijah prays to Israel's covenant God (v. 36a), Yahweh sends fire that burns up the burnt-offering and everything else (v. 38). That sort of thing had happened before. Aaron and his sons had been ordained as priests and Aaron had just pronounced the benediction at the first tabernacle service when

> fire came forth from Yahweh's presence and consumed the burnt-offering and the fat pieces on the altar; and all the people saw and shouted and fell on their faces (Lev. 9:24).

---

[21] H. L. Ellison, 'I and II Kings,' *The New Bible Commentary*, 2nd ed. (Grand Rapids: Eerdmans, 1954), 315.

[22] This authorization is important since Elijah's is a solitary altar outside of Jerusalem. Some scholars think the editors of Kings would be very nervous about such a non-centralized altar. But I doubt it. Much depends on how one brings together Exodus 20:24-26 and Deuteronomy 12. On this see Richard E. Averbeck, NIDOTTE, 2:890-97, and 4:1006-7. In any case, believers in the north lived under exceptional circumstances. 'In fact, the split between the north and the south ca. 930 BC created a situation where the Lord once again seems to honor worship at exclusively Yahwistic solitary altars in the north (see e.g., 1 Kgs 18:30 with 19:10), since the people there were cut off from the temple in Jerusalem (1 Kgs 12:25-29)' (Averbeck, NIDOTTE, 2:897).

Burnt-offering, fire, people on their faces: the same as verses 38-39 in this passage. Leviticus 9 reports the inauguration of the tabernacle worship, and the sudden fire (apparently from Yahweh's glory-cloud) signals Yahweh's acceptance and validation of the sacrificial system of worship he had prescribed. Again, during the scourge on Israel and Jerusalem, David sacrificed, as ordered, at Araunah's (called Ornan in Chronicles) threshing-floor:

> And he called to Yahweh, and he answered him with fire from heaven upon the altar of burnt-offering (1 Chron. 21:26).

David then declared that this very spot where Yahweh had both authorized and accepted his sacrifice would be the location of the future temple (1 Chron. 22:1). When in Solomon's regime that temple was finally completed and dedicated,

> fire came down from heaven and consumed the burnt-offering and the sacrifices; and the glory of Yahweh filled the house (2 Chron. 7:1).

Divine fire blazed at the two major liturgical moments in Old Testament life, at the inauguration of both the tabernacle and the temple worship. That fire was Yahweh's green light, indicating that he would accept this worship and that Israel should proceed to approach him in this way.[23]

Now back to 1 Kings 18 with its savage flames and smoking cinders. In light of its Old Testament parallels the miraculous fire shows that *Yahweh has accepted Elijah's sacrifice* (cf. v. 36, 'and that I am your servant'). Is this not Israel's hope? Does this not hint to Israel that there is a way back?[24] How? Via the means of

---

[23] We must never forget that the Old Testament sacrificial system was Yahweh's *gift* to Israel (Lev. 17:11). In fact, the Book of Leviticus is the answer to the question, 'How can a sinful people maintain fellowship with a holy God?'

[24] Verse 37b ('And *you* [emphatic] have turned their heart back') would support this positive view if the words are meant positively. Montgomery (*The Books of Kings*, International Critical Commentary, 305) denies this, but Alan J. Hauser in *From Carmel to Horeb* (Sheffield: Almond, 1990), 49-50, argues for it.

grace and reconciliation Yahweh has already provided. By way of the old, rugged altar. Is it too wild to think that God is saying to Israel, 'You have an altar, a place of atonement, where I will receive you'? If this is so, then the Carmel contest proves not only that Yahweh is truly God but that he is truly gracious. He is not only the real God but the reconciling God. Yahweh's fire is both an overt proof and a subtle invitation.[25]

Surely I needn't say that the same – and yet a better – provision holds for covenant people now? Whether flagrantly rebelling or stupidly wandering, the road to restoration leads straight to the altar at Golgotha. As my colleague Knox Chamblin delights to point out, the Lord never allows us to leave the cross or to get beyond the cross, but takes us more deeply into the cross.

The severity of the real God is so condemning (v. 40)
The smoke clears (v. 38) and Israelites are on their faces, confessing that Yahweh is the real God (v. 39).

> Then Elijah said to them, 'Grab the prophets of Baal; don't let a man of them escape.' So they grabbed them and Elijah brought them down to the Wadi Kishon and slaughtered them there (v. 40).

Some readers now sigh with disappointment. We have had a perfectly marvelous day on Mt. Carmel, and now Elijah goes and spoils it all. Here we go, wading into the gore of another 'moral problem' in the savage Old Testament. Is that what we have here? Elijah giving vent to his vindictiveness? Must we chalk it up to his 'fanatical tendency'?[26]

However, this Kishon slaughter was not an act of personal

---

[25] I owe thanks to Graeme Goldsworthy for a hint in his *Gospel and Kingdom* (Carlisle: Paternoster, 1994), 117, that stimulated my thinking in this section.

[26] So John J. Bimson, '1 and 2 Kings,' *New Bible Commentary*, 4th ed. (Leicester: Inter-Varsity, 1994), 359. Ronald Wallace refuses to belittle but somewhat apologizes for Elijah: God's servants do not always respond as God planned, but he works with them in any case amidst the superstitions and hatreds of their times (*Readings in 1 Kings* [Grand Rapids: Eerdmans, 1996], 124).

revenge but of capital punishment in line with the Torah. Elijah was carrying out the sanctions of Deuteronomy 13: those who woo Israel to worship another god (whether a successfully wonder-working prophet, a member of one's intimate circle, or the citizens of a whole town) forfeit their lives. Remember Israel was a theocracy; what we call church and state functioned as one. And here Elijah simply carries out Israel's constitution, the provisions of Yahweh's covenant law, relating to solicitation to apostasy.[27]

Remember the heading for this section: the severity of the real God is so condemning. It does not condemn God, nor Elijah – but us. How does it condemn us? It condemns us whenever we look at verse 40 and simply don't get it.

Red army troops were overrunning Berlin in the spring of 1945. Some of these troops were Russian peasants unfamiliar with amenities of modern life. Bathroom plumbing mystified them. They sometimes used toilets to wash and peel potatoes. Since they didn't know what bathrooms were for and couldn't locate outhouses, they left excrement and urine everywhere.[28] A Red soldier might stare at a German toilet, but he just didn't get it.

That is the way Christians too often look at verse 40. We read it and go into moral hysterics. We simply don't get it. The problem is not with Elijah or the Old Testament but with us. We react the way we do because, in our subliminal view, apostasy is not that big a deal. We simply don't understand Yahweh's violence against rebellion in his people. He uses surgery not breath mints on cancer. The problem is not God's lack of refinement but our lack of sanctification. If our thinking were holy, we would understand such texts. The nasty episode at the Kishon testifies that we have

---

[27] See the discussion of K. C. W. F. Bähr, *The Books of the Kings*, Lange's Commentary on the Holy Scriptures, in vol. 3, *Samuel-Kings* (1868; reprint ed., Grand Rapids: Zondervan, 1960), 209. Claus Schedl also points out that 'the annihilation of devotees to the bull cult, by sword and blood, already had a precedent in Moses' (see Exod. 32:27 in context). Hence Elijah 'was simply imitating the zeal of the great Moses' (*History of the Old Testament*, 5 vols. [Staten Island: Alba House, 1972], 4:63).

[28] Cornelius Ryan, *The Last Battle* (New York: Simon and Schuster, 1966), 494.

little horror of sin and calls evangelical Christians in particular to repentance.

The real God stood up that day on Mt. Carmel, but the real God has also come down (John 1:1, 14) and calls you to serve him. You'll find him the same: using such different servants, making such disturbing demands, liberating you from your recurring pagan thinking, lacing his severity with grace, and exposing your shoddy level of holiness.

Chapter 23

In Prayer and on the Run

1 Kings 18:41-46

The deity contest on Mt. Carmel is not the main event of 1 Kings 18. It is only the prelude. There Yahweh shows he is the real God, but he must still show he is the giving God, as he promised in verse 1 ('I will give rain'). This he does in verses 41-46. These verses depict two contrasts and contain two themes. The contrasts are between king and prophet. In the one Ahab dines while Elijah prays (v. 42); in the other Ahab rides while Elijah runs (vv. 45b-46). Elijah expends more energy. The passage breaks down into two sections. In the first we enter the school of prayer (vv. 41-45a), and in the second we watch the drama of grace. The exposition develops these themes.

Prophetable Prayer (vv. 41-45a)

Elijah is still calling the shots on Mt. Carmel. He commands Ahab to 'go up, eat and drink' (v. 41) and the king complies (v. 42a).[1] 'But Elijah went up to the top of Carmel, crouched down to the ground, and put his face between his knees' (v. 42b). Though the text does not overtly use a 'pray' verb, Elijah's body language says it all. This is the posture of intense, concentrated prayer.

Its Humiliation

It seems a bit ironic to see the brash Baal-buster of verses 21-40 turned into the humble supplicant of verse 42. Elijah has been the one giving orders, using imperative verbs throughout the story. Now, however, he humbles himself to beg Yahweh's favor.

---

[1] I do not think Ahab's eating and drinking is a covenant meal and/or a parallel to Exodus 24:4, 11. It may signal celebration (cf. Ecc. 5:18 and 9:7) in anticipation of the end of the drought (see v. 41b) and the renewal of covenant blessing.

Ah, but he is used to that. In chapters 17-18 Elijah is repeatedly reduced to the helplessness of prayer, though readers may fail to observe it. Elijah prays for life in 17:20-21, for fire in 18:36-37, and for rain here in 18:42. Alec Motyer reminds us of Elijah's prayer for 'dismissal' in 19:4.[2] Elijah has no power to produce any of these changes. We may think he is super-prophet, but only if we ignore the whole testimony of the text. He is always confessing his inability because he resorts to begging Yahweh for what he can in no way bring about. We must hold to the biblical picture: for all his seeming dynamism and charisma, his assertiveness and control, his gumption and boldness, Elijah has no magic, no ace up his sleeve to play in a pinch. He can call upon no sleight of hand by which he slithers out of tight spots and dead-end dilemmas. Elijah can only confess his helplessness; that is, he can only pray. Prayer is most humiliating work.

Its Principle

Elijah seems so sure. He tells Ahab to get his supper, 'for there is a rumbling of [approaching] rain' (v. 41, NJPS). Was Elijah's certainty presumptuous? Brash? If he is so certain rain is coming, why does he pray for it in verse 42?

We can be sure that Elijah is sure. He could have had a *general confidence* on the basis of 1 Kings 8:35-36:

(35) When the heavens are shut up and there is no rain, because they have sinned against You, and they pray toward this place and confess Your name and turn from their sin when You afflict them,

(36) then hear in heaven and forgive the sin of Your servants and of Your people Israel, indeed, teach them the good way in which they should walk. And send rain on Your land, which You have given Your people for an inheritance (NASB).

One could view Elijah's prayer here as piggybacking on Solomon's prayer there. Granted, Israel as a whole may not be

---

[2] See Motyer's fine discussion in *The Message of James*, The Bible Speaks Today (Leicester: InterVarsity, 1985), 205-206.

petitioning Yahweh, but Elijah as prophetic intercessor is. But Elijah has more than this. He has a *particular promise*. In 18:1 Yahweh had assured him, 'I will give rain upon the face of the ground.' Yahweh had promised (v. 1); now Elijah prays for the promise to be fulfilled (v. 42b). Put it together: Yahweh wills to send rain – and he wills that his will come to pass through Elijah's prayer.

If we generalize further we can state the principle of 'prophetable' prayer: God's will is certain, but he delights to do his will in answer to the prayers of his people. The prayers of the saints constitute the appointed channel by which God works his will. He is not limited to this channel, but, we might say, he highly prefers it. The Bible bristles with this thinking. In Ezekiel 36:37-38 the Lord says:

> (37) This also I will let the house of Israel ask me to do for them: to increase their men like a flock. (38) Like the flock for sacrifices, like the flock at Jerusalem during her appointed feasts, so shall the waste places be filled with flocks of men (RSV).

The population explosion will certainly come (v. 38), but Yahweh 'will let the house of Israel ask' him to bring it about (v. 37). Prayer nearly clips the heels of Jesus' promise in Revelation 22:20. No sooner does he assure, 'Yes, I am coming soon,' than his people beg, 'Amen, come, Lord Jesus.' The word is dogmatic: 'The earth shall be full of the knowledge of Yahweh as the waters cover the sea' (Isa. 11:9); yet the command is insistent: pray 'thy kingdom come' (Matt. 6:10).

It is a matter of what we call ends and means. Today farmers put up alfalfa in huge round bales, which they either leave in the field or move with a tractor and lift. A few years ago, however, humanly manageable rectangular bales were common. A hay wagon would be hitched behind the tractor and baler and the hay would be stacked on the wagon as it was baled. The wagon could then be pulled to the barn, the bales placed on a conveyor belt of sorts; they would chug their way up to the hay mow where sweaty fellows would stack them for future use. If a farmer had put his thinking into words at a time like that, he might have said: 'I am going to get my hay into the barn; I'm going to hire three college boys to do it.' The end and the means. Too bad if it sounds crass but God seems to work that way. He declares his will and then he says, 'Now I am going to move my people to pray for that.'[3] That is the way at Carmel: Yahweh says, 'I will give rain' (v. 1), and Elijah prays it down (v. 42).

Doesn't God's *modus operandi* give dignity to prayer? We take his promises and turn them into prayers in order that the promises may come to pass. What honor God confers on us, not as robots, but as servants who should have no higher ambition than to pray down his will.

Its Mystery

It began to look like opposing Baal's prophets was not nearly so arduous as pleading with Yahweh.

> 'Now go up', he told his servant, 'and look out to sea.' He went up and looked. 'There is nothing at all,' he said. Seven times Elijah told him to go back. The seventh time, the servant said, 'Now there is a cloud, small as a man's hand, rising from the sea' (vv. 43-44a, NJB).

These verses form the tension-point of the episode, as any reader naturally senses. As soon as the servant reports, 'There is nothing at all,' suspense reigns. This suspense stands at the heart of the passage as a sketch can show:

---

[3] Thomas Manton observed that 'when God meaneth to bestow blessings, he stirreth up the hearts of the people to pray for them' (*An Exposition of the Epistle of James* [Marshalltown, DE: National Foundation for Christian Education, n.d.], 471; on James 5:18). See also William Greenhill, *An Exposition of Ezekiel* (1645-47; reprint ed., Edinburgh: Banner of Truth, 1994), 737-38. For 1 Kings 18 Ronald Wallace (*Readings in 1 Kings* [Grand Rapids: Eerdmans, 1996], 125) has put it nicely: 'We are meant to notice, in this incident, that even though God had already promised to send rain, and was going to do so, he nevertheless waited till Elijah prayed earnestly for it to happen. In the Bible it always seemed to be of real pleasure and value to God to do things for his people on earth, if he could first stir up people to pray for these things. He indeed found such pleasure in answering prayers that he loved even simply to give way to human praying. He even allowed himself at times to be actually pushed into complying with what his people prayed for (Gen. 18:22-23, Ex. 32:9-10, 14, Gen. 32:26-30).'

Breakdown of 1 Kings 18:41-46

Prophet's command, 41
    King dines, 42a
        Prayer begins, 42b
            Go up and look for a sign, 43a
                Disappointment & repeated returns, 43b
                Seventh time – little cloud, 44a
            Go up and order king, 44b
        Rain comes, 45a
    King rides, 45b
Prophet's service, 46

However, no one needs a structural layout to smell a dilemma. Elijah crouches down but repeatedly gets the same report: 'There is nothing at all.'

How differently Yahweh responds to *one* servant's prayers! He sent an immediate and warm answer (v. 38) to Elijah's previous prayer on Carmel (vv. 36-37), but here puts him through an agonizing process before sending his delayed and wet answer. We think we can understand the momentary response in verse 38 – Yahweh's reputation over the claims for Baal must be visibly and decisively clear. But why a different manner in verses 42-44a? Ultimately, I don't think we can know; but, clearly, there is nothing monolithic about Yahweh's ways.

Before General Stonewall Jackson became 'Stonewall' or a general, he was Major Jackson, teaching cadets at Virginia Military Institute in Lexington. He taught 'natural and experimental philosophy,' something akin to our physics. The course included electricity, magnetics, acoustics, and optics. Jackson's pedagogy, however, was less than inspiring. Each afternoon he would commit the next day's lecture material (i.e., paraphrasing the textbook line by line) to memory. After supper, for at least two hours, he would sit totally erect or stand rigidly facing the wall, while he reviewed the material he would teach. Apparently, his presentation was just as unbending. If cadets did not understand, Jackson could only repeat it, line-upon-line. Drawing upon an analogy or offering extempore explanation was beyond his ken.[4] For Jackson teaching was done in this way and in no other.

Yahweh obviously regales his people with more variety, not least in the ways he answers their prayers. This proves both more interesting and more mystifying. He answered Elijah immediately in one case (vv. 36-38) and, apparently, after extended pleading in another (vv. 42-44a). In another case, he will refuse Elijah's request altogether (19:4). We must simply live with the mystery – and allow it to teach us caution. I think especially of those saints who are so keen to write God's script for him and seem to assume that he provides a one-size-fits-all 'conversion experience,' or that he has a uniform way of answering prayer (if only one has enough 'faith'), or that he follows one pattern in giving guidance in circumstantial matters. But Yahweh is not so dull. Sometimes prayer is relatively effortless (vv. 36-38), sometimes extremely agonizing (vv. 42-44a). And who really knows why?

Its Benefits

'Then a heavy rain came' (v. 45). Rain meant life, water for soil, people, and livestock, grain for food, grass for animals (cf. 18:5). Yahweh then is the God of dramatic intervention (vv. 31-39) and of daily provision. Israel's apostasy and divided mind had forfeited these material benefits (Deut. 11:16-17; 28:23-24; Lev. 26:19-20). Now Yahweh graciously restores them. Wallace is right: 'Israel is to learn again this day that the God who sends fire to convert their hearts will also send rain to refresh and feed their bodies.'[5] Yahweh is the God of the spectacular and of the routine, who sends both fire and food (see Ps. 65:9-13). Whenever we fail to acknowledge these latter down-to-earth provisions as Yahweh's gifts, we apostatize to naturalism (a more contemporary, sophisticated form of Baal worship). Whenever we begin to assume that they are ours by some inalienable right, we have become blind to the Father's hand. We forget that the common is special.

---

[4] James I. Robertson, Jr., *Stonewall Jackson: The Man, the Soldier, the Legend* (New York: Macmillan, 1997), 118-20.

[5] Ronald S. Wallace, *Elijah and Elisha* (Grand Rapids: Eerdmans, 1957), 41.

I had never given it any thought – the misery country dwellers faced in the late 1800s. From bugs. The summer invasion of flies, mosquitoes, and their ilk. The foreign legion of insects swarmed through open windows of the farm house, assembling about the stove and ceiling, sticking on fruit, swimming in milk crocks, floating in soup. Night was no different: unless one preferred to sweat and boil, one opened the window – and in came the pests. But then in the 1880s something new was introduced: window screening. Someone philosophized that such screening was 'the most humane contribution the nineteenth century made to the preservation of sanity and good temper.'[6] Who would think of it that way? Window screening. So common – yet such a gift.

That is the way we must train ourselves to look upon Yahweh's basic, common gifts. By Yahweh's gracious intention (v. 1) and Elijah's tenacious intercession (v. 42), the crass, earthy, material benefits were Israel's again. How crucial to understand that both holiness and harvests are his gifts, that he is the God who consumes altars and serves oatmeal.[7]

Incredible Grace (vv. 45b-46)

The knees bent in prayer are now running track. Elijah has gone from worship to aerobics. His feet are pounding the ground out in front of Ahab's chariot with something like seventeen miles to

---

[6] Otto L. Bettmann, *The Good Old Days – They Were Terrible!* (New York: Random House, 1974), 52.

[7] I have developed this section under the theme of prayer because I think there is an implicit theology of prayer in the text and because that is the theme James 5:16b-18 highlights. However, I have not brought James 5 explicitly into the exposition, because this is an exposition of 1 Kings 18 and not of James 5. For a lucid and helpful exposition of the latter, see that of Alec Motyer cited in note 2. More properly perhaps the theme of our text is 'covenant benefits restored,' which occurs not because Israel has demonstrated lasting repentance (cf. v. 39) but because of Yahweh's grace (v. 1) and Elijah's prayer (v. 42). Here Elijah is the covenant intercessor (though in chapter 19 he becomes covenant prosecutor). Israel then enjoys covenant favor because God's mercy extends it (v. 1) and because an intercessor (mediator?) wins it (vv. 42-44a). Sounds rather New Testamentish.

cover.[8] The text informs us that this is no mere feat for feet but due to the Lord's hand:

> Ahab mounted his chariot and made for Jezreel. But the hand of Yahweh had come on Elijah and, hitching up his clothes, he ran ahead of Ahab all the way to Jezreel (vv. 45b-46, NJB).

Let's step back a moment and take in all that Ahab receives on Carmel Day. From Carmel Ahab has:

(1) The reality of Yahweh proven (vv. 1-40)
(2) The blessings of Yahweh restored (vv. 41-45a)
(3) The appeal of Yahweh extended (vv. 45b-46)

It is the third item we want to discuss in this section.

What does Elijah's running in front of Ahab's chariot signify? Since it was the 'hand of Yahweh' that equipped Elijah for this exploit, we should assume God had something he wanted to communicate by this strange race. Hence we should not worry overmuch about what may have been going on subjectively in Elijah's head. Who knows what he was thinking?[9] But: what does it seem Yahweh wanted to depict for Ahab through his running prophet?

I agree with Van't Veer that we should consider Elijah and Ahab here primarily in terms of their respective offices, i.e., as prophet and king. When we do so, I propose that Yahweh is putting before Ahab an offer, a demand, and a decision.

The fact that Elijah runs before Ahab as a herald or forerunner suggests that Yahweh's prophet may be a servant rather than an opponent of the king. The king and prophet could work in unity in an ongoing reform. There is no inherent reason that the prophet must always be a burr in Ahab's saddle. The king could have the prophet as his willing servant instead of his glowering adversary.

---

[8] In support of historicity, see James A. Montgomery, *A Critical and Exegetical Commentary on the Books of Kings*, International Critical Commentary (New York: Scribners, 1951), 307.

[9] I think Van't Veer is right on this score (see *My God Is Yahweh* [St. Catharines, Ont.: Paideia, 1980], 314-15).

So they ride/run together, prophet *with* king, and *going before* him.

Yet if Elijah is running before Ahab it means that Ahab is *following* Elijah. Is this significant? Some would say so. 'The final image, of the prophet racing on foot before the king on his chariot, symbolizes the restoration of the proper order in Israel: king follows prophet.'[10] Van't Veer sees it that way:

> That was the exact relationship Yahweh wanted at that moment: the king on the way to his residence, that is, his throne, preceded by the bearer of the Word of the Lord. God's Word leads the way gloriously! The Word of prophecy must show the king the path to follow![11]

If these inferences are valid, then Yahweh is placing a demand upon Ahab. The king must not operate in his own autocratic way but submit to the divine word. Royal power must seek prophetic direction.

All this leaves Ahab with a decision. The people had faced one that day (vv. 21, 39). Now it is Ahab's turn. Here is his moment of opportunity; here is a pictorial appeal from Yahweh.

I have dubbed this section 'incredible grace'. I don't like to use that adjective, simply because it is overused in our day to describe items that are not really incredible. Is Yahweh's appeal, Yahweh's grace, incredible here? So much so that it may anger you. Ahab is the one who permitted Baal worship, who approved the construction contracts on Baal's altar and temple, and who even participated himself in that worship (16:31-32). Ahab is the gutless wonder who stood by and allowed his wife to butcher Yahweh's prophets (18:4) and – apparently – her ruffians to pull down Yahweh's altars (19:10, 14). He is the one who seethed with murderous hatred against Yahweh's premier servant (18:10, 17). Yet now Yahweh offers this swine a gospel opportunity, showing him the road to repentance and offering him the help of the servant of the word. We can hardly object, however, because

---

[10] Robert L. Cohn, 'The Literary Logic of 1 Kings 17-19,' *Journal of Biblical Literature* 101 (1982): 341.

[11] *My God Is Yahweh*, 317.

we must agree with John Brown of Haddington near the end of his life:

> Oh! to have my heart stirred and set in an eternal flame of love to that dear Son of God, of whom I think I can say, 'He loved me and gave Himself for me'; and I am sure, in point of worthlessness, He might as well have loved Beelzebub himself.[12]

So who dares object when grace is extended to Ahab? And of course it's incredible. There is no other kind.

Imagine that crucial yet fleeting scene. Elijah stops bent one-quarter over, heaving for oxygen. Momentarily, Ahab's chariot comes barreling past and turns down the lane leading to his summer residence. Elijah and Ahab can both see it: there's a light in the queen's quarters. Ahab has an offer of grace in his hand, but his feet will soon stand in the devil's bedroom.

---

[12] Robert Mackenzie, *John Brown of Haddington* (London: Hodder & Stoughton, 1918), 297.

Chapter 24

Shall the Psychotherapists Win?

1 Kings 19:1-18

Apologies to Harry Emerson Fosdick for corrupting his famous sermon title.[1] However, the doctored chapter title reflects my concern over the proper interpretive approach to 1 Kings 19 – in my view, one of the most important chapters in the Old Testament, and one, again in my opinion, most consistently misinterpreted.

I want to tackle this passage a bit differently. Usually we jump to exposition as soon as possible. However, since I want to dispute a prevalent approach that dominates both popular and scholarly treatments of this passage, and since I am convinced that many biblical sleuths have passed over crucial clues, I think we should take time to wallow in the problems. In short, I plan to pull you through the hermeneutical slime and mire. As a sovereign reader you can choose to avoid all this and run immediately to the expository observations in the last section. You will not, however, understand the basis on which those observations are made. There is simply no substitute for getting dirty in the text.

The Quest for the Historical Elijah
We are strangely, perhaps perversely, fascinated by weaknesses in prominent people. Peter the Great was fearless of assassins but petrified by cockroaches. The latter are, admittedly, despicable creatures (as are assassins), but it is a bit amusing to ponder Peter's massive bulk trembling before such scurvy specimens. We lesser mortals, however, receive secret comfort from seeing a point of weakness in a man of fabled strength. Perhaps this tendency

---

[1] Fosdick preached 'Shall the Fundamentalists Win?' on May 21, 1922, at the First Presbyterian Church in New York City; cf. Bradley J. Longfield, *The Presbyterian Controversy* (New York: Oxford, 1991), 9-11.

accounts for the fascination interpreters of all stripes have for this passage. In any case, scarcely has the fire died on Carmel's altar (1 Kings 18) before a horde of expositors and scholars jump with both feet all over Elijah in chapter 19. There seems to be such a huge contrast between the Elijah of Carmel and the Elijah of Horeb – and expositors are quick to exploit it.

Note how Ronald Wallace depicts the failure (chap. 19) in the midst of victory (chap. 18):

> Elijah cracked up. As we read on we see the man at whose courage all Israel had marvelled fleeing before the threat of a mere woman! We see the man who had spoken as if he had but to raise his hand and God would send legions of angels to aid him in the battle now floundering about for some prop by which to hold himself up. We see the man who had been the most spectacular political success suddenly sink into a mood of despondency and gloom.[2]

Similarly, A. W. Pink affirms that up to this point Elijah 'had been sustained by faith's vision of the living God, but now he lost sight of the Lord and saw only a furious woman.' This merely underscores the 'disastrous consequences of walking by sight.' Pink stresses the fact that Elijah 'went for *his life*' (v. 3) but 'not for God, nor for the good of his people; but because he thought only of self.'[3]

Sometimes observations border on sarcasm or contempt. Brueggemann reacts to Elijah's response in verse 10 with: 'The response is self-serving. One would imagine he came to Horeb simply to celebrate his personal faithfulness.'[4] Merrill F. Unger exclaims, 'What a contrast! Elijah the hero on Carmel victorious over Baalism! Elijah the coward of unbelief at Horeb, self-

---

[2] Ronald S. Wallace, *Elijah and Elisha* (Grand Rapids: Eerdmans, 1957), 45. Jezebel was certainly an unscrupulous and vicious woman, but I doubt anyone ever considered her a *mere* woman! Wallace has modified his view in his later *Readings in 1 Kings* (Grand Rapids: Eerdmans, 1996), 129-31, but I still think he draws too much from the mind of Elijah than from the text of Kings.

[3] A. W. Pink, *The Life of Elijah* (London: Banner of Truth, 1963), 197.

[4] Walter Brueggemann, *1 Kings*, Knox Preaching Guides (Atlanta: John Knox, 1982), 89.

occupied, utterly discouraged, wishing to die ..., praying against rather than for God's people.'[5]

But these are rather popular expositions. Does the picture not change when we turn to literary critics who engage in 'close reading'? Not really. Russell Gregory avers that words like 'I am left, I alone' (vv. 10, 14) 'reveal once more Elijah's arrogance.'[6] In the same volume, Alan Hauser holds that Elijah is 'transformed by Jezebel into a whimpering defeatist,' that he 'has not come to Horeb to do Yahweh's will' but is still 'fleeing from Jezebel and seeking Yahweh's pity,' and that God's question ('What are you doing here?') 'implies that Elijah really ought not to be at Mt. Horeb complaining, but rather back doing what he was sent to do among the people of Israel.'[7] Bernard Robinson seems to have slithered inside Elijah's own head when he writes:

> ...[T]he panic that came over him when Jezebel issued her threat against his life has punctured his inflated image of himself. He has always seen himself as *sui generis*, and cannot live with the realization that has come upon him during his flight that he is as other men.[8]

But these are literary critics. Can we not run to evangelical commentators and find a more balanced view? Hardly. Donald Wiseman opines that Elijah 'exhibited symptoms of manic depression, wishing for death, together with loss of appetite [in the text?], an inability to manage and with excessive self-pity.'[9]

---

[5] Cited in Ronald Barclay Allen, 'Elijah the Broken Prophet,' *Journal of the Evangelical Theological Society* 22 (1979): 196.

[6] In Alan J. Hauser and Russell Gregory, *From Carmel to Horeb* (Sheffield: Almond, 1990), 124.

[7] Pp. 60, 67, 71.

[8] Bernard P. Robinson, 'Elijah at Horeb, 1 Kings 19:1-18: A Coherent Narrative?,' *Revue Biblique* 98 (1991): 517.

[9] Donald J. Wiseman, *1 and 2 Kings*, Tyndale Old Testament Commentaries (Leicester: Inter-Varsity, 1993), 171. Richard D. Nelson warns that 'guessing at the psychological motivations of characters in narratives is usually a serious exegetical mistake' and proceeds to do so in Elijah's case! Apparently there are so many explicit symptoms that an interpreter cannot help himself (*First and Second Kings*, Interpretation [Louisville: John Knox, 1987], 126).

John Bimson is sure that on Mt. Horeb

> we see him weak, mistaken and in need of God's rebuke. God's
> opening question shows that, although God's own messenger had
> enabled Elijah to make the journey, Elijah should not really have
> been there. Elijah's answer completely devalued what had happened
> on Mt. Carmel. He ignored God's victory over Baal as though it had
> achieved nothing. By implication, he dismissed the people as utterly
> faithless. He disregarded the faithful Obadiah and the possibility that
> there might have been many more like him.[10]

Patterson and Austel seem very clear on Elijah's condition. They
lament that just 'when God needed him most, the divinely trained
prophet was to prove a notable failure'. They go on to make such
statements as:

> God's subsequent tender dealings with his prophet were to bring his
> spiritual problem to light. His God-given successes had fostered an
> inordinate pride (cf. vv. 4, 10, 14) that had made him take his own
> importance too seriously. Moreover Elijah had come to bask in the
> glow of the spectacular. He may have fully expected that because of
> what had been accomplished at Mount Carmel, Jezebel would
> capitulate and pagan worship would come to an end in Israel – all
> through his influence!

> Yet here he was, alone and seemingly deserted in this desert
> wasteland, the very symbol of a wasted life.

In their view God sent Elijah back to the northern kingdom, the
'place where he had veered off the track with God in his spiritual
life.'[11]

I propose that we continue our quest for the historical Elijah
but that we do so on a different road.

---

[10] John J. Bimson, '1 and 2 Kings,' *New Bible Commentary*, 4th éd.
(Leicester: Inter-Varsity, 1994), 360.

[11] R. D. Patterson and Hermann J. Austel, '1 and 2 Kings,' *Expositor's
Bible Commentary*, 12 vols. (Grand Rapids: Zondervan, 1988), 4:148, 149,
150-51.

The Path to Hermeneutical Sanity

I propose that there are some steps we can take which will probably cast a different light on this episode. Let me outline them.

1. Weigh the text. In the traditional Hebrew text the first word of verse 3 is a form of the verb *rā'āh* and may be rendered, 'And/ then he saw,' or 'When he saw (that).' However, a few Hebrew manuscripts read a form of *yārē'*, 'to fear, be afraid.' The LXX and derivative versions follow this latter reading. This reading ('Then he was afraid') seems to fit so naturally that most all modern English versions adopt it (e.g., NIV, NASB, NRSV; the last does not even indicate 'he saw' as an alternative). These two verbs look very much alike, especially in the 'imperfect' verb form used here, and so can be easily confused. Which was likely original? How can we tell? Ask which reading better explains the other. That is, is it more reasonable to assume that 'fear' was original and was changed to 'see', or that an original 'see' was changed to 'fear'? If 'fear' (*yārē'*) were original we have a problem, for it fits so naturally after Jezebel's threat in verse 2 that we can't imagine any scribe ever changing it to 'see' (*rā'āh*) and that reading then appearing in the bulk of Hebrew manuscripts. But if 'he saw' were original we can easily understand someone looking at that and thinking that the text must have meant to use the very similar looking 'he was afraid.' (At this point I am *afraid* to ask if you *see* that!) The upshot is that 'see' is more likely the true text.

Supposing then that 'he saw' is the original reading, how does it fit the context, coming as it does between Jezebel's threat in verse 2 and the following clauses of verse 3 ('he rose and went for his life')? We must remember chapter 18, where Yahweh, in living color and on turf known to be sacred to Baal, had publicly and irrefutably shown Baal to be the non-god he was; by both fire and rain Yahweh had proven he was the only real God – and the people had confessed as much (18:39). Ahab, of course, told Jezebel all about this and about Elijah's execution of the prophets of Baal (18:40). Then Jezebel sent her death-threat to Elijah (19:2). Hence Elijah *saw* that in spite of the Carmel Apologetic nothing was going to change in Israel; Jezebel was still wearing not only the pantyhose but the pants in the kingdom and calling the shots. Since he was not required to be meek meat under Jezebel's guillotine, Elijah left the kingdom, but not because he was afraid of dying. Rather,

> He wanted to die, for he was broken. He did not wish to die at Jezebel's hand, for that would be judged her victory – hence his flight. But south of the proverbial southernmost city of the southern kingdom, in the wilderness of Judah, where none would give Jezebel credit for his death – there he begged Yahweh to take his life.[12]

I think Allen is right. Elijah *was* broken. But one can be broken without being psychotic.

2. Watch the map. When Elijah arrives at Beersheba he is roughly 100 miles south of Jezreel, in the Dixie of Judah, and surely secure from Jezebel's clutches. When he therefore goes a day's travel into the wilderness (v. 4), it can hardly be for fear of Jezebel. Instead of the death he pleads for, Yahweh sustains his life (vv. 5-7a; cf. 17:4, 9), and the Angel of Yahweh himself suggests the impending journey to Elijah (v. 7b), which, in time, brings him to Horeb (v. 8). If we accept the traditional location in southern Sinai, Elijah is at Horeb some 200 miles south of Beersheba. Geography undercuts a good bit of the fear-interpretation. To use a very rough (American) analogy: if Jezebel is in Philadelphia, one could understand Elijah's fleeing to Washington, D.C.; but why go all the way to Raleigh, North Carolina, if you only want to get away from Jezebel? The map suggests we are dealing with plan rather than panic.

3. Ponder parallels. Elijah arrives at Horeb (v. 8), Moses' Place, Covenant Mountain. The Moses-Elijah parallels may not be tight but are nevertheless obvious. Horeb/Sinai was where the covenant was both given and broken (see Exod. 32-33; here, vv. 10, 14); the 'forty days and forty nights' (v. 8) were the time of Israel's

---

[12] Allen, 'Elijah the Broken Prophet,' 200. His argument effectively answers those (like Walsh) who claim that if Elijah truly wished to die he had no need to flee from Jezebel, since she would have gladly accommodated him.

unfaithfulness (Exod. 24:18; Deut. 9:9, 11) and of Moses' intercession (Deut. 9:18, 25; cf. Deut. 10:10 and Exod. 34:28). Here Yahweh 'passes by' ('*ābar*, v. 11) as he promised Moses (Exod. 33:19, 22).[13] Both occasions focus on covenant business: in Exodus, covenant intercession by Moses (chaps. 32-33) leads to covenant renewal and restoration (chap. 34), whereas in 1 Kings, to anticipate, covenant accusation (vv. 9-14) results in covenant judgment and restriction (vv. 15-18). Such parallels suggest that at the very least we may be dealing with matters of redemptive-historical moment and not merely with a whining prophet.

4. Believe angels. In verse 7 we are told that the angel of verse 5 is actually 'the angel of Yahweh.' He tells Elijah to eat and drink again 'for the journey is too much for you' (NIV). Verse 8 indicates that the angel is anticipating the trip to Horeb and not reflecting on the journey taken from Jezreel. If so, then Elijah goes to Horeb *with divine authorization*, a fact which should control how we construe Yahweh's question in verses 9b and 13. Which brings us to the need to....

5. Consider options. The interpretation of this text reminds me of the way John Wesley once reflected on his preaching. At the end of a Sunday's work in which he had preached three times, Wesley declared, 'I believe it pleased God to bless the first sermon most, because it gave the most offence.'[14] Was the offence a sign that God was blessing or only that Wesley himself was obnoxious? Apparently, Wesley could not conceive of the latter possibility.

That of-course-we-know-what-this-means attitude has plagued this passage. Yahweh's question (vv. 9b, 13) is consistently taken as an implied criticism of Elijah. Yahweh is 'rebuking his faint-heartedness'[15] or is conveying 'to the prophet the inappropriateness

---

[13] We cannot be certain that 'the cave' (v. 13) refers to the very spot Moses occupied in Exodus 33:21-22, though some think so.

[14] Arnold A. Dallimore, *George Whitefield*, 2 vols. (Westchester, IL: Cornerstone Books, 1979), 1:197.

[15] James A. Montgomery, *A Critical and Exegetical Commentary on the Books of Kings*, International Critical Commentary (New York: Scribners, 1951), 314.

of his being where he presently in fact is.'[16] Robinson says that when Elijah arrives at Horeb, Yahweh 'twice tells him that he ought to be elsewhere.'[17] Hence Robinson infers that neither Yahweh nor his messenger (=angel) wanted Elijah at Horeb; rather, the 'journey' the angel had in mind was Elijah's trip back to Israel, but somehow Elijah ventured off in the other direction.[18] Can no one consider Yahweh's question as an *invitation* rather than a rebuke? In light of the context (see items 2, 3, and 4 above), it seems to me that this is the correct alternative, as if Yahweh says, 'What are you doing here, at Moses' Place, at the Covenant Connection, Elijah, where I myself [v. 7] have led you to come?' And therefore Menken may also be right when he says that this was

> a question of tender kindness, to relieve the full, burdened heart of the prophet, that he, to whom the great privilege of being able to complain of his sorrow had so long been denied, might be moved to reveal his desire, to pour out his whole heart before the Lord.[19]

6. *Listen to prophets.* I make the naïve and novel proposal that Elijah may be telling the sober truth in verses 10 and 14. The usual diagnosis charges him with 'inflexibility and egocentrism.'[20] By the way, I am not troubled by the doubling of the question-

---

[16] W. J. Dumbrell, 'What are you doing here: Elijah at Horeb [1 Kgs 19],' *Crux* 22/1 (1986): 12.

[17] Robinson, 'Elijah at Horeb,' 518.

[18] Robinson, 519, 522. Jerome Walsh takes the same position (*1 Kings*, Berit Olam [Collegeville, MN: Liturgical, 1996], 270, 272). There are two problems with it: it is not the more natural way of reading the text, and it does not make sense. How could a trek back to Israel be called a 'journey too much for you' (v. 7)? He had made it south of Beer-sheba, hadn't he? Surely going back to Israel with settlements along the way would not require special sustenance, but going in 'Moses-time' (forty days and forty nights) all the way to Moses' Place (Horeb) through bleak and desolate country was another matter.

[19] Quoted in K. C. W. F. Bähr, *The Books of the Kings*, Lange's Commentary on the Holy Scriptures, in vol. 3, *Samuel-Kings* (1868; reprint ed., Grand Rapids: Zondervan, 1960), 219.

[20] Gregory, *From Carmel to Horeb*, 134.

response in verses 9-10 and 13-14, for the chapter deals in pairs – two stages of Elijah's journey (vv. 3, 4), two episodes of angelic provision (vv. 5-7). I take verses 9-10 as a sort of preliminary hearing and verses 13-14 as a formal statement of the charges.[21] But back to Elijah's answer. Is it too wild to consider that Elijah, finding himself in the shuddering presence of the Almighty, may have been speaking the truth?

> I have been terribly jealous for Yahweh, God of hosts,
> for they have abandoned your covenant – the sons of Israel,
> your altars they have thrown down,
> and your prophets they have killed with the sword,
> and I am left, I alone,
> and (now) they seek my life, to take it (v. 14).

Elijah claims he is upset for God's sake, for God's cause. The Hebrew underscores this by placing the emphasis on the direct objects, especially 'your altars' and 'your prophets.' Note that Elijah only mentions his own case as illustrative, as a confirmation of the general Prophets' Liquidation Programme.[22] It sounds like Elijah is charging Israel with apostasy rather than crying over a

---

[21] Verse 11a implies that after the theophany of vv. 11b-12 Elijah would be 'before Yahweh' (=in Yahweh's presence) in a way in which he was not in verses 9-10, and so charges would be lodged 'officially' at that point.

[22] Expositors tend to accuse Elijah both of whining and inaccuracy. Elijah had made the same 'I only' statement on Mt. Carmel (18:22) and most don't accuse him of self-pity there. But how could Elijah make such a statement when he knew there were, for example, a hundred prophets of Yahweh sheltered and sustained by Obadiah (18:4, 13)? But they were in caves. It's not wild to understand Elijah's statements in 18:22 and 19:10 and 14 as meaning 'I am the only prophet openly and visibly opposing the Baal machine.' But surely Elijah is uncharitable in so accusing the Israelites (so Walsh, *1 Kings*, 273), for it is as if he ignores their conversion in 18:39 and must dispute its sincerity. We probably don't have enough data to clear up this matter. Yet when Elijah saw (19:3) that Ahab was effecting no changes post-Carmel and that Jezebel was still running the show, he likely knew there would be no large-scale or public change among the people. What evidence we do have shows that Jezebel's sway turned Israelites into pliable toadies (21:11-14).

failed ministry. Indeed I think verses 13-14 constitute a formal lawsuit against Israel. After the covenant Lord comes, he puts the formal question to the prosecutor (v. 13b), who then levels the formal charges against the accused (v. 14). In my view, *Elijah's mission at Horeb was to bring covenant accusation against Israel for breach of the covenant.*[23]

7. Connect the context. The following context (=vv. 15-18) throws a shaft of light upon verses 9-14. In verses 15-18 Yahweh places Elijah in charge of anointing Hazael, Jehu, and Elisha. These two kings and one prophet will be Yahweh's *instruments of judgment* upon Israel (note the terminology of v. 17, 'sword,' and 'slay'), though even in this wrath Yahweh will remember mercy (v. 18).[24] This (vv. 15-18) is Yahweh's response to Elijah's accusation (v. 14). We might catch the flavor via a paraphrase. It is as if Yahweh says, 'You're absolutely right, Elijah! I agree with your assessment and your charges are true. Therefore, I am going to bring covenant judgment, and I want you to return and to set apart my instruments of judgment. And yet there will be a remnant that I will keep faithful.' Yahweh does not rebuke Elijah but *agrees* with him; he does not condemn Elijah but confirms his diagnosis![25] Claus Schedl is right on the money:

---

[23] On Elijah as covenant prosecutor, see W. A. VanGemeren, *The Progress of Redemption* (Grand Rapids: Zondervan, 1988), 257-58, 449-50, and his *Interpreting the Prophetic Word* (Grand Rapids: Zondervan, 1990), 36-38.

[24] 'Judgment would come through (1) internal political forces in Israel, represented by Jehu; (2) external military forces, represented by the Aramean Hazael; and (3) the prophetic ministry, symbolized by Elisha' (VanGemeren, *Interpreting the Prophetic Word,* 37).

[25] Yet expositors commonly ignore this connection between verse 14 and verses 15-18. They tend to interpret verses 15-18 in isolation as if Yahweh administers reality therapy for the prophet's alleged depression. To Fretheim God is saying: 'Quit the pity party, go back home, much work remains to be done, and here are a few starters; besides, you're not alone' (*First and Second Kings*, Westminster Bible Companion [Louisville: Westminster/John Knox, 1999], 110). My hunch is that most interpreters don't take Elijah's words in verse 14 seriously because they look upon him

The theophany is thus not meant to chide the prophet; quite the contrary, it is a full endorsement of his zeal in behalf of Yahweh's sole kingship.[26]

These seven considerations do not resolve every dilemma in this text, but they do, in my opinion, point us in the right direction, a different direction from those who prefer to keep Elijah on the couch.

Can Hermeneutical Mountains Be Moved?

We come to a thrilling but teasing text. I refer to verses 11-12. How are we to understand this text in its context? Can we get at the heart of these lines? One can scarcely read these verses without feeling the grip of their climax, 'And after the fire a still small voice' (KJV). Intuitively one feels that here is a great text! There is only one problem: what does it mean?

I prefer to translate the last phrase of verse 12, *qôl dĕmāmâ daqqâ*, as 'a voice, a low whisper.' The quietness or silence was not absolute, for Elijah heard it (v. 13a); and, although *qôl* can also mean 'sound' or 'noise,' in this context it is important to construe it as 'voice' (more on this below).[27]

How then are we to understand this theophany? One commonly meets with the *didactic view*, i.e., it was didactic for Elijah, especially that it was 'an implied rebuke of much in Elijah's

---

as a psychological basket case who obviously can't assess matters in their true colors. Why then would God give a rational response to a neurotic like Elijah? But if for once interpreters would take off their clinical white coats and listen to Elijah's charges, they ought to see that Yahweh in his response *concurs* with the prophet. But amateur psychotherapists die hard.

[26] Claus Schedl, *History of the Old Testament*, 5 vols. (Staten Island: Alba House, 1972), 4:67.

[27] J. Lust argues that verse 12b should be rendered 'a crushing and roaring sound'; see 'Gentle Breeze or a Roaring Thunderous Sound: Elijah at Horeb, 1 Kings 19:12,' *Vetus Testamentum* 25 (1975): 110-15; also his 'Elijah and the Theophany on Mount Horeb,' in *La notion biblique de Dieu* (Leuven: LUP, 1985), 91-99. Jeffrey Niehaus, *God at Sinai* (Grand Rapids: Zondervan, 1995), 248, follows him here. I still think the text intends a contrast and remain unconvinced by Lust's argument.

methods.'[28] De Vries waxes applicatory and holds that the Horeb experience is 'a rebuke not only for the biblical prophet, but for all religionists who rely on shoutings and flurries of action, while neglecting the way of quiet love, simple piety, and persuasive kindness.'[29] B. B. Warfield alleged that 'Elijah could not understand that the ends of God could be gained unless they were gained in the path of miracles of manifest judgment' and so the Lord corrected him.[30] There may be some truth in this view, but surely the Lord was not merely advocating a kinder, gentler prophecy or prophet.

Others press for a *polemic view*: Yahweh's *not* being in the wind, earthquake, and fire is a broadside at Baal worship. These fireworks are associated with Baal as a storm and nature god. By not being 'in' them Yahweh is refusing to use these Baal-modes of revelation. Here these phenomena only herald the coming of Yahweh. Hence the purpose of the deafening explosions versus the quiet voice may be to show that Yahweh possessed all the attributes of a rain and storm god but was not part of nature; instead he was above it and controlled it.[31] I find the polemical view attractive but think it pulls more data from backgrounds than from the text. I think the polemics are more convincing in connection with chapters 17 and 18.

I would therefore downplay the polemics and advocate a *revelatory view*, that is, the text is teaching that Yahweh is present especially in his word (which the following context will show to be a word of judgment and of grace). Yahweh was not in the wind,

---

[28] H. L. Ellison, *The Prophets of Israel* (Grand Rapids: Eerdmans, 1969), 32. He goes on to say, however, that 'it was a rebuke of the exaggerated in them, and God immediately accepted the accusation against Israel as fundamentally correct' (pp. 32-33).

[29] S. J. De Vries, *1 Kings*, Word Biblical Commentary (Waco: Word, 1985), 237.

[30] B. B. Warfield, *Faith and Life* (1916; reprint ed., Edinburgh: Banner of Truth, 1974), 12.

[31] Leah Bronner, *The Stories of Elijah and Elisha as Polemics against Baal Worship*, Pretoria Oriental Series (Leiden: Brill, 1968), 63; Frank Moore Cross, *Canaanite Myth and Hebrew Epic* (Cambridge, MA: Harvard, 1973), 190-94.

earthquake, and fire (vv. 11b-12a). The wind is most extensively described; it is 'great and strong, splitting mountains and shattering rocks'; and it does this 'before Yahweh' – this last is presumably true for the earthquake and fire as well. These phenomena are precursors of Yahweh's arrival, but he is 'in' none of these. After the fire, however, there is 'a voice, a low whisper' (v. 12b). The text does not say that Yahweh *was* 'in' the voice, but, clearly, this is the signal to Elijah that Yahweh is present (note v. 13a). The text is not saying Elijah must be more gentle; if anything, it says Yahweh must be gentle if his prophet is to have dealings with him. How can the prophet survive wind, earthquake, and fire? If anything is to transpire, Yahweh must restrain himself. Thus 'a voice, a low whisper.' Even so, Elijah must wrap up his face – just as a glimpse of Yahweh's 'after-effects' must have been trauma enough for Moses (Exod. 33:23).

Now let us trace the thread of the text: The 'voice' (*qôl*) of verse 12b appears again in 13b, where the *qôl* asks Elijah the what-are-you-doing-here question. In verse 9b the same question had been asked by 'the word of Yahweh'. I assume then that the 'voice' in 13b is to be identified with the word of Yahweh. The following context seems to confirm this, for after the voice (*qôl*) asks the question in 13b and Elijah answers in 14, verse 15 begins with 'Then Yahweh said to him,' and proceeds to announce both judgment (vv. 15-17) and grace (v. 18). Perhaps we are to see a contrast: you may not find Yahweh in the spectacular explosions of 'nature', but you can be sure he is present in his quiet word given to his prophet(s), a word that directs history (vv. 15-17) and preserves a people (v. 18).[32] Allow this discussion to simmer on the back burner and we will build upon it in the next section.

From Horeb to Homiletics

Much ink has been spilt arguing for a proper approach to and interpretation of 1 Kings 19. This has been necessary because the passage has been – for the most part and in my view – grossly misinterpreted. One can understand this. We as readers seem to identify so readily with Elijah's situation and perhaps with how he must have felt that we are almost sure that we understand what's happening from the start. And so, almost immediately, we become fixated on prophetic feelings rather than on biblical text. I know. In my first pastorate I preached 'The path to spiritual depression' from this passage and offered useful psychological advice baptized in biblical narrative. But I have repented. And I have dragged you through pages arguing for a more excellent way. But does it all make any difference? Does the chapter provide teaching or only stir debate? Hence we must move on to the teaching and preaching points of the text, and I propose that our 'covenantal' interpretation yields richer applications than the usual 'psychological' approach.

Remember the drift of this study. I have agreed with Ronald Barclay Allen that Elijah was not terrified by Jezebel but broken by her unrepentant paganism and by her continuing power throughout the nation. Keep the redemptive-historical situation in mind, especially the significance of Horeb. Elijah was meeting

---

[32] The structure of verses 9-18 falls into two symmetrical parts:

> Elijah stays in the cave, 9a
> > Yahweh's question, 9b
> > (And behold! – the word of Yahweh to him, and he said ...)
> > > Elijah's answer, 10
> > > > Yahweh's command, 11a
> > > > (And he said, Go forth and stand)
> > > > > Three destructive precursors, 11b-12a
> > > > > A surprising contrast, 12b
> Elijah in entrance of cave, 13a
> > Yahweh's question, 13b
> > (And behold! – to him a voice, and he said ...)
> > > Elijah's answer, 14
> > > > Yahweh's command, 15a
> > > > (And Yahweh said to him, Go, return)
> > > > > Three instruments of judgment, 15b-17
> > > > > A faithful remnant, 18

We should not press correspondences too far. VanGemeren (*Interpreting the Prophetic Word*, 37) would relate the wind, earthquake, and fire (11b-12) to the three instruments of judgment (Jehu, Hazael, and Elisha, 15b-17), but would we then want to say that Yahweh 'was not in' the judgments he authorized?

God at Moses' Place; Yahweh's own nudge had directed him there. And Elijah's mission there was to bring accusation against Israel for ongoing breach of covenant. In light of this the text teaches ...

1. The limitations of evidence, or, the 'frustration' of revelation (vv. 1-3)

Just because there has been clear proof on Carmel (chap. 18) doesn't mean Jezebel will receive that proof or that such clear evidence will change her. One can imagine the semi-apocryphal scene. Ahab mildly protests, 'But Jezebel, honey, when Elijah prayed to Yahweh, fire came down and zlurped up everything right there in front of our eyeballs!' The queen glares through mascara-laden lashes at Ahab and with that familiar derisive turn of Revlon-tended lips retorts, 'So?' This response surprises us if we have swallowed the education fallacy that pervades our culture and governments, i.e., get people the right information and it will change them.

But it doesn't. In one of his columns Don Feder reviewed Japan's attack on Pearl Harbor on December 7, 1941. While paying tribute to the heroism of many American servicemen he bemoaned the stupidity that allowed it to happen. He cited the evidence. American cryptographers had cracked the Japanese diplomatic code and on November 22, 1941, intercepted a message to the Japanese envoys negotiating with Roosevelt that in about a week 'things are automatically going to happen'. In January 1941, the U. S. ambassador to Japan reported he had heard a lot of talk that in case of a break with the U.S., Japan was planning 'a surprise mass attack on Pearl Harbor'. Days before Japan's attack the FBI reported that the Japanese consulate in Honolulu was burning its diplomatic papers. There was more, but this is adequate. There were all these indications, all these telltale evidences. And yet the U.S. (or somebody therein) paid no heed. It changed nothing.

Sometimes Christians slip into thinking that if we only get the truth to people or press upon them our most rigorous and cogent arguments, then.... But let Jezebel be your teacher about what the human heart is like. There was a blaze of light on Mt. Carmel, but unless Yahweh grants internal light to see his external light the darkness remains. Yahweh's fire consumed everything (18:38) except the blindness in Jezebel's mind and the recalcitrance in her will. 'And this is the judgment, that the light has come into the world and men loved darkness rather than light...' (John 3:19). This realization must temper all our expectations in our evangelism, counseling, and preaching.

2. The tenderness of God toward his desponding servants (vv. 9, 13)
Many interpreters would see these verses as God's rebuke for his arrogant or self-pitying servant. I do not take a different view because I have a passion to defend biblical characters, but because I think Elijah has gotten a raw deal from the hermeneutical media. Clearly, verses 4-8 already show Yahweh's kind sustenance for the prophet's need. 'Why, at his head there was a cake [*'ugâ*] baked on coals and a jug [*ṣappaḥat*] of water' (v. 6). The terms conjure up the previous provision story in chapter 17, where the same words occur: Elijah begs the widow for a 'little cake' (17:13) and Yahweh insures there is always oil in her 'jug' (17:12, 14, 16). But I would suggest Elijah receives not only provision but understanding. There is an implicit tenderness in Yahweh's famous question, 'What are you doing here, Elijah?' (vv. 9, 13). I contend that Yahweh's query is not reproof but invitation. It is a double invitation – an invitation to state the case against Israel and, in so doing, to unburden his own soul. Yahweh's question is both covenantal and pastoral. It is an act of kindness, offering Elijah the opportunity to spill his concerns. Since verses 15-18 show Yahweh's agreement with the prophet's charges, a positive view of Yahweh's questions becomes all the more likely. This kindness, of course, is vintage Yahweh. And I must confess that in my despair I would far rather fall into the hands of Elijah's God than into the clutches of his interpreters.

3. The one holy passion that should stir God's servants (vv. 10, 14)
As noted, the common view is that these verses patently and plainly show Elijah wallowing in self-pity or even engaging in prophetic bellyaching of the most reprehensible sort. Perhaps we have a vested interest in insisting that Elijah is whining. If we grant that

in the presence of God he is carefully speaking the truth, then does he not condemn us? Do we not hear in Elijah's answer a theology and experience that disturb us? Could you or I earnestly say such words?[33] Do we really care that much about the infidelity of the professing church? Do its doctrinal indifference and idolatrous pragmatism ever get us upset *for God's sake*? But then if we think Elijah is only a psychological mess ready for the fellows in the white coats – well, then, we'll never have to face that question, will we?

Late in September 1781, Prince William Henry (George III's son, who would reign as King William IV) arrived in New York. His arrival stirred the English into a flurry of activity. There was a 21-gun salute. There were parties, receptions, parades, tours of the city, reviews of German and English regiments, dinners with prominent citizens, an evening concert by a military band. Down in Yorktown life was not so frivolous. Lord Cornwallis was impounded with Colonial and French troops in his front and the French fleet in the bay in his rear, awaiting relief from New York. In New York General Clinton held councils of war but didn't move; the navy repaired its ships but didn't sail.[34] They should have been making war but they were entertaining the prince, as lassitude reigned in New York. They had no passion for what mattered.

Clearly, Elijah did – if we can take his words at face value. Is he depressed? Is he despondent? I think so. Over what? Over Yahweh's interests – his covenant, his altars, his prophets. Such intensity and God-centeredness seem strange to us; indeed it exposes our frivolity by comparison. But if we can construe Elijah as a semi-whacko 'covenanter' we can more easily justify ourselves. But if Elijah's answer to Yahweh is not swept aside, you are left with unnerving questions. What is it that you get despondent about? Do you ever get depressed for God's sake?

---

[33] The usual interpretation does not allow you even to raise this issue because it has already presumed that Elijah's 'outburst' is not to be taken seriously.

[34] Barbara W. Tuchman, *The First Salute* (New York: Knopf, 1988), 278-79.

4. The hiddenness of Yahweh's work and presence (vv. 9-14)

I find it difficult to let go of the tantalizing contrast between Yahweh's not being 'in' the wind, earthquake, and fire, and his apparent presence in the quiet voice (vv. 11-12). Might this suggest that Yahweh will not be giving many dramatic, overt proofs of his reality, as at Carmel (chap. 18), now that such revelation has been officially rejected? Instead his presence and reality will primarily be seen in his ongoing work of judgment (vv. 15-17) and grace (v. 18), which through his voice and his word he has disclosed to his prophet (see Amos 3:7-8). The 'quietness' of Yahweh's work does not mean he is not at work, but rather that the kingdom of God has gone into its mustard-seed mode.[35] I was reminded of this several weeks ago when we sang one of Margaret Clarkson's hymns in public worship:

> God of this morning, gladly your children
> worship before You, trustingly bow:
> Teach us to know You always among us,
> *Quietly sov'reign* – Lord of our now.[36]

There is a spillover from the text to our own day. Christians may crave signs but will seldom find Christ in the wind, earthquake, and fire. It is Baal worship that works up orgasms (cf. 18:28-29); biblical faith is content with the word.

5. The stubbornness of the covenant-keeping God (v. 18)

This climactic declaration puts a thrill into one's theological bones. 'And/but I shall leave seven thousand in Israel....'[37] It is the Old Testament equivalent of Jesus' 'I will build my church' (Matt. 16:18). Grace *will* have a remnant. The God of grace insists on it. Yahweh, so the text teaches, will always have a people, even an

---

[35] Cf. H. L. Ellison: 'If we grasp the inner significance of Elijah at Sinai we shall understand the work of his followers better. They strove not so much to save the state as to increase the size of the remnant, for there are probably few who will regard the 7,000 as anything other than a symbolic number' (*The Prophets of Israel*, 33).

[36] 'God of the Ages,' stanza 2 (emphasis mine).

Israelite people (Rom. 11:1-6), to worship him upon the earth. He has decided that he will have a true people, and he will have them and keep them, and there is nothing any Jezebel can do about it. It is the infectious assurance, the defiant certainty, the holy dogmatism, of this text that keeps some of us on our feet.

Elijah has not been Yahweh's last broken servant. There are cases also in these new covenant days. It is hardly a state to be desired, and yet surely 1 Kings 19 teaches you that you needn't fear being a broken servant when you have such a kind and adequate God.

---

[37] The verb should be translated as an English future (not as a present, as in NIV, nor as a past, as in NKJV) since verse 18 is anticipatory as with all of verses 15-17. The point is that as Yahweh will be executing judgment he will also *in that judgment* be preserving a true church.

Chapter 25

Leaving the Farm

1 Kings 19:19-21

Lest we think this passage invites us to enjoy a nostalgic visit to the family farm, we must remind ourselves what it depicts. This episode is like a homeowner who discovers a little dampness or some slight dribbles of water in the pan or on the floor under the water heater in his/her house. Nothing to panic about. But it should be monitored, for it may become a small puddle with some flecks of rust idling about. It indicates the water heater is rusting out and, if left untended, the climactic day will come when the contraption gives way and a domestic flood gushes out. Elisha's call corresponds to those first dribbles of water. Elisha, remember, was to prove an instrument of judgment upon Israel (vv. 16-17), and so Elijah's claiming Elisha for Yahweh's service constitutes the very first and faint fulfillment of Yahweh's decreed process of judgment (outlined in vv. 15-17).[1] Israel's fate then hangs behind Elisha's call. We must keep this in mind even though we focus just now on that call.

---

[1] Cf. Burke O. Long, *1 Kings*, Forms of the Old Testament Literature (Grand Rapids: Eerdmans, 1984), 206 (under 'Intention'). According to verses 15-17, Elijah was to *anoint* Hazael, Jehu, and Elisha. Elijah actually anointed none of them: he threw his mantle upon Elisha (v. 19), Elisha's deputy anointed Jehu (2 Kings 9:1-10), and Elisha predicted (apparently apart from actual anointing) Hazael's rise to kingship (2 Kings 8:7-15). Some would say this shows Elijah less than obedient, but I think H. L. Ellison is nearer the mark: 'For Elijah to anoint those who were to carry on his work, whether he did it personally or by proxy, is rather to stress with what authority they would act, when they brought judgment and destruction on Israel' (*The Prophets of Israel* [Grand Rapids: Eerdmans, 1969], 33).

How Suddenly God's Call May Come (v. 19)

> So he went from there and found Elisha son of Shaphat, while he was plowing. Twelve pairs of oxen were in front of him – he himself was with the twelfth. And Elijah crossed over to him and threw his mantle upon him (v. 19).

Howard Hamer had just taken off in his homemade plane from the airfield in Chiloquin, a high desert town in Oregon. Almost immediately the single-engine plane lost power and Hamer decided to attempt an emergency landing on northbound route U.S. 97. Filiberto Corona Ambriz was minding his own business this particular Thursday. He was driving his rig, a flatbed truck, north on U.S. 97. Unknowingly he drove his flatbed truck under Hamer's plane at the very moment the latter was trying to settle his craft down on the highway. Hamer, the pilot, never saw the truck since he was watching out for southbound traffic and trying to keep the plane's nose up. Ambriz knew nothing of the plane until he felt a bump and heard a loud bang. The propeller caught on the truck's sleeper and the plane's nose remained there, while the tail dropped down on the flatbed trailer. The 'landing' was successful and neither man was injured.[2]

Now that usually doesn't happen to most truck drivers. There is no way Mr. Ambriz could have guessed that would happen. He did not say, 'You know, I'll bet while I'm driving north on U.S. 97 today some plane will use my flatbed for a runway.' No, he was simply doing what he normally does and, literally, out of the blue a plane landed on his truck.

That is precisely how Elisha must have remembered this day. He was simply doing what farm lads must regularly do, in his case working the ground on Shaphat's farm near Abel-meholah.[3] How could he have guessed that Elijah the Tishbite would come walking across the field and throw his mantle on him? Elisha knew what that meant (v. 20a), but he hardly anticipated it when he

---

[2] An Associated Press story, appearing August 12, 2000, in our local newspaper.

[3] Location not definite but usually placed in the Jordan Valley west of the river, ten miles south of Beth-shan.

woke up that morning. Wallace reminds us that others have been so surprised: Moses while tending his daddy-in-law's flocks (Exod. 3:1-2) and Matthew in the midst of collecting tolls (Matt. 9:9).[4]

The call may be sudden, but that does not mean it is unplanned, as though the kingdom of God were a seat-of-the-pants operation, bumping along from one nervous synapse to another. Yahweh had disclosed his decision to use Elisha at Horeb (v. 16). So what appeared sudden to Elisha was already settled with God. 'God had decided all this even before Elisha was given the opportunity of deciding.'[5] Suddenness is the wrapping paper in which sovereignty sometimes arrives.

Careful Bible readers (as we try to be) are quick to note that Elisha is a special case. His call is unique: he is called to be Elijah's successor much as Joshua was Moses' successor (cf. Num. 11:28; Deut. 31:14; Josh. 1:1). Yahweh calls Elisha to the prophetic office and to the special capacity as Elijah's successor, and so we may surmise that the text holds no claim on us at the John-and-Jane-Christian level. If so, we would be wrong. For, in one sense, Elisha's call is *not* all that unusual, for it simply depicts what God is always entitled to do (command our obedience) and what we are always obligated to acknowledge (that he has the right to do so). A particular call (like Elisha's) only dramatizes in a unique case the general attitude that ought always to pervade God's people, namely, that they are servants ready to do their Master's will.

How Joyfully God's Call Is Obeyed (vv. 20-21a)

(20) And he left the oxen, ran after Elijah, and said, 'Please let me kiss my father and my mother, and I will come after you.' Then he said to him, 'Go, return; but what have I done to you?'
(21a) So he turned back from after him, took the pair of oxen, and slaughtered them; and, using the implements of the oxen, he boiled them, that is, the meat; then he gave it to the people and they ate.

---

[4] Ronald S. Wallace, *Readings in 1 Kings* (Grand Rapids: Eerdmans, 1996), 136.

[5] See Wallace, *Elijah and Elisha* (Grand Rapids: Eerdmans, 1957), 56.

Elisha's response does not indicate unwillingness but a clear recognition of what is demanded ('I will come after you') and an obvious desire to comply.[6] His following actions point to his intention to make a complete break with his former work. Why did Elisha use the oxen's gear for firewood?

> [C]ertainly not because there was no other wood at hand…, but rather in order to indicate that he gave up for ever his previous calling.[7]

And people ate steak to celebrate it.

Sometimes Elisha has received less than favorable reviews because people allow Luke 9:61-62 to color their reading of our passage. Because of the similar trappings and coloring of the two texts one wonders if interpreters don't view the volunteer of Luke 9:61-62 as Elisha's alter ego and therefore impute to Elisha an inferior commitment.[8] The fellow in Luke 9 is far different from Elisha. Jesus' comment in verse 62 pictures one who has resolutely

---

[6] The last clause of Elijah's response to Elisha is difficult: 'For/but what have I done to you?' These words may emphasize the permission in 'Go, return,' i.e., 'Of course you may; what have I done to prevent that?' (so Keil). Or (taking the particle *kî* adversatively), they may suggest a caution: 'Yes, you may, but remember what I've done to you and what it signifies' (so Gray).

[7] K. C. W. F. Bähr, *The Books of the Kings*, Lange's Commentary on the Holy Scriptures, in vol. 3, *Samuel-Kings* (1868; reprint ed., Grand Rapids: Zondervan, 1960), 223. So too R. S. Wallace: 'The slaying of the oxen was a sign that he was sacrificing to God what was most precious in his former way of life. The destruction of the yokes was a sign that never again would he come back and take up this work' (*Readings in 1 Kings* [Grand Rapids: Eerdmans, 1996], 137).

[8] Cf. the remarks in Darrell L. Bock, *Luke*, IVP New Testament Commentary (Downers Grove: InterVarsity, 1994), 186; and F. W. Danker, *Jesus and the New Age* (Philadelphia: Fortress, 1988), 211. I recognize Luke 9 presses home the urgency of commitment in light of the 'already' presence of the kingdom in Jesus, but that is no reason to dub Elisha's request as 'temporizing' (Danker). Taking time to ponder the Old Testament text on its own terms and in its own context often prevents such questionable comparisons.

taken up a task (the plow) only to be continually looking back.[9] That is, he has a divided mind. Luke 9:61 has only a formal similarity to 1 Kings 19:20. In Luke 9 saying good-bye is an obstacle to kingdom commitment, whereas in 1 Kings 19 it functions as the entry into kingdom service. Elisha goes back to *sever* his connections, not to delay his commitment. He does not return to hold back but to cut loose.[10]

Our text clearly shows that Elisha faced the cost of his call in the area of *affections*: 'Please let me kiss my father and my mother.' He knew going after Elijah would forever subordinate such relationships (cf. Luke 14:25-26). But he had to kiss *security* good-bye as well. The fact that Shaphat may have twelve pairs of oxen suggests a comfortable level of wealth on the family homestead. Even if some of this stock 'belonged to neighbors who had turned out to help, the field must have been a big one to be thus ploughed'.[11] Shaphat's farm offers a degree of earthly comfort that Elijah's mantle can't touch. Perhaps (for this is not so obvious) he had to turn from the lure of *familiarity*. Naturally, some are not lured by familiarity. But some of us who think that tedium and routine are cousins of joy understand. There is something strangely reassuring in knowing what will generally be on your plate. Life is not predictable, but the familiar can give you the illusion that it is. Farm, soil, livestock, crops – such was the ordered tradition of the customary. Elijah offered nothing so stable.

As we think with Elisha's sandals on we should realize that even as Jesus' disciples we don't live in a different bailiwick. We must consider the hindrances, obstacles, and difficulties that may or do stand in the way of whole-souled commitment to Jesus. Affections, security, familiarity – don't we find ourselves repeatedly having to count the cost precisely in these 'Elishan'

---

[9] Note the decisive action implied in the aorist *epibalōn*, followed by the ongoing action of the present *blepōn*; M. Zerwick and Mary Grosvenor, *A Grammatical Analysis of the Greek New Testament*, 4th ed. (Rome: Pontifical Biblical Institute, 1993), 217.

[10] A truer New Testament parallel might be Luke 5:29 (and context), where Levi's party was not incompatible with a previous call to discipleship.

[11] Ellison, *The Prophets of Israel*, 43.

areas? Don't we find our favorite idols arising from these domains, even if we've never been lured by Baal worship?

For Elisha, Yahweh's call must dominate everything. For some perverse reason the claim of this text reminds me of a brief aside Walker Percy makes in one of his novels:

> There is one sure cure for cosmic explorations, grandiose ideas about God, man, death, suicide, and such – and that is nausea. I defy a man afflicted with nausea to give a single thought to these vast subjects. A nauseated man is a sober man. A nauseated man is a disinterested man.[12]

A bit disgusting but lucid. Given the situation, nausea preempts all other considerations. The fellow with such a malady can only say, 'I am a man with nausea and my nausea controls everything – I can give attention to nothing else.' A sick analogy perhaps, but that is the way God's call must dominate God's servants. And it did so in Elisha's case. With Elijah's mantle over his shoulders, Yahweh's call before him, and perhaps much to keep him, he willingly cried, 'I will come after you.'

How Ingloriously God's Call Begins (v. 21b)

The farewell dinner is over. Now Elisha 'rose up and went after Elijah and served him.' I do not want to bleed every detail of the text for significance, but might it be worth pointing out that that is not very glamorous labor for one who has been specially designated by Yahweh (v. 16)? A few years later after Elijah's departure a coalition of kings, prodded by Judah's Jehoshaphat, wanted to obtain direction from one of Yahweh's prophets. A servant of the king of Israel knew of one available: 'Elisha the son of Shaphat is here, who used to pour water on the hands of Elijah' (2 Kings 3:11, NASB).[13] Elisha used to plow fields. Then Yahweh called

---

[12] Walker Percy, *The Second Coming* (New York: Farrar, Straus, Giroux, 1980), 213.

[13] 'The custom of washing hands before and after eating is well attested; pouring water over the hands on such occasions was a gesture of respect shown by a servant to his master or by a host to his guest' (G. H. Jones, *1*

him, and he poured water on Elijah's hands. Not a very outstanding piece of ministry. Simply a personal servant of Elijah.

But this snatch of a verse, with its companion from 2 Kings 3, should not be wasted on us. Is it perhaps the very check we need to receive in the church in the west just now? Do we not often find ourselves wanting to ascend the ministry scale, not necessarily in remuneration but in recognition? Don't we sense, if we know our own twisted hearts, that we are soul brothers with James and John in our quest for ministerial supremacy (Mark 10:35-37)? However, when the Holy Spirit exposes my darkest secrets, I must confess that I would not be content with sitting at the right or left of the Son of Man; I would have *more* than that. It is frightening to realize that Christ has called you and that you still find the lure of Genesis 3:5 so overwhelming. We are not naturally servants (cf. Mark 10:43-45).

Yet if our idolatry needs this text, so does our discouragement. Yahweh calls Elisha and 'he rose up and went after Elijah and served him.' Pretty mundane stuff. But at that time that was Yahweh's call. If it is Yahweh's call, then what is wrong with a 'no frills' ministry, perhaps somewhere in the backwater? If Yahweh calls us to pour water on the hands of Elijah and we do so, are we not doing his will? Does anything else matter?

---

and 2 Kings, New Century Bible Commentary, 2 vols. [Grand Rapids: Eerdmans, 1984], 2:395).

Chapter 26

Getting Clear about God

1 Kings 20

Reading the Bible may be like staying in someone else's house. Imagine you must be in a certain locale for a week or so, and some people currently out of town have offered you the use of their house during that time. They may be your friends or only friends of your friends. Anyway, you will have the run of their house and enjoy welcome savings on lodging costs. During your tenure in their home you may think that – if it were your place – you would have arranged it differently. Perhaps you'd prefer a lighter color on the walls, a different style of furniture, and the weight-lifting apparatus moved out of the dining room. But it's not your place – it's theirs. They have arranged items as they, presumably, want them and as a temporary guest you must simply accept their arrangement. So with the Bible: we may prefer another arrangement but our task is to work with what we have been given.

We must therefore realize how the Bible writer has arranged the last three chapters of 1 Kings. As he united chapters 17–19 around the 'God war', so he combines chapters 20–22 into another triad in which each chapter emphasizes the *failure of Ahab* and how the word of God stands opposed to him. Because of Ahab's spineless moderation, both Ahab and Israel stand under doom (20:42); because of his heartless oppression, his household will be exterminated (21:21-24); and because of his thick-headed obtuseness, his life is forfeit (22:19-23, 29-38). No other king receives such a literary battering from the sacred writer, but no other king the likes of Ahab had come along (21:20, 25; cf. 16:30, 33). Chapters 20-22 then intend to display Ahab's repeated (and fatal) opposition to the word of Yahweh.

So much for orientation to chapters 20–22. What about chapter

20 and its historical background? We cannot be sure precisely when the events related in chapter 20 occurred. One might not be far wrong to assume that the Aramaean incursion came about 860 BC, or shortly afterwards, under Ben-hadad II.[1] Discussing the chapter's critical problems will be next to useless,[2] but surveying its structure will help us to grasp the coherence and development of the story.

General Structure of 1 Kings 20

Syrian threat (against Samaria), 1-12
  Prophetic intervention, 13-14
    Israelite victory, 15-21
      Aftermath: Prophetic counsel, 22
                            Syrian theology, 23-25

Syrian threat (at Aphek), 26-27
  Prophetic intervention, 28
    Israelite victory, 29-30
      Aftermath: Syrian probing, 31-32a
                            Royal clemency, 32b-34

Preparation: dangerous word, 35-37
Confrontation: prophetic ruse, 38-40
Disclosure: divine decision, 41-42
Aftermath: royal response, 43

---

[1] For positing a Ben-hadad II, see K. A. Kitchen, NBD, 3rd ed. (1996), 129. W. S. LaSor provides a feasible reconstruction: 'The dating of this chapter [20] is a problem. The battle of Qarqar occurred in 853 BC; at that time Ahab was allied with Damascus and nine other Aramaean city-kingdoms against Shalmaneser III of Assyria.... Ahab was fatally wounded fighting against the king of Damascus at Ramoth-gilead c. 852 BC [1 Kings 22]. It would seem that the victories over Ben-hadad of Syria were several years earlier and that the treaty with Ben-hadad (20:34) was a step toward a coalition against the Assyrians. After the battle of Qarqar we assume that Israel and Damascus were again at war' ('1 and 2 Kings,' *New Bible Commentary*, 3rd ed. [Leicester: Inter-Varsity, 1970], 345-46).

We needn't spend much time with this structure just now. Note, however, that although the first two major sections vary significantly in bulk (25 and 9 verses, respectively), they are parallel in pattern. So first we read two chunks of narrative that develop the very same way. At the end of the second major section (v. 34) everything seems to be resolved and sewed up – only to be torn apart by the 'punch line' section of the chapter (vv. 35-43), when an unnamed prophet denounces the architect of the 'Chariot Summit.' Now, on to exposition.

The Marvel of Yahweh's Grace (vv. 1-22)

It is at once hopeless and pathetic. Ben-hadad, the Aramaean king, has penetrated Israel all the way to Samaria and put Ahab's capital under siege.[3] Ben-hadad has glued together a coalition of thirty-two kings, i.e., leaders of tribal groups with their respective levies, and so has a formidable force at his command. Relishing his advantage he imposes his terms (v. 3) and Ahab tamely acquiesces (v. 4). Perhaps thinking that he had been far too reasonable, Ben-

---

[2] I am aware that some scholars hold that the events of chapter 20 took place some fifty years later in the time of Jehoash and that Ahab did not figure in them at all. Why then does the text specify Ahab as the king of Israel (vv. 2, 13, 14)? Ah, they say, a later redactor inserted his name. Is there substantial, objective *textual* evidence of this? No. How then do critics know this? By literary analysis (the convenient mantra). Cf. Wayne T. Pitard, ABD, 1:339-40; cf. also W. Thiel, ABD, 1:101. I would agree that meshing Aramaean and Israelite historical data can be elusive, but doctoring the text in the absence of textual evidence is not the path to progress.

[3] Yigael Yadin held that Ben-hadad had not shut off Samaria but only threatened it (at this point) from a distance. He takes his clue from verses 12 and 16 where the term *sukkôt*, usually translated 'booths' or 'shelters,' is used. Yadin argued that this was a place name, Succoth, east of the Jordan, and not a common noun (see his *The Art of Warfare in Biblical Lands*, 2 vols. [New York: McGraw-Hill, 1963], 2:304-310). I am not convinced but agree with Herzog and Gichon: 'In the days before the telephone it would not have been feasible for a commander to direct troops from a headquarters thirty-nine miles distant from the field of action.' See their whole treatment of the maneuvers in 1 Kings 20: Chaim Herzog and Mordechai Gichon, *Battles of the Bible* (New York: Random House, 1978), 107-115 (quote above from p. 232).

hadad decided he preferred Ahab's humiliation over simply his submission; hence back came his lackeys with another message:

> Here's what Ben-hadad says: True, I sent to you, saying, 'Your silver, your gold, your wives, and your children, you must give to me'; but at this time tomorrow I will send my servants to you, and they shall go over your house and your servants' houses, and everything you value they will place in their hand and carry off (vv. 5-6).

Some interpreters think that Ben-hadad's first demand (v. 3) may have involved no more than Ahab's accepting vassal status, which the latter was willing to do (v. 4). In any case, Ben-hadad soon made it clear that he had more than formalities in mind (vv. 5-6). Ahab, after conference, decided he had to draw the line at Ben-hadad's fresh demand (v. 9). This snip of Israelite spunk reaps a nasty Aramaean oath and threat: Ben-hadad vowed there wouldn't be 'enough dust in Samaria for each of my followers to have a handful' (v. 10, NJB).[4] Ahab is powerless. He can only muster a wisecrack, something like: Better do it before you blow off about it (v. 11). It's a bleak day for a helpless people.

Suddenly hope comes into this helpless situation by *a word of promise* (vv. 13-21). Out of the blue[5] a prophet approaches Ahab:

> Why, a certain prophet drew near to Ahab king of Israel and said, 'Here's what Yahweh says: "Have you seen all this vast army? See – I'm giving it into your hand today, and you shall know that I am Yahweh"' (v. 13).

Not unnaturally Ahab has a question or two. Who will be the human catalysts in this? The prophet answers: 'Here's what Yahweh says: "By the young servants of the district leaders"' (v. 14a). These young fellows may not have been militarily trained at

---

[4] 'The threat is twofold: it vaunts the size of Ben-hadad's army, and it forebodes total destruction of Ahab's capital' (Jerome T. Walsh, *1 Kings*, Berit Olam [Collegeville, MN: Liturgical, 1996], 298).

[5] The Hebrew implies this with the first form in verse 13, *wĕhinnēh*, traditionally translated, 'And behold' (cf. NASB); NIV's 'Meanwhile' is too weak. I try to capture the element of surprise with 'Why,...' (cf. NKJV's 'Suddenly,' which fits nicely here).

all (contrary to NIV).[6] Ahab himself is to coordinate or 'pull together' the plan of battle (v. 14b).[7]

Let's pause for several observations. Note that the prophet came unsolicited. Ahab did not seek out this prophet. This unnamed prophet took the initiative in coming to Ahab with this word of hope. And note how, through this prophet, Yahweh threw Ben-hadad's arrogance back in his teeth. Twice when the Aramaean king announced his demands on Ahab he had begun, 'Here's what Ben-hadad says' (vv. 2, 5; traditionally, 'Thus says Ben-hadad'). But Yahweh's prophet uses a double formula too that more than counters the king's: 'Here's what Yahweh says' (vv. 13, 14). Thus says Ben-hadad, and thus says Yahweh – and we'll see whose word carries the day. It will not be the cocky claim of the strutting Syrian but it will be Yahweh's word that determines history. Finally, note that this staggering, 'unreal' promise of verse 13 is *announced beforehand* (i.e., it's a 'predictive' prophecy), so that when Israel's triumph occurs there will be no hermeneutical guesswork about Who brought it about or why it occurred.

True to Yahweh's word, Israel enjoys a smashing victory (vv. 19-21). One wonders if Syrian port didn't contribute. Ben-hadad and his cronies were drinking themselves under the table when the Israelite attack began (v. 16). When Ben-hadad's lookouts tell him they've spotted some men coming out of the city, the king issues the inane orders of verse 18. Notice especially the last half of the verse: 'or if they have come out for war, take them alive.' That order could only come from someone with suds on the brain. A panicky horse ride will sober him up (v. 20b).

If, as stated, hope comes by a word of promise, verse 22 shows that security comes through *a word of warning*. The same prophet approaches Ahab again, giving him a vital piece of intelligence: next year the king of Aram will be coming up against you again.

---

[6] See discussion in Iain W. Provan, *1 and 2 Kings*, New International Biblical Commentary (Peabody, MA: Hendrickson, 1995), 155.

[7] Ahab's second question is, literally, 'Who will bind [or, tie up] the battle?' The verb *'āsar* is frequently rendered 'begin' here. However, the literal sense may be apropos if we understand that Ahab is asking who is responsible for 'tying together' the battle.

Victory is sweet but vigilance is essential. Ben-hadad will be back; prepare to meet him. Here is more grace, Yahweh's protective revelation to shield his people.

All this help – the promise, the direction, the warning – is purely Yahweh's gift. Ahab never seeks a lick of it; it is God-initiated and prophet-imposed. And utterly baffling. When viewed in the larger context we are thrown for a loop. Why is such kindness shown to the Ahab of chapters 17-19? Why does this king of 16:29-34 receive any goodness from the Lord? We can't say it's amazing grace. That would be redundant. Grace is by definition amazing. And here it is, in possibly its most offensive form.

The grace of 1 Kings 20, however, is not only marvelous but demanding. It does not mean for Ahab and Israel to remain untouched. They are held accountable for responding to this grace. The prophet makes this clear in verse 13: 'Have you seen all this vast army? See, I am giving it into your hand today, and you shall know that I am Yahweh.' The 'you' is singular here: 'You, Ahab, shall know.' In the next segment, in verse 28, the 'you' in 'you shall know that I am Yahweh' is plural, likely referring to Israel at large. The idea is not that Ahab or Israel will know that Yahweh is the true God. That was the Mt. Carmel issue (1 Kings 18). 'You shall know that I am Yahweh' means: when I do what I have predicted, then you will have clear evidence that I, Yahweh (and no other), have acted, in grace or judgment as the case may be, and that you are accountable for responding appropriately.[8] In the victories over Aram Ahab and Israel are to see that Yahweh is there in saving help, unasked, undeserved – and that both king and people should acknowledge and adore. If the Lord has been on site, dare we yawn and go on as before?

John Croumbie was a merchant in Haddington (Scotland), probably in the 1770s. He had gunpowder stashed in a cellar beneath his shop. One summer evening, as he labored over his ledger by the shop window, an apprentice went down to the cellar

---

[8] See this in Pharaoh's case in Exodus 7:1-7. This 'recognition formula' appears repeatedly in Ezekiel's prophecies; see the concise summary in Daniel I. Block, *The Book of Ezekiel: Chapters 1-24*, New International Commentary on the Old Testament (Grand Rapids: Eerdmans, 1997), 39.

with a lighted candle. A spark from the sputtering flame fell on an exposed barrel. Then an immediate, horrific explosion. The lad was killed instantaneously; Croumbie was shot into the air, carried up the street about thirty yards, and dumped among the debris without a scratch. An experience hard to forget. And he didn't. Every year for the rest of his life Croumbie 'scrupulously observed its anniversary, shutting himself within his bedchamber the whole day long, pouring out his thanksgivings for his preservation.'[9] He was impressed; grace left its mark. Croumbie understood its claim. And Ahab? From all we can tell, a different process: grace – undeserved, unasked, unacknowledged.

The Scope of Yahweh's Power (vv. 23-30)

All the Aramaeans were sober now. In their post-battle debriefing they planned for the next campaign, which they would also lose. Why? Bad theology.

Actually both religion and politics entered the counsels of war after the aborted siege of Samaria. Ben-hadad's advisors pressed him to shake up the military structure, removing the bevy of petty kings from command, replacing them with provincial military officers (v. 24).[10] They may have believed this arrangement would allow a more integrated, cohesive chain-of-command. Then, of course, total mobilization was necessary to replace all the men and material lost in the recent debacle (v. 25). But these advisors claimed insight into divinity in addition to their degrees from the war college:

> Their gods are gods of the hills – that's why they were stronger than we; however, we will fight with them on level ground – surely we will prove stronger than they (v. 23).

One admires their integrated world view. These Aramaeans were no crass secularists; they had no qualms about combining military strategy with theological insight. Fallacious theology, however,

---

[9]Robert Mackenzie, *John Brown of Haddington* (London: Hodder and Stoughton, 1918), 163-64.

[10] G. H. Johnston, NIDOTTE, 3:602.

will only replay disaster. We will re-visit this Syrian theology momentarily.

The prophet (v. 22) had given King Ahab reliable counsel (v. 26). Come spring, the Aramaeans amass at Aphek for battle. There are several Apheks in the Old Testament; this one is generally located a little to the east of the Sea of Chinnereth/Galilee along a major road between Damascus and Beth-shan.[11] Israel was there, not impressively so, but camped 'like two little flocks of goats' (v. 27, NASB) before the Syrian hordes. Human weakness rides again.

Precisely at this point the king of Israel receives a divine promise and fresh assurance. For the third time in the narrative a prophet or man of God 'draws near' (*nāgaš*; vv. 13, 22, and now 28) to give Ahab an encouraging promise or protective counsel. These gracious intrusions constitute the Lord's goodness to Ahab as already noted. Here the man of God tells him:

> Here's what Yahweh says: 'Because Aram has said, "Yahweh is a god of the hills and not a god of the valleys," I shall give all this vast army into your hand, and you [plural] shall know that I am Yahweh' (v. 28).

Consider the argumentation. By the coming victory Yahweh will both show goodness to Israel and get glory for himself. The latter is the primary concern in verse 28. Syrian stupidity has distorted the truth about Yahweh, casting him in the image of a humdrum pagan deity. When Israel levels them on level ground Yahweh shall have exposed their theological nonsense for what it is. After disaster number two (vv. 29-30)[12] what an opportunity Syrians have to see the truth, if they will. However, the man of God stresses the impact the prophecy and the victory should have

---

[11] See Carl G. Rasmussen, *Zondervan NIV Atlas of the Bible* (Grand Rapids: Zondervan, 1989), 27-28, 129, and John Gray, *I & II Kings*, Old Testament Library, 2nd ed. (Philadelphia: Westminster, 1970), 427-28.

[12] On the large numbers (100,000 and 27,000) in verses 29-30, see, to begin, the discussion in William Sanford LaSor, David Allan Hubbard, and Frederic William Bush, *Old Testament Survey*, 2nd ed. (Grand Rapids: Eerdmans, 1996), 103-106.

upon Israel: 'and you shall know that I am Yahweh.' Frequently, it is God's professed covenant people who most need convinced of Yahweh's power and omnipotence. We may stand within Israel's camp but keep lapsing into Syrian modes of thinking.

It is too easy to smirk at the pagan fellows from Aram, who think Yahweh's power doesn't extend to plains and valleys. Our paganism may be more refined and hence less obvious, yet no different in principle. Sometimes Syrian theology appears in a deistic strain, as when Benjamin Franklin wrote to George Whitefield:

> I rather suspect, from certain circumstances, that though the general government of the universe is well administered, our particular little affairs are perhaps below notice, and left to take the chance of human prudence or imprudence, as either may happen to be uppermost.[13]

That is, God governs and controls the big show but doesn't get himself dirty in the mucky details of our lives. It's the God-of-the-hills-but-not-of-the-valleys all over again. God operates in the broad strokes of the universe but don't expect him to micro-manage. Franklin was an Aramaean. Or sometimes we operate on the reverse heresy: we have a god of personal need but not of historical order. We become so transfixed on God's help for our dilemmas and Aunt Sarah's gall bladder surgery that we lose the God of Psalm 24:1-2.

Syrian theology simply says that there is some turf beyond the reach of Yahweh's power. And we easily slip into this mentality, contrary to our expressed beliefs. We may catch ourselves assuming that God is at work in religious things but not in routine things. Or some have had a wretched and perverse past that has left multiple scars; they are such victims of their experiences that they can expect, they say, no change, no deliverance. The Holy Spirit may regenerate and sanctify more kosher folks, but, one of these will say, he cannot do anything with the absurd medley of genetics, environment, and folly that have made me the twisted

---

[13] Arnold A. Dallimore, *George Whitefield*, 2 vols. (Westchester,IL: Crossway, 1980), 2:452.

mass of hopelessness that I am. Yahweh is only the god of the hills. And then one sometimes meets this attitude in a small church of forty or fifty members, most of whom are age sixty and above: we can't expect God to do anything in us or among us; we are growing older, we've no younger couples or children; we can't muster up any revival starter-kit like larger churches can do. We can't expect God to stir us – he's not a god of the valley.

Such thinking reminds me of my own thinking on a shameful occasion in my boyhood. I had had an altercation with an older boy in our neighborhood. I don't remember the cause of the dispute; I only remember that as around a ten-year-old I had a cadre of theological vocabulary at my command and I wielded it with some gusto upon this other lad. He chased me with retribution in mind but couldn't catch me (though he was older). I escaped into the woods. It was early Wednesday evening and from my vantage point in the woods I saw my parents walking to church for Mid-week Prayer Meeting. Normally, I would have been with them but I had run into this difficulty and was hiding in the woods. And then I saw my antagonist intercept them as they passed his house. He was talking to them and I knew what he was telling them: line upon line of every nasty syllable I had used on him. He ratted on me. I was almost sure I was doomed but had a sliver of hope. I ran home, ascended to my bedroom on the third floor of our old, spacious manse, and hopped into bed. If I could get to sleep I might be spared. My reasoning was that if my father found I was in bed when he and my mother returned, he might decide not to spank me Wednesday evening. Perhaps he would conclude he would deal with me on Thursday and perhaps Wednesday's wrath would cool a bit by then. Especially if I were asleep I entertained hope, for even wicked children look endearing when they're sleeping. All, however, was ineffective: the sound of paternal feet on the stairs was followed by the application of his hand where it was required. I had thought that an apparently sleeping child already in bed would be considered beyond reach. It was childish – Syrian thinking always is.

The Announcement of Yahweh's Judgment (vv. 31-43)

The tables are turned. Here in the rubble of Aphek one no longer hears a strident 'Thus says Ben-hadad' (vv. 2-3, 5). Ahab is no longer the pliant servant (v. 9); but Ben-hadad speaking by proxy through his cronies calls himself Ahab's servant and begs for his life to be spared (v. 32). The Aramaean negotiating team hopes they can be just that. They eat humble pie, backing it up with body language and wardrobe: sackcloth, the duds of penitence, and ropes about their heads or necks, a sign of servitude. Ahab seems a bit surprised that Ben-hadad has survived, but without batting an eye he declares, 'He is my brother' (v. 32b). Like most politicians Ben-hadad's servants had their antennae up and were fishing for any clue to indicate what was going on in Ahab's victorious head. The 'brother' blurb was the sort of saving signal they were looking for. Hence Ben-hadad came out of hiding; Ahab welcomed him into his chariot; they had a royal chat about territorial sovereignty and economic concessions (v. 34); and Ben-hadad set out for home.[14] Ahab had spared the enemy, or, as he would put it, his brother.

One might imagine that verse 34 could adequately conclude the story. Everything seems resolved at this point. Such is not the case, however. Verse 35 opens the whole thing up again – and in a rather bizarre fashion. Let me exaggerate only a bit: in 1 Kings 20, verses 1-34 are a long introduction to the main section of the story (=vv. 35-43; see the structural outline earlier in this chapter). And what does one meet in this climactic section? Another prophet (v. 35a). Interesting: Ahab cannot get free of the word of God!

But we meet this prophet before Ahab does and in his very first vignette he depicts for us *the seriousness of Yahweh's word* (vv. 35-37). Before this unnamed prophet encounters the king of Israel, he orders a companion to strike him. The text clearly states that this order was given 'by the word of Yahweh' (v. 35), i.e., the prophet made clear that this command was not some whacko idea he had dreamed up but was, strange as it sounded, a demand authorized and ordered by Yahweh. The man refused to strike

---

[14] The text of verse 34 is a bit rough but its general import is clear.

him. The prophet did not thank him for being considerate but condemned him for not listening to the voice of Yahweh (v. 36). He announced the fellow's judgment: as he goes away a lion will meet him and 'strike' him – mortally (v. 36b). Shades of 1 Kings 13. And so it happened. The next candidate cooperated and bashed the prophet with desired severity (v. 37).

We may complain, if we want, about how weird and strange this episode is. That would be both true and beside the point. Instead we should confess the clip is both clear and frightening. It is not safe to ignore the word of Yahweh. That is the point. The disobedient companion (vv. 35-36) becomes a preliminary paradigm of the disobedient king (v. 42); 'if disobedient prophets cannot escape God's judgment, then disobedient kings certainly will not.'[15]

The next scene (vv. 38-40) shows us *the manner of Yahweh's word*, at least in this case. The prophet accosts Ahab much as Nathan did David in 2 Samuel 12:1-7. He disguises himself with some sort of covering or bandage over his eyes, waits for the king to come by on his return, then cries out for the king to redress his alleged dilemma. He was, he claims, in the thick of the recent battle. One of the other Israelite troops brought him an Aramaean prisoner to guard. If the POW came up missing, he was told, 'your life will pay for his, or else you will have to pay one talent of silver' (v. 39, NJB).[16] I have always enjoyed the prophet's lame excuse: 'And as your servant was busy here and there, he was gone' (v. 40a, RSV). One imagines that Ahab must have chafed, being badgered with such a flimsy case. It was a no-brainer: 'There's your verdict! You yourself have decided it' (v. 40b). Ahab walked right into the prophet's plan: let the judge judge the matter and so judge himself.

---

[15]Iain W. Provan, *1 and 2 Kings*, New International Biblical Commentary (Peabody, MA: Hendrickson, 1995), 156. See also B. O. Long, *1 Kings*, Forms of the Old Testament Literature (Grand Rapids: Eerdmans, 1984), 220.

[16] A talent of silver would be about 3,000 shekels. This was a hundred times the price of a slave (cf. Exod. 21:32) and would be an impossible amount for an ordinary soldier.

Off comes the disguise and the king's heart sinks (v. 41). The king recognizes this prophet and hears his word:

> Yahweh says this, 'Since you have let the man escape who was under my curse of destruction, your life will pay for his, your people for his people' (v. 42, NJB).

Yahweh here labels Ben-hadad, literally, 'the man of my destruction [*ḥerem*].'[17] Ahab had spared the man Yahweh meant to destroy; he had been 'busy here and there' (v. 40) preening his image as the moderate, temperate, reasonable victor, and had let Yahweh's prisoner escape. Hence the destruction designed for Ben-hadad will fall upon Ahab and his people. This is *the import of Yahweh's word*. Ahab begins by sparing his enemy (vv. 31-34) and will end by destroying his people (v. 42). The prophet's wounding stood as a sign: to 'show to Ahab symbolically what he had to expect from Ben-hadad whom he had released.'[18]

Some may wonder if Yahweh was fair to Ahab. Yahweh had not explicitly told him to liquidate Ben-hadad. Isn't it arbitrary to fault him for something that was not made clear beforehand? Many commentators, however, hold Ahab had all the light he needed about Ben-hadad's funeral, and that in freeing him he had violated the rules for holy war (cf. Deut. 20:10-18; 1 Sam. 15:17-24).[19] And, though one hesitates to appeal to it, clear thinking should have pointed out the right way, as Bähr has argued:

> If ever a man ought to have been made harmless once for all, it was this Ben-hadad, who had twice wantonly commenced war for the mere sake of robbing and exercising power ... and who proposed to

---

[17] The term 'involves the exclusion of an object from the use or abuse of humanity and its irrevocable surrender to God. Surrendering something to God meant devoting it to the service of God or putting it under utter destruction [as here]' (Jackie A. Naude, NIDOTTE, 2:277). Persons can sometimes be/become *ḥerem* (see Deut. 7:26; Josh. 6:17; and here).

[18] C. F. Keil, *The Books of the Kings*, Biblical Commentary on the Old Testament (1876; reprint ed., Grand Rapids: Eerdmans, 1965), 268.

[19] So, e.g., Terence E. Fretheim, *First and Second Kings*, Westminster Bible Companion (Louisville: Westminster/John Knox, 1999), 114-15; and Provan, *1 and 2 Kings*, 153-54.

change Samaria into a heap of ruins and utterly exterminate Israel. This is no question of relations between private individuals; just as Ahab was not so much victor as Jehovah, so Ben-hadad was not Ahab's but Jehovah's prisoner. Ahab had then no right to let him go free and unpunished, for by so doing he arbitrarily interfered with the righteous decision of God, and instead of being an instrument of divine justice he became the toy of his own foolishness and imbecility.[20]

If Ahab had been bothered over the matter he could surely have asked for prophetic guidance. Instead, a little sackcloth, a little bootlicking (or, 'kissing up', as they say in the American south), and Ahab is talking about brotherhood. Not that he didn't have his reasons: if he could charm Ben-hadad with his leniency, Aram would remain in place as a buffer state between Ahab and the rising scourge Assyria.[21] Justice may be right, but expediency is convincing. Ahab was happy to win but no need to be fanatical about it. Let's not be too thorough.

Ahab's policy resembles the argument of Confederate prisoners after the Federal victory at Forts Henry and Donelson in 1862. The Federals were trying to organize, disarm, and get their captives on transports headed for northern prison camps. The Confederates had stacked their arms when directed, but they insisted that they should be permitted to keep their knives, which, they claimed, were part of their personal property. Federal officers noted that

---

[20] K. C. W. F. Bähr, *The Books of the Kings*, Lange's Commentary on the Holy Scriptures, in vol. 3, *Samuel-Kings* (1868; reprint ed., Grand Rapids: Zondervan, 1960), 238-39. Keil argues much to the same effect: 'To let a cruel and faithless foe go unpunished, was not only the greatest harshness to his own subjects, but open opposition to God, who had announced to him the victory, and delivered the enemy of His people into his hand. Even if Ahab had no express command from God to put Ben-hadad to death, as Saul had in 1 Sam. xv.3, it was his duty to punish this bitter foe of Israel with death, if only to secure quiet for his own subjects; as it was certainly to be foreseen that Ben-hadad would not keep the treaty which had been wrung from him by force, as was indeed very speedily proved (see ch. xxii.1)' (*The Books of the Kings*, 267-68).

[21] Cf. Merrill F. Unger, *Israel and the Aramaeans of Damascus* (Grand Rapids: Baker, 1980), 66-67.

every Confederate seemed to have one, most made from files and saw blades, some with lethal-looking blades two inches wide and eighteen inches long. The Federals wisely ordered all knives dropped into baskets as the prisoners got aboard the transports.[22] Can you imagine the alternative? 'Stack your muskets, but you may all keep your knives; you never know when you'll need one in prison camp.' No, disarming must be a total affair. So Ahab was to destroy evil, not make treaties with it. And, strangely and sadly, we who pamper evil rather than purge it understand him all too well.

Yet some Christian readers may wonder: Is this our God in verses 31-43? The God who wants an Aramaean king executed and who announces judgment on Ahab for not doing so? Is it not embarrassing to claim this God? Should we not rather commend Ahab for his enlightened magnanimity and admirable restraint?[23] We may be tempted to think Ahab is more like Jesus than Yahweh is. If so, we only show that we have never really heard Jesus (e.g., Mark 9:42-43, 45, 47-48). It may be that you need a strong dose of 1 Kings 20: you need to see that Yahweh holds the right to judge, and, if you will not have this God, you will not have the God of the Bible.

First Kings 20 then teaches me that I must get clear about God: about his grace (vv. 1-22) – it surprises me, for I don't understand it, held out as it is even to the likes of Ahab; about his power (vv. 23-30) – it rebukes me, because, Syrian-like, I try to limit it; about his judgment (vv. 31-43) – it should sober me, even though, like Ahab and my own culture, I try to dismiss it.

We are at the close of the first chapter of this triad (chaps. 20-22) that highlights Ahab's relation to the word of Yahweh. The prognosis is not encouraging: 'so the king of Israel went to his

---

[22] Bruce Catton, *Grant Moves South* (Boston: Little, Brown, 1960), 182.

[23] As some have done, calling Ahab's decision 'an act which did honor to his heart,' a token of a 'naturally very noble mind,' reflecting his 'natural kindness of heart and confiding disposition' (cited in Bähr, *The Books of the Kings*, 238).

house rebellious and furious' (v. 43a).[24] As Matthew Henry says, he was 'not truly penitent, or seeking to undo what he had done amiss, but enraged at the prophet, exasperated against God'.[25] The word of God had stirred him but had not tamed him. However, this was not the failure of the word of God but the failure of Ahab.

---

[24] The last phrase is interesting. I have retained a rather wooden 'rebellious' for *sar* (from *sārar*, to be stubborn, rebellious); perhaps 'resentful' might reflect the internal attitude better (cf. BDB, 711). 'Furious' renders *zā'ēp*; although the root may refer to dejected or unsatisfactory appearance (Gen. 40:6; Dan. 1:10), it usually denotes rage of some sort (cf. BDB, 277). Hence RSV's 'sullen' and TEV's 'depressed' are likely a bit weak; NIV's 'angry' is better.

[25] Matthew Henry, *Commentary on the Whole Bible*, 6 vols. (New York: Fleming H. Revell, n. d.), 2:693.

Chapter 27

Getting Clear about God's Justice

1 Kings 21

They were only announcements. The clip in the newspaper said so. But in Paris, Tennessee, the high school's Christmas concert was cancelled over them. A brawl erupted in the Music Department of Henry County High School: the chorus teacher apparently smashed the band director in the face with a chair. The chorus teacher was freed on $1,000 bail after the band director filed aggravated assault charges. But why the disharmony between musicians? The men allegedly got into a fight over who would make announcements at the concert. Only announcements, but a lot of fall-out.

That is the way it is in 1 Kings 21. It's only a vineyard. The king wants the vineyard. But the king does not need the vineyard. And the owner is unwilling to part with the vineyard. Yet that is not the end of it, for coveting and sulking combine with power and cruelty to produce oppression and destruction. All for a vineyard. It seems strange that a mere vineyard stirs up such a ruckus.

The focus of the text, however, is not viticulture but theology. It means to speak more about Yahweh's justice than about Naboth's vineyard. Yahweh, our God, is a God who sees that his people get justice, as this case of gross injustice in 1 Kings 21 shows. Jesus himself nicely sums up the promise of this chapter in Luke 18:7: God will bring about justice for his chosen ones, who cry out to him day and night. That is the main proposition; now we may flesh out the teaching of the text in terms of certain principles.

God's people must expect to suffer injustice in this world (vv. 1-16)
I want to walk through this section of the story first, describing
and explaining; afterwards I will highlight some of its implications.
Verses 1-16 constitute a (nearly) self-contained section by
themselves, and it will be useful to appreciate how they depict the
unfolding drama. We may summarize the story's movement in
four segments:

> Problem, vv. 1-4
> Conversation, vv. 5-7
> Action, vv. 8-14
> Resolution, vv. 15-16

The problem is Ahab's – it only became Naboth's later. Ahab
had – as kings could – a second residence in Jezreel (cf. 18:45-
46), about twenty miles north-northeast of Samaria and a little
over eight miles (mostly) east of Megiddo. It was Naboth's lot to
own a vineyard immediately adjacent to the royal estate. Perhaps
his landscape architect had suggested it; at any rate, the idea
fastened upon Ahab's mind. Naboth's bordering vineyard would
make a superb plot for a vegetable garden. Ahab's offer was the
soul of reason: he would swap Naboth a better vineyard in
exchange or pay him the price in cash (v. 2). That struck a nerve.
'Yahweh forbid that I should give you the inheritance of my
fathers!,' Naboth exclaimed (v. 3). Strong words. No deal.

What was the basis for Naboth's refusal? I assume Naboth's
thinking was shaped by teaching found in Leviticus 25:23-28 and
Numbers 36:7-9.[1] There was no absolute prohibition; under certain
emergencies an Israelite might sell land (see Lev. 25).[2] But these
conditions did not apply in Naboth's case. He does not seem to be
suffering from any grinding poverty necessitating his selling land.

---

[1] On Leviticus 25, see, briefly but helpfully, C. J. H. Wright, 'Leviticus,'
New Bible Commentary, 4th ed. (Leicester: Inter-Varsity, 1994), 153-54.

[2] Cf. Raymond B. Dillard, *Faith in the Face of Apostasy* (Phillipsburg,
NJ: Presbyterian & Reformed, 1999), 69: 'Because the land represented the
fruit of the nation's redemption, God commanded that it remain in the hands
of the families to whom it was originally allotted. The land had been provided
by God as part of his grace toward Israel; therefore, no one was to take the

If he need not sell, then he should not sell. Hence his refusal. He treasures Yahweh's land-gift passed down via his ancestors more than making bucks or placating kings. Naboth, in my view, is not nasty but definite; his refusal (v. 3) is couched in strong language but one cannot say he was obnoxious. He had a perfect right to refuse Ahab's offer. He did so because his thinking was covenantal rather than pragmatic. Note that in his reply Naboth identifies himself as a man subject to Yahweh and caring about his law. Naboth's refusal, however, enrages Ahab. He goes off 'rebellious [resentful] and furious' (v. 4a; same phrase as in 20:43) and then settles down for a good pout (v. 4b). And it was only a vineyard.

Enter Jezebel. She wants to know why Ahab is so upset and didn't come down for dinner (v. 5). Ahab tells her of Naboth's rebuff (v. 6).[3] The grammar of Jezebel's retort is a bit touchy: Is it a question? An exclamation? At any rate, NJB nicely captures the sense:

> Some king of Israel you make! Get up, eat and take heart; I myself shall get you the vineyard of Naboth the Jezreelite (v. 7).

'Ahab, are you a king or are you a wimp? No local-yokel grape picker is going to stand in the way of *this* regime! Your problem, Ahab, is that you still think of a king as subject to law; you must get it through your head that what the king wants *is* the law.' This was the Phoenician world-view. Ahab's conduct simply baffled

---

land of another away from him. The law provided that the land could be leased for a period, but that it could never be sold outright (Lev. 25:13-17, 25-28).'

[3] In this royal therapy session Ahab quotes Naboth's refusal as 'I will not give [sell] you *my vineyard*'; he did not use Naboth's own term, 'the inheritance of my fathers.' There are at least two possible explanations: (1) Ahab may have been playing spin doctor for himself; dropping the religious-social rationale from Naboth's words makes his refusal seem more like sheer bull-headedness (Ahab may have counted on this stirring Jezebel's blood and, conceivably, 'using' Jezebel could have been part of his ploy – but this is speculation); or (2) Ahab may have known Jezebel wouldn't care a lick about Israelite views of ancestral land and so simply gave her a paraphrase of Naboth's answer.

Jezebel. She'd never seen her daddy put up with such resistance from a mere subject. If folks resist your will, you simply run over them. '*I* will give you the vineyard' (v. 7c, emphasis in Hebrew). So Ahab orders some lunch and Jezebel strides off to the executive suite.

She goes into action. Using Ahab's letterheads she sends letters to the elders and nobles in Naboth's town (v. 8) with explicit instructions (vv. 9-10): proclaim a fast, make Naboth sit at 'the head of the people,'[4] have two lowlifes come in and accuse him of cursing God and the king;[5] then take him out and stone him.

As Jezebel was accustomed, local leadership carried out her plan precisely (vv. 11-13). They proclaimed a community 'Day of Prayer.' It may be injustice but it will be *religious* injustice. Perhaps the community or a part of the country was under some sort of scourge and the fast day was to discover the reason for it. It may be injustice but it will be *legal* injustice: Jezebel insisted upon at least two witnesses, just as the law required (Deut. 17:6-7; 19:15; Num. 35:30). The appropriate penalty followed (cf. Lev. 24:13-16). That motionless form, that pulverized mass of flesh and bone, is mute testimony to what happens to those who won't play ball with the government.

Verses 15-16 read like all has been resolved. Naboth has been disposed of; the king can now claim the vineyard. Jezebel has been nothing if not thorough: 2 Kings 9:26 notes that Naboth's

---

[4] This expression may indicate a position of honor (Gray) or the position of the defendant (Keil).

[5] The Hebrew text literally reads, 'You *blessed* God and the king,' but this is usually taken as a euphemism for its opposite, i.e., 'cursed,' as seems to be the case in Job 1:5, 11; 2:5, 9; Ps. 10:3 (see NASB on this last text). They allege then that Naboth has transgressed something like Exodus 22:28. Francis I. Andersen suggests that Jezebel's charge may have been a deliberate falsification of Naboth's oath in verse 3, i.e., she charged that Naboth had gone on oath in Yahweh's name *to sell* the vineyard and had reneged on the deal. Taking such an oath in God's name and backing out makes the oath a 'vain' one and is tantamount to cursing God ('The Socio-juridical Background of the Naboth Incident,' *Journal of Biblical Literature* 85 [1966]: 46-57, esp. 53). It may be; we simply can't be sure. We know what we need to know: Naboth was framed on a capital charge.

sons were also liquidated, likely to 'free up' the inheritance from family interference. It was slick work. And it only cost a little postage.

Did you notice a certain *heartlessness* about the way verses 8-14 read? I don't mean the writer himself was so, but that the way he writes up the account conveys a sense of the heartlessness of the deed. Look over verses 8-14 again. See how matter-of-fact it all is. Here is what the queen wrote; here is what her toadies did. Just the hard facts, that's all. All that mattered was that Naboth was dead (a fact mentioned five times in vv. 13-16). God's people must expect to suffer injustice in this world.

Now what implications might we draw from this narrative thus far?

First, here we find *a true picture of the lot of the people of God in this world*. Of course the story is about Naboth and Jezebel, but it is not *merely* about Naboth and Jezebel. It is a representative, typical narrative: it says, 'Now this is the sort of treatment remnant believers can expect from the rulers of this age.' 'Beloved, do not be surprised at the fiery ordeal which comes upon you to prove you, as though something strange were happening to you' (1 Peter 4:12, RSV) – that is the point of 1 Kings 21. It is what Jesus said would be the case (Mark 13:9-13). It is difficult for Christians in the west to grasp this because we are constantly pummeled with other propaganda. One televangelist has written: 'He promises to heal *all* – every one, any, any whatsoever, everything – all our diseases! That means not even a headache, sinus problem, not even a toothache – nothing! No sickness should come your way.'[6] If God yearns to pamper us with total dental health, then why does a kangaroo court frame his servant and bash him to death outside Jezreel? I am not advocating pessimism but realism. The Bible's portrayal of believers' lot in this world is so refreshing precisely because of its sober realism, a realism missing from much 'Christian' telecasting because the cross has been deleted from its gospel.

Second, *such injustice will often be inflicted by the government*

---

[6] Benny Hinn, cited in Hank Hanegraaff, *Christianity in Crisis* (Eugene, OR: Harvest House, 1993), 242 (emphasis in original).

and/or its courts. Here it came via a passive king and an activist queen. In Daniel 3 it will come from the king of Babylon, in Daniel 6 from the government and civil service cronies of Medo-Persia. Or it will come from some Roman official enforcing emperor worship (cf. Rev. 2-3). Government does have a God-ordained role (Rom. 13:1-7), but, historically, governing authorities have repeatedly made themselves the adversaries and oppressors of the people of God. John MacArthur tells of two young female students in Wisconsin who advertised for a third roommate to share their private residence. They rejected one applicant who told them she was a lesbian. Because of that they were forced by the state Human Rights Commission to pay the lesbian applicant $1,500 for causing her distress. The Commission also ordered a public letter of apology and required the two girls to attend a 're-education class' taught by homosexuals.[7] Who was behind that power play? The Wisconsin Human Rights Commission. Ordinarily we are to submit to government; always we should beware of it.

Third, *we have a 'Naboth' who understands*. There is a Naboth in the New Testament. One can hardly read 1 Kings 21 and Matthew's Passion account without seeing that Jesus stands in Naboth's very position:

> Now the chief priests and the whole council sought false testimony against Jesus that they might put him to death, but they found none, though many false witnesses came forward. At last two came forward, and said... (Matt. 26:59-61a, RSV).

Two false witnesses. Jesus walks where Naboth walked (cf. Isa. 53:7-8a). Now what if this should come to you? What if you should suffer in this way? It means you will not be isolated in it. The Christ who has shared in Naboth's suffering is surely united to you in yours (cf. 2 Cor. 1:5).

---

[7] John F. MacArthur, Jr., *The Vanishing Conscience* (Dallas: Word, 1994), 68-69.

God's servants must be prepared to pay the price of standing for justice (vv. 8-14)

It could have been stopped; it was not necessarily a 'done deal'. Jezebel's scheme, however, goes like clockwork. We read nothing of any protest on the part of anyone or of any attempted defense of Naboth.[8] By this 'omission' the writer means to depict Jezreel's leadership negatively for their slobbering subservience to the queen. These local magistrates should have stood their ground. Instead, like bureaucratic robots, they played right along. Why didn't they take a stand against Jezebel, warn Naboth, and expose the whole Vineyard-gate mess?

What would have happened had they refused? They knew. Jezebel was not used to being refused. We can sympathize with their dilemma. If any of them considered defending Naboth certain considerations came instantly to mind. They had families, livelihoods, a desire to live. Who knows what the Mafia in Samaria might do if they failed to toe the line?

We may understand the magistrates' dilemma but that does not justify them. The text is telling us that *injustice flourishes not only by wickedness but by weakness, not merely from a lack of goodness but by a lack of guts*. These fellows were willing to bend the rules the whole way, especially considering they wiped out Naboth's sons as well (remember 2 Kings 9:26). When we shuck it all down to the bone the problem is simply one of our favorite idols: the fear of man – or, in this case, of woman. Jesus has warned us about this: 'You will even be brought before governors and kings for my sake' (Matt. 10:18); and has given us a word of assurance and terror to hold us fast: 'Do not fear those who kill the body but are unable to kill the soul; but rather fear Him who is able to destroy both soul and body in hell' (Matt. 10:28, NASB). This is a matter we must settle. We can't simply stand off and shake our heads over the flaky fellows in Jezreel City Hall. This is our decision as well.

---

[8] Johannes Fichtner, *Das erste Buch von den Königen*, Die Botschaft des Alten Testaments, 2nd ed. (Stuttgart: Calwer, 1979), 318.

God will intervene to bring justice to his wronged people (vv. 17-26)
At the end of verse 16 everything seems sewed up. The Naboth case has been closed. Jezebel likely congratulated herself on such a clean job – in line with her definition of that adjective. Ahab, her ever-obedient husband, had gone down to claim his vineyard.[9] Then the word of God invades and disturbs the 'peace' (vv. 17ff.).

I want to pause and look at the 'lay of the text' in the rest of 1 Kings 21. I will not treat all the details of these sections in the exposition, but we should be alert to the content and shape of the whole passage. As for content we find mainly: (1) Yahweh's commission of Elijah with the word of judgment on Ahab himself (vv. 17-19); (2) Elijah's announcement of the disaster Yahweh will bring on Ahab's whole household (vv. 20-24);[10] (3) the writer's own exclamation over the unparalleled wickedness of Ahab and his regime (vv. 25-26);[11] and (4) a report of Ahab's remorse and Yahweh's postponement of the disaster on his house (vv. 27-29).

Structurally, the passage looks like this:[12]

---

[9] 'Some interpreters have held that Ahab had a collateral right of inheritance to Naboth's vineyard, which he could legally exercise after the owner's death. There is no evidence, however, to contravene the view that the land was appropriated for the crown by simple royal confiscation. Elijah was surely correct in denouncing a double crime [i.e., murdering *and* taking possession] (I Kings 21:19)'; so J. M. Ward, IDB, 3:495.

[10] Note the 'omission' between vv. 19 and 20. The writer does not begin verse 20 with, 'So Elijah rose up and went down...and he found Ahab in the vineyard...,' and then repeat through Elijah's mouth the exact words of Yahweh in verse 19. Instead, the writer makes you catch up with Elijah in the vineyard. He assumes you will know that Elijah obeyed Yahweh's directions; and instead of reporting the exact message of verse 19, he reports Elijah's announcement of an (apparently) additional portion of that message dealing with Ahab's house (vv. 20b-24). This reflects the economy Hebrew narrative sometimes uses; the writer assumes you will mentally supply what happens between verse 19 and verse 20; he assumes you will understand that Elijah did not omit the word of verse 19 but that he spoke more than simply that word. See the similar omission of details between 2 Kings 1, verses 4 and 5.

[11] That Jezebel 'incited' Ahab to evil (v. 25) does not lessen but aggravates Ahab's guilt, for it shows he was not only wicked but weak, not simply sinful but spineless.

Word of Yahweh to Elijah: judgment on Ahab himself, 17-19
    Ahab's reaction: resistance, 20a
        Sold out to evil: disaster for Ahab's house, 20b-24
        Sold out to evil: perversions of Ahab's reign, 25-26
    Ahab's reaction: remorse, 27
Word of Yahweh to Elijah: postponement of judgment on Ahab's house, 28-29

Though this whole passage consists of several segments it does not seem to have been sloppily arranged. For this reason I treat it as a unity, and my hunch is that the unity was original.[13] With this overall orientation let us go back and allow the main force of verses 17-26 to hit us.[14]

It looks, by the end of verse 16, like the classic perfect crime has been carried off. The Samaria machine has run over the Jezreel fool; Jezebel has instructed Ahab in politics, the art of the possible; and Ahab is ambling about his new vineyard, perhaps expecting his Buildings and Grounds superintendent to arrive momentarily as per orders. And then ...

---

[12] Jerome Walsh's suggestion helped me to consider this passage structurally (see his *1 Kings*, Berit Olam [Collegeville, MN: Liturgical, 1996], 328), though my proposal differs a good deal from his.

[13] Party-line criticism looks on the section as a patchwork of various contributions. In its view, verse 23 (about Jezebel) is a very late editorial insertion; verses 21-22, 24 are heavily doctored by deuteronomistic redactors (editors working over two centuries after the events); and both verses 25-26 and verses 27-29 were additions from deuteronomistic redactors (see the commentaries by John Gray or G. H. Jones). Apparently not satisfied with Elijah's original confrontation of Ahab, the spin doctors of the 'Deuteronomistic School' keep supplementing and inserting over the years until it all comes out to someone's satisfaction. Old Testament scholars seem able to conjure a deuteronomist out of the semi-historical haze whenever needed. Tracing such a process is highly complex, apparently scholarly, and largely guesswork. When this approach is fed to seminarians, one can almost forgive them for giving up on the Old Testament. I am, however, unrepentant; I still think that if a text has an overall unity as it stands, such coherence is more likely the product of an author at one time than of an ongoing series of editors each tweaking the text to his liking.

[14] We will discuss the fulfillment of 21:19 in connection with 22:38.

Then the word of Yahweh came to Elijah the Tishbite, saying, 'Rise, go down to meet Ahab king of Israel who lives in Samaria. See! He's in Naboth's vineyard; he's gone down there to possess it' (vv. 17-18).[15]

How quietly the Bible makes the most massive assumptions! Surely you see it: no one is exempt from the scrutiny and judgment of God's word. In Israel, like it or not, the prophet as bearer of Yahweh's word stands above and over the king and queen. No one, whatever his status, whatever her success, can wiggle, squirm, or run beyond the boundaries of that jurisdiction.

Isn't this the reason this passage is such consolation to Yahweh's people who have been pushed and shoved and squashed all along the time-line of history? 'The word of Yahweh came to Elijah the Tishbite' (v. 17). 'Have you murdered and also taken possession?' (v. 19a). 'In the place where the dogs licked up Naboth's blood, the dogs will lick up your blood – yes yours!' (v. 19b). 'I have found you because of your selling yourself to do what is evil in Yahweh's eyes' (v. 20). Are these not wonderful words of life to God's people who have been kicked, beaten, and left for dead along life's way?

When you begin reading at verse 17 you must understand this did not occur because of a news leak. The speaking God in verse 17 is the omniscient God who saw. It looked like a slick job, with an air-tight cover-up. Jezebel's letters had already been put through the shredder at city hall; none of the shady details came out in the papers. Elijah himself apparently didn't know until Yahweh told him. 'Then the word of Yahweh came.' Yahweh did not let it pass. He saw and intervened (Exod. 3:7-8a). Naboth bites the dust as a helpless victim, yet Yahweh is the God who sees his hapless Naboths and their lifeless forms amid the stones.[16]

---

[15] Yahweh's command to Elijah in verse 18 is couched as an ironic play on Jezebel's command to Ahab in verse 15. She orders Ahab to *qûm rēš* (Rise, possess), while Yahweh orders Elijah to *qûm rēd* (Rise, go down).

[16] 'The frequency with which Naboth's name appears throughout the story is striking. Even after his death, he is named six times in three verses (21:14-16); he haunts the scene like a ghost that will not be laid to rest' (Jerome T. Walsh, ABD, 4:978). Naboth may be dead—but not to Yahweh.

The Naboths are legion, even – especially – in our own time. Recently, a World Relief Commission newsletter related the story of Clementine, who, about six years ago was a beautiful seventeen-year-old. One day militia troops came down on her village; she and her family took refuge in a church. No safety there; the troops gunned down people right before her eyes; their blood flooded the floor. This was Rwanda, 1994. Clementine tried to run but soldiers grabbed her. They drove her into the bush for torture and rape – and to leave to die. After hours a compassionate soul found her and took her to a hospital. But it was understaffed; she received no treatment for her wounds nor care for her rape and torture. But a Belgian doctor flew Clementine to Europe where she had surgery. There the doctors discovered Clementine had only endured part of the horror: the soldiers left her HIV-positive. It wasn't that long before she had full-blown AIDS. At the time the story was passed on, her death was imminent. Back in Rwanda, she had received care and assistance, and, through a Christian worker's witness, had come to Christ. That matters. But still she will die, because wicked, powerful, diseased men destroyed her.

Such true tales may seem to shrink 1 Kings 21 into pretty meager consolation. For Yahweh did not intervene to prevent Clementine's horror in the bush. Yet that is part of the problem in 1 Kings 21 itself, for it doesn't look like Yahweh protected Naboth either. The word of Yahweh invades and nails Ahab with his word of judgment. But Naboth was dead. If Yahweh has such a passion against injustice, why was his justice so late in arriving? This is the mystery of God's restraint that pervades the Bible. Why did Yahweh so marvelously preserve the infant Moses from Pharaoh's post-natal disposal programme (Exod. 2:1-10), though seemingly there was no intervention in numerous other cases (Exod. 1:22)? Again, the toddler Jesus escapes by God's timely providence (Matt. 2:13-15) but Herod's police massacre the other youngsters around greater Bethlehem (Matt. 2:16). Even Messiah's forerunner received the Naboth treatment because of another gutless king, Herod Antipas (Mark 6:14-29). And Herod Agrippa executes James (Acts 12:1-2) while Peter enjoys an angelic jail break (Acts 12:6-11). Why does Yahweh often hold back his hand (Ps. 74:11a)?

Such a question can't help but nag the reader of 1 Kings 21. Yet the flow of the narrative, the way the word of Yahweh tracks down Ahab, shows that Yahweh comes as Naboth's defender. We may wonder about the timing, but the text remains an immense comfort. The Naboth episode, we can say, is no guarantee of immunity, only of justice – and that not necessarily this October. But come it will, for 1 Kings 21 is a preview of 2 Thessalonians 1:6-7. We have the narrative in 1 Kings 21; we have the doctrine in 2 Thessalonians 1. God will intervene to bring justice to his wronged people.

We mustn't allow our quandary over the timing of Yahweh's justice to eclipse our comfort over the fact of it; indeed, the way Yahweh takes up the cudgels here for his wronged people is what, in part, makes him such an attractive God. This struck me several years ago when I read an anecdote Chris Wright passed on in an editorial in *Themelios*.[17] He had been speaking at a conference in India. After one session a fellow (now a doctor of science and university lecturer in chemistry) came up to tell him how thrilled he had been to hear Wright would be preaching from the Old Testament at the conference, because, he said, he had become a Christian through reading the Old Testament. Let Dr. Wright tell the rest:

> He grew up in one of the many backward and oppressed groups in India, part of a community that is systematically exploited and treated with contempt, injustice and sometimes violence. The effect on his youth was to fill him with a burning desire to rise above that station in order to be able to turn the tables on those who oppressed him and his community. He threw himself into his education, and went to college committed to revolutionary ideals and Marxism. His goal was to achieve the qualifications needed to gain some kind of power and thus the means to do something in the name of justice and revenge. He was contacted in his early days at college by some Christian students and given a Bible, which he decided to read out of casual interest, though he had no respect at first for Christians at all.
>
> It happened that the first thing he read in the Bible was the story

---

[17] Volume 17/2 (Jan.-Feb., 1992): 3.

of Naboth, Ahab and Jezebel in 1 Kings 21. He was astonished to find that it was all about greed for land, abuse of power, corruption of the courts, and violence against the poor – things that he himself was all too familiar with. But even more amazing was the fact that God took Naboth's side and not only accused Ahab and Jezebel of their wrongdoing but also took vengeance upon them. Here was a God of real justice. A God who identified the real villains and who took real action against them. 'I never knew such a God existed!' he exclaimed. He read on through the rest of OT history and found his first impression confirmed. This God constantly took the side of the oppressed and took direct action against their enemies. Here was a God he could respect, a God he felt attracted to, even though he didn't know him yet, because such a God would understand his own thirst for justice.

'I never knew such a God existed!' That was his virgin reaction to the Naboth story; he got the point immediately. He wasn't converted yet, but the Holy Spirit's first nudge came via 1 Kings 21. Would that the long-converted could see with the same clarity and thrill that Naboth's God is the true consolation for a fragile church in a brutal world.

God delights to exercise mercy while imposing his justice (vv. 27-29)
The last time Ahab 'heard' something was of Naboth's death in verse 16a; there he responded by grabbing Naboth's vineyard (v. 16b). But when Ahab 'heard these words' (v. 27a), that is, Yahweh's horrors with Ahab's address on them (=vv. 20b-24), he reacted quite differently. He 'tore his clothes and put sackcloth over his bare flesh; he fasted, lay in the sackcloth, and went about dejectedly' (v. 27b, NRSV). That rather surprises us. But what really surprises us is Yahweh's response to Ahab's response,[18] when he asks/tells Elijah: 'Have you seen how Ahab has humbled himself before me? Because he has humbled himself before me I will not bring the disaster in his days – in the days of his son I will

---

[18] Verses 28-29 cannot be taken as a trivial footnote closing off the narrative, for verse 28 begins with the word-of-Yahweh-came formula; in fact, verse 28 is identical to verse 17. There the formula introduces a word of accusation and judgment; in verse 28 it leads into a word of restraint and mercy. Both alike are Yahweh's word.

bring that disaster upon his house' (v. 29).

There seems a mixture of delight and excitement in Yahweh's words. The question is nearly an exclamation. I don't mean it irreverently, but it is as if the Almighty nudges Elijah in the ribs and exclaims, 'Did you see *that*?' We may wonder: Is Yahweh naïve? Is he gullible? Has Yahweh gone soft? Is he like a crusading politician who, once elected, goes to his nation's capital and soon becomes a toothless 'team player'? Yahweh had it right in verses 17-24. Why should he cut Ahab any slack – this scuzzball from Samaria whose wife does his human meatpacking for him? Surely Yahweh doesn't mistake Ahab's torn clothes and drooping head for genuine repentance, does he? What are we to make of this?

Early this fall a major college football game was to be played in Blacksburg, Virginia. Georgia Tech was to play Virginia Tech in the latter's stadium. As a rule, nothing ever prevents a football game; they play in cold, rain, mud, and snow. But this game was not played; it was not the rain but the lightning that was the culprit. Too dangerous. Then came something else, perhaps nearly as unusual: the game was cancelled. That meant the game never would be played. Some folks wanted the game to be postponed and to re-schedule it for later in the season (say, in early December). But apparently the two coaching staffs did not want to burden their schedules with an extra game late in the season. So the game was cancelled.

What does Virginia Tech have to do with Ahab? Just this: it is essential to distinguish between postponement and cancellation. In verse 29 Yahweh postpones the judgment against Ahab's dynasty or household, but he does not cancel it. He changes the timetable but does not remove it from the agenda. Sometimes Yahweh, in answer to human repentance, will delay the arrival of his judgment. The prophecy of Huldah to King Josiah (2 Kings 22:8-20) is a premier example of this phenomenon (cf. also Jer. 18:7-8). Yahweh does that here: in light of Ahab's response (v. 27) Yahweh will not obliterate his whole household as soon as he had threatened. He will do it; you can read all about it in 2 Kings 9-10. But he will not do it now. Now is a moment of opportunity granted to Ahab.

But, someone may ask, surely you don't think that Ahab's 'repentance' was sincere? Judging from verse 27 Yahweh's word of judgment made quite an impression on Ahab. He doesn't seem merely to be acting. I hold that his 'repentance' is sincere at the moment but not lasting; it was serious but temporary.[19] Apparently he did not relinquish his claim on Naboth's vineyard and yet certainly he was profoundly moved by Yahweh's threat. When the wash is all done perhaps we would call it remorse rather than repentance.

Where does all this lead us? Back to Yahweh, hopefully. Don't you see your God here? Can't you sense Yahweh's enthusiasm for mercy as he asks Elijah, 'Have you seen how Ahab has humbled himself before me?' Don't you suspect his readiness to relent when he assures, 'I will not bring the disaster in his days'? Don't go around muttering about Ahab's shabby and passing repentance (most of ours is such). Isn't Yahweh's mercy (i.e., this delay of judgment here) itself an appeal to Ahab to go on into a deeper repentance? For if Yahweh so responds to Ahab's initial expressions of remorse, how much more mercy might he find should he persevere in repentance? Who is a God like Yahweh with such gusto for mercy? One is tempted to join Chris Wright's friend (see above) and say, 'I never knew such a God existed!'[20] And that mercy never changes. Otherwise, why does Jesus hang around Laodicia, knocking on doors (Rev. 3:20)?[21]

---

[19]So C. F. Keil, *The Books of the Kings,* Biblical Commentary on the Old Testament (1876; reprint ed., Grand Rapids: Eerdmans, 1965), 273.

[20] In one chapter we meet one God, who is both trenchant in justice (vv. 17-26) and tender in mercy (vv. 27-29).

[21] Matthew Henry has a concise and helpful treatment of vv. 27-29; see his *Commentary on the Whole Bible*, 6 vols. (New York: Revell, n.d.), 2:698-99.

Chapter 28

Getting Clear about God's Word

1 Kings 22:1-40

It's all Jehoshaphat's fault. At least he's the one who raised the matter in the first place. He said they needed to have the light of the word of God on their plans (v. 5). That request not only sets off a whole chain of episodes that form 1 Kings 22:1-40 but also provides the primary theme for that whole passage, i.e., the word of Yahweh. Remember that this passage is now the third in a series of Ahab's judgment-encounters with the word of God (see my remarks introducing 1 Kings 20). First, an unnamed prophet rebukes him (1 Kings 20:35ff.); next, Elijah denounces him (21:17ff.); and now Micaiah pronounces his doom (22:17ff.). This passage then depicts Ahab's third failure in relation to the word of God. In broad terms the passage consists of two major sections: (1) the repudiation of Yahweh's word (vv. 1-28); and (2) the fulfillment of Yahweh's word (vv. 29-40). The principal contention of the passage is that *the word of God destroys the man who defies it*. The whole story gives us a mini-theology of the word of God, which the exposition will seek to develop. Naturally, some may wonder why we need worry ourselves with such a basic item as 'getting clear about God's word.' Well, because Ahab was not so clear about it and ran straight into ruin because of it.

Before we move to exposition, take a moment to become familiar with the literary shape of 22:1-40.

Proposed Structure for 1 Kings 22:1-40
Setting, 1-4

Inquiry, 5-6a
  Approval, 6b
    Dissatisfaction, 7
      Hated prophet, 8-9
        Throne scene: emphatic assurance, 10-12
          True prophet and clear pressure, 13-14

Inquiry, 15a
  Approval, 15b
    Dissatisfaction, 16
      Hated message, 17-18
        Throne scene: certain disaster, 19-23
          True prophet and overt suffering, 24-28

The king's disguise, 29-30 (fear)
  Deliberate plan of king of Aram, 31-33
  'Accidental' fulfillment of Yahweh's word, 34-36
The king's death, 37-38

Summary, 39-40

Observe that two major sections (vv. 5-14 and vv. 15-28) of the first part of the narrative follow the same general pattern of development. Note too certain points of what I would call ironic contrast. I have tried to make these visible in the outline, e.g., in the two 'throne scenes' (vv. 10-12 and 19-23), and in the designations given for verses 31-33 and 34-36. This is a sad but entertaining story, carefully and artfully told. Now on to the theology of the text.

The Candor of Yahweh's Word (vv. 1-8)
The brief time of peace (v. 1) probably came in the wake of Ahab's previous pact with Ben-hadad (20:32-34). The date is 853/852 BC. Ahab has likely just returned from the Battle of Qarqar (or Karkar),

where he was a part of a twelve king coalition that fought Assyrian king Shalmaneser III to a standstill. Ahab, according to Shalmaneser's annals, had contributed the second largest army and over half the chariots to the anti-Assyrian bloc.[1] Perhaps Ahab's battle blood was up. In any case, he must have kept troops mobilized for a bit of war against his recent ally, Aram. He suggested the venture among his advisors when Jehoshaphat of Judah came down to pay Ahab a state visit (v. 2). Jehoshaphat scored high in piety but low in sense. He had concluded a stupid marriage alliance with Ahab: Jehoshaphat's son Jehoram was wed to Ahab's daughter Athaliah (2 Kings 8:18; 2 Chron. 18:1).[2] So Jehoshaphat has painted himself into Ahab's corner. Now he hears Ahab's agenda, floated among his courtiers: 'Do you know that Ramoth-gilead belongs to us? But we keep doing nothing about taking it away from the king of Aram!' (v. 3).

True, Ramoth-gilead belonged to Israel. But shekels probably weighed more heavily than rights in swaying Ahab's policy. Ramoth-gilead (probably=Tell Ramîth) stood twenty-five to thirty miles east of the Jordan, astride the north-south King's Highway leading to Damascus in the north. A road also ran westward from Ramoth-gilead to Beth-shan and other points west of the Jordan. Incense and spice caravans trucked through Ramoth-gilead. That meant whoever controlled the site collected 'caravan transit revenues'.[3] In short, it's a shame to have a turnpike running through a place if you aren't sitting in the toll booth.

Ahab then turns to ask Jehoshaphat if, in view of the justice of the cause, he would join Israel in regaining Ramoth-gilead. With diplomatic gusto Jehoshaphat replies, 'I am as you are, my people as your people, my horse as your horses' (v. 4), which, translated, means: Yes. And then (the order of things is interesting), pious

---

[1] Alfred J. Hoerth, *Archaeology and the Old Testament* (Grand Rapids: Baker, 1998), 312-13.

[2] Athaliah was Ahab's daughter, but whether by Jezebel or one of his other wives (cf. 2 Kings 10:1) we cannot be sure. In any case, 2 Kings 11 shows she is a Jezebel clone.

[3] Carl G. Rasmussen, *Zondervan NIV Atlas of the Bible* (Grand Rapids: Zondervan, 1989), 127.

king that he is, Jehoshaphat asks Ahab to obtain the word of Yahweh on this matter (v. 5). That, of course, is no problem, for Ahab retains the services of a good number of prophets for just such occasions, so he asks his collection of clergy the essential question: 'Should I go up to Ramoth-gilead for battle or should I hold back?' (v. 6a). These unanimously approved the venture (v. 6b). Jehoshaphat is uneasy. He smells a problem. Perhaps it was too neat. He presses the matter: 'Is there not here yet a prophet belonging to Yahweh that we may inquire from him?' (v. 7). Jehoshaphat wants to hear the voice of orthodoxy, and he knows he has not heard it. Whatever we make of Ahab's prophets they are not prophets of Yahweh in the way Jehoshaphat defines such.

A brief tangent then. Although the number of Ahab's prophets (400, v. 6) reminds us of the four hundred prophets of Asherah who were possibly no-shows on Mt. Carmel (18:19, 22), they are not Asherah or Baal prophets. These are prophets who speak in Yahweh's name (v. 11), claim to have Yahweh's Spirit (v. 24), promise Yahweh's success (v. 12, cf. v. 6), and can apparently deliver Yahweh's word (v. 5). One might surmise they were prophets connected with the syncretistic Jeroboam cult with its veneer of Yahwism mixed with bull worship (see 1 Kings 12:25-33), 'who practised prophesying as a trade without any call from God, and even if they were not in the pay of the idolatrous kings of Israel, were at any rate in their service.'[4]

In any case, Jehoshaphat wanted to hear from a bona fide prophet of Yahweh. Do you still have any of that ilk, Ahab? Ahab is blunt. 'There's still one man from whom one can inquire of Yahweh, but *I* hate him, for he never prophesies what is positive about me but what is disastrous – Micaiah son of Imlah' (v. 8, emphasis in Hebrew). Jehoshaphat attempts a soothing response, the equivalent of 'I say, let's not be quite so negative' (cf. v. 8b). But Ahab was right. Micaiah was no sycophant longing for royal favor, no cooperative evangelical begging his colleagues in ministry to confer respectability upon him.

---

[4] C. F. Keil, *The Books of the Kings*, Biblical Commentary on the Old Testament (1876; reprint ed., Grand Rapids: Eerdmans, 1965), 274.

Ahab hated Micaiah; he hated the word he spoke. Why? He could not stomach the frankness of the word, its candor. The king's fixation, however, was not upon what was true or false but upon what was supportive or non-supportive. 'He never prophesies what is positive about me.' And so Ahab interprets Micaiah's fidelity as contrariness. He does this in verse 18, when he turns to Jehoshaphat, and so much as says, 'See? I told you so. The guy has a personal vendetta against me. How can one take his word seriously when it labors under such obvious bias?'

Note the sad irony in Ahab's statement in verse 8. Ahab admits 'there is yet one man' (NASB). What a boon! What a kindness that there is yet one man through whom Ahab has access to truth. Ahab is not totally cut off from the word of Yahweh. But Ahab does not see it that way. He takes shelter behind a smokescreen of prophetic animosity; he does not see the relentless truthfulness of Yahweh's word as God's being stubbornly faithful to him by repeatedly telling him what he does not want to hear.

The candor of the word is not always so fruitless. During John A. Broadus' student days at the University of Virginia he once wrote a note in Greek to a fellow student: *Hen se hysterei* (one thing you lack). They are the words of Jesus from Mark 10:21, his analysis of the condition of a religious, moral man who was blissfully unaware of the idol he worshipped. This admonition eventually led to the friend's conversion.[5] But, though kind, it was a direct and blunt word.

One sometimes wonders if the church is drifting back to an Ahab mind-set, or, if not hostile toward the candor of the word at least embarrassed by it. I have received church advertisements in my mail. A new church is forming in our area. It is going to feature, among other attractions, a 'non-judgmental atmosphere' to attract me. I know, I mustn't over-interpret. But what does that mean? Likely that the church means to eschew negativism, refrain from making folks 'feel guilty', or – the ultimate contemporary sin – feel bad about themselves. What will the ministry of the word be

---

[5] David S. Dockery, 'John A. Broadus,' *Bible Interpreters of the Twentieth Century*, ed. Walter A. Elwell and J. D. Weaver (Grand Rapids: Baker, 1999), 39.

like in such a church? Will it ever press home the word of God in its searing honesty? Or must that be sacrificed lest it destroy the non-judgmental ambiance? Ahab would love such a place.

The Freedom of Yahweh's Word (vv. 9-14)
One can imagine hearing the snap of Ahab's fingers, followed by his curt order to a court official: 'Quick! Micaiah ben Imlah' (v. 9). The messenger hurries off and the entertainment continues. What takes place in verses 10-12 helps us see what tremendous pressures Micaiah will face should he go against the united voice of the establishment.

The scene is vivid. The two kings are sitting on temporary thrones in all their regalia at the gate of Samaria (v. 10a). Everyone knows it's a council of war. One can almost hear the sound track from 'Chariots of Fire' pulsating from a nearby boombox. And all the prophets go on prophesying before the kings with their heartening propaganda (v. 10b). Suddenly Zedekiah son of Chenaanah takes center stage, sporting a pair of iron horns and performing a goring-ox charade (v. 11).[6] Church was so much fun when Zedekiah was there!

Don't think Zedekiah is some weird prophet from the lunatic fringe. Prophets frequently combined parabolic action with verbal declaration (see, e.g., 2 Kings 2:19-22 and Jer. 19:1-13, among many). And Zedekiah is not merely horning in but is likely trying to make an application of Scripture. Zedekiah accompanies his antics with a prophetic word: 'With these [i.e., the horns] you will gore Aram until they are finished off' (v. 11b). Zedekiah may well have Deuteronomy 33:17 in mind.[7] That text is part of Moses' blessing upon the Joseph tribes, Ephraim and Manasseh, the tribes that constituted the heart and core of the northern kingdom in

---

[6] Zedekiah did not manufacture these iron horns on the spot. He must have brought them with him. He obviously made them or had them made ahead of time. His prophecy has then a premeditated look about it. Cf. H. L. Ellison, *The Prophets of Israel* (Grand Rapids: Eerdmans, 1969), 41.

[7] See Keil, *The Books of the Kings*, 275. Keil adds, 'But the pseudo-prophet overlooked the fact that the fulfilment of the whole of the blessing of Moses was dependent upon fidelity to the Lord.'

Ahab's time. These tribes, Moses says, have horns like those of a wild ox, and 'with them he [=Joseph, represented in Ephraim and Manasseh] gores the peoples.' Zedekiah picks up Moses' verb *nāgaḥ* (to gore) in his prophetic pronouncement to Ahab in verse 11. He is not, he might have said, simply speaking out of the blue – his prophecy has *a Scriptural basis*. Zedekiah is only applying the biblical text to a fresh situation. Can we not believe, he says, that when Moses speaks of Joseph's goring 'peoples,' the present day Aramaeans are to be among the gored? Zedekiah speaks from a biblical text not out of thin air. Ahab should proceed because Zedekiah has given him a slip out of God's promise-box.

Perhaps we can now appreciate the weight of Micaiah's opposition. These prophets, especially Zedekiah, speak with parabolic action (v. 11a), using the prophetic formula (v. 11b, traditonally, 'Thus says Yahweh'), anchored in a biblical promise (v. 11c; cf. Deut. 33:17), and with multiple attestation (v. 12, 'And all the prophets kept prophesying that way').

We now rejoin the king's messenger who has just arrived to conduct Micaiah to court. This emissary seems to know of Micaiah's party-pooping reputation and so counsels the prophet not to sour the perfect prophetic unanimity that had been reached. He urges Micaiah to fall in with the majority for once and 'speak positively' (lit., 'good'; v. 13b). Micaiah can recognize pressure when he hears it and shoots back a solemn retort: 'By the life of Yahweh, what Yahweh says to me – that's what I'll speak' (v. 14).

Micaiah has just nailed something which neither Ahab nor his messenger understands. Look back at Ahab's words in verse 8 and the messenger's in verse 13. What do both assume about the word of Yahweh? They assume that the prophet controls or can control that word. Ahab's remark in verse 8 implies that Micaiah didn't have to be such a purveyor of doom-saying, anti-Ahabian sentiment. If he wanted to, he could speak a kinder, gentler word. The messenger assumes that Micaiah could agree with the prophetic caucus if only he would (v. 13). They do not understand Micaiah's position, which he states in verse 14: He is in bondage to the word of God. Hence, the word of God is free and cannot be manipulated by kings or messengers or (even) slick prophets. Whatever word Yahweh gives a prophet, that is what the prophet must speak. The prophet is not at liberty to massage or shape or bend, let alone pervert, that word. The word of Yahweh is a given and must be passed on as given. *The true prophet of God is in bondage to the uncoercible word of God.* The word of Yahweh is free; the servant of Yahweh is in bondage to it. Ahab cannot comprehend the sovereign freedom of Yahweh's word.

He is not alone. You are a pastor. Before you sits a nice, romantic, post-modern couple who want you to perform their marriage. One of them, a professing Christian, is a member of the church you serve; the other, you have divined by question and conversation, is not a Christian. You tell the latter so and then inform the couple that Scripture does not allow you to join them in marriage (inferring from 1 Cor. 7:39, for example). But, they say, they were going to attend church here (the suggestion being that now they won't do so). You realize, don't you, that the member's family [also members] will be irate over your refusal? Don't you know there are other clergy who have no such scruples? While you may have your opinion about what the word of God requires, why do you have to be bound by that? Aren't a lot of these things open for reinterpretation? On it goes. Men and women still don't understand that the word of God is not under your control but that, contrariwise, you are in bondage to it. This blows them away. The pressure to compromise the word of God may come at the gate of Samaria – but it repeatedly comes in the pastor's study. Micaiah would understand, for he knew that the loneliness of Yahweh's man is the corollary of the freedom of Yahweh's word.

The Irrelevance of Yahweh's Word (vv. 15-18, 19-23)

Micaiah arrives and Ahab asks him about Operation Ramoth. Like a natural-born yes-man Micaiah answers, 'Go up and succeed, and Yahweh shall give it into the king's hand' (v. 15b). His counsel is precisely the same as that of the four hundred in verse 12. In my view, some puzzle needlessly over verse 15. As readers, of course, we cannot hear tone of voice. But I've no doubt Micaiah spoke in sarcasm in verse 15b, and Ahab's response in verse 16 supports my view. The usual translation of verse 16 is clear enough, but let me provide a somewhat fuller one:

> Then the king said to him, 'How many times must I keep on putting you on oath that you not speak to me anything but truth in the name of Yahweh?'

The rather unwieldy 'keep on putting you on oath' translates a participial form of the verb, which often, as here, indicates continuing action. This is something Ahab keeps having to do. Combine this consideration with the initial 'how many times' and one has all the clues. This sort of interchange *has happened repeatedly in the past*. It's an almost stock routine Micaiah goes through with Ahab. Ahab asks Micaiah for counsel; Micaiah spouts the party line of Ahab's bootlickers; Ahab puts Micaiah under oath to tell the truth; then Micaiah turns from sarcasm to sobriety and tells Ahab true truth. As he does in verse 17, where he so much as says, All right, you want the real truth? 'I saw all Israel being scattered to the hills like sheep without a shepherd; and Yahweh said, "These have no master; let them each go back to his house in peace."' If Israel has no shepherd, no master, it means that Ahab will be eliminated in battle. Note also the biting implication: when Ahab is dead, Israel can have 'peace'. There you have it, O king. Should you go up to Ramoth-gilead? What do you think?

Now why did Micaiah play these prophetic games with Ahab? Doesn't such sarcasm seem too flippant for Yahweh's prophet? Yet it is not a flippant but a sad sarcasm Micaiah uses. Micaiah spouts the party line in verse 15 *because it doesn't make any difference what the word of Yahweh is* – since Ahab will not heed it. Ahab has come to the point where it doesn't matter whether Micaiah speaks truth, falsehood, or gobblelygook. If Ahab is beyond following truth why should he have it in the first place?[8]

---

[8] Having said all this, one still sees in verse 16 the strange contradiction in the natural man: he hates the truth yet must have the truth. He does not want the truth in order to follow it but only to know it. In this narrative, Ahab hates the truth (v. 8) and refuses the truth – and yet *fears* the truth (v.

He may seek it as a mere formality but it will not determine his path. The word of Yahweh is an irrelevance for him. Can you conceive of anything more alarming?

Let us look briefly at verses 19-23. This is the last chunk of Micaiah's message. The first installment was the sarcasm of verse 15, then the 'revision' of verse 17, and now the doom of verse 17 is fleshed out in more detail in this strange vision of verses 19-23. However, let me state here that verses 19-23 do nothing but reinforce the point made in verses 15-18, i.e., Ahab is beyond the point of responding obediently to Yahweh's word.

Micaiah claims to give Ahab a replay of what took place in Yahweh's council room. Clearly our writer wants us to see verses 19-23 as the antithesis of verses 10-12. Both sections depict 'royal' scenes with kings upon their thrones. In the one, two earthly kings in all their regalia listen to the prophetic cheerleading of Zedekiah & Co. In the other, the sovereign King of all determines the manner in which he will dispose of Ahab. Is there any doubt as to which king's decision will shape history?

Micaiah portrays Yahweh conducting a kind of contest in the heavenly council. 'Who,' Yahweh asks, 'will lure Ahab, that he might go up and fall at Ramoth-gilead?' (v. 20). Three times a form of the verb *pātāh* (to lure, entice, seduce, deceive) occurs (vv. 20, 21, 22). That is the task: who can lure Ahab to his destruction? Several inadequate suggestions are submitted (v. 20b). Finally, a particular spirit claims he can succeed (v. 21) by being a lying spirit in the mouth of all Ahab's prophets (v. 22a). Yahweh acclaims his plan as a prize ruse and commissions him to go to work. Since Micaiah has 'seen' this planning, he announces its execution: 'And now, look! Yahweh has placed a lying spirit in the mouth of all these prophets of yours' (v. 23a). So that Ahab cannot claim the message is fuzzy, Micaiah adds a terse summary: '*Yahweh* [emphatic in Heb.] has declared disaster against you' (v. 23b).

I grant that verses 19-23 startle our usually prosaic western

---

30). Theologically, 1 Kings 22 is a next door neighbor to Romans 1-3. Cf. the anger-cum-attraction Herod Antipas had toward John the Baptist's preaching (Mark 6:17, 20).

imaginations and probably unsettle our puny theological minds. Leave aside, however, your speculative questions (that all begin with 'But why would God ...') and stick with the main point. Some questions will immediately lead you astray. Some may ask, 'Is it not unfair of Yahweh to deceive Ahab?' Wrong question. Someone didn't read the text. There is *no* deception, for Yahweh clearly tells Ahab exactly what is going on, that is, that he is being lured to ruin by his own prophets. Yahweh candidly tells Ahab what he, Yahweh, is doing. Yahweh cannot be charged with deception when he clearly tells Ahab about the deception by which he is deceiving him! How could Yahweh be clearer, more transparent? The point is that it will make no difference; Ahab is beyond the point of heeding Yahweh's word, however clear, full, and detailed it may be. Micaiah might as well say 'Go up and succeed' (v. 15) for the word of God is an irrelevance for Ahab.

Or perhaps I should say the word is a mere formality for Ahab. He does insist that Micaiah level with him (v. 16); oddly, Ahab wants Yahweh's word for the record, we might say. But it is simply a formality. Ahab's stance calls to mind the anecdote told of Lord Bolingbroke, sometime hearer of Whitefield but a notorious infidel, reading Calvin's *Institutes* one day when a clergyman came in to visit him. Bolingbroke said, 'You have caught me reading John Calvin; he was indeed a man of great parts, profound sense and vast learning; he handles the doctrines of grace in a very masterly manner.' The clergyman, no friend of the 'doctrines of grace' himself, expressed his disdain for them. Bolingbroke then countered, 'I am surprised to hear you say so, you who profess to believe and to preach Christianity. These doctrines are certainly the doctrines of the Bible; and if I believe the Bible I must believe them.'[9] But of course he didn't. He could admire Calvin and discern doctrine but would 'not receive the love of the truth so as to be saved.' Who knows at what point God will send upon such folks 'a deluding influence so that they will believe what is false' (2 Thess. 2:10-11, NASB)? When the word of Yahweh becomes a mere formality we should be scared to death.

---

[9] See Arnold A. Dallimore, *George Whitefield*, 2 vols. (Westchester, IL: Crossway, 1980), 2:268n.

The Humiliation of Yahweh's Word (vv. 24-28)

True to his oath (v. 14) Micaiah had spoken what Yahweh had told him to speak. What reward does the faithful prophet receive? He gets cuffed on the cheek by his rival (v. 24) and thrown in the slammer by the king, with orders to keep him on the most meager of rations (vv. 26-27). With royal bravado Ahab implies he will return from Ramoth-gilead victoriously and/or safely (v. 27b). Micaiah does not quit: if Ahab comes back a living king then he himself is a false prophet (v. 28). Here the servant of the word suffers humiliation, which means that the word of Yahweh suffers humiliation.

Note that Zedekiah raises a critical issue in this humiliation section: 'Which way did the spirit of the LORD pass from me to speak to you?' (v. 24, NRSV).[10] How is it that Yahweh's Spirit should suddenly flit from me to you so that you speak such a contradictory word? Zedekiah is claiming to speak by the Spirit of Yahweh and insinuating that Micaiah does not. How does one know the authentic word of Yahweh? How can we tell if a prophet speaks Yahweh's true word? Because, like Zedekiah, he makes a claim to inspiration? If he says the Lord 'spoke' to him? If he has an authoritative tone or demeanor? Micaiah does not think so; his answer is 'Wait and see' (v. 25).[11]

---

[10] One can assume that Zedekiah is referring to the lying spirit Micaiah had previously mentioned. If so, Zedekiah is sarcastically accusing Micaiah of lying, i.e., 'If I was speaking via a lying spirit, as you say, how did that lying spirit leave me so that you have now spoken by it?' See Terence E. Fretheim, *First and Second Kings*, Westminster Bible Companion (Louisville: Westminster/John Knox, 1999), 125, for this view. I prefer to take Zedekiah's remark as an implicit claim that he himself spoke by 'the Spirit of Yahweh' and cannot fathom how Yahweh's Spirit who moved his prophecy could so quickly leave him and inspire Micaiah with a directly opposing word.

[11] His actual words to Zedekiah were: 'Look, you're going to see on that day when you go from room to room to hide yourself' (v. 25). 'All will come clear, Micaiah claims, when the disaster that he is predicting does eventually fall' (Iain W. Provan, *1 and 2 Kings*, New International Biblical Commentary [Peabody, MA: Hendrickson, 1995], 163). Precisely how that disaster would engulf Zedekiah, I do not know. Conceivably, the fall of

This is essentially Micaiah's answer to Ahab as well (v. 28). If you come back breathing and walking, Ahab, then you'll know Yahweh has not spoken by me. But if you come back in a box – or in the bottom of a chariot, you may not know but others will know that Yahweh has spoken through me. Micaiah does not rev up his rhetorical intensity and make a counter-claim to divine inspiration. He simply says, 'We'll see how things turn out.'[12] Micaiah willingly submits himself to the prophetic test: if a prophet speaks in Yahweh's name and the prediction does not come to pass, Yahweh has not spoken by that prophet (Deut. 18:21-22).[13]

This is a slow test but an accurate one. Probably in the late 1240s a certain Brother Arnold put forth a manifesto in Swabia which anticipated 1260 as the year when, among other last-day events, a great social revolution would occur in which the wealth of the Church of Rome would be confiscated and distributed to the poor. The Emperor Frederick was the one who would bring about this grand reversal. Unfortunately, in 1250 Frederick suddenly died, a decade shy of his projected finale. Wait and see – you'll see. Or what is one to make of Thomas Müntzer standing among a horde of peasants in Thuringia in 1525 and declaring that God had spoken to him and had promised him victory against the forces of the princes? He himself, he said, would catch the enemy's cannon-balls in his cloak's sleeves, and in the end God would transform heaven and earth rather than allow his people to perish. At this point a rainbow appeared, an obvious sign of divine favor, since a rainbow was the symbol on Müntzer's banner. What could be clearer? Müntzer's company was singing 'Come, Holy

---

Ahab would lead to the elimination of all Ahab loyalists and Zedekiah would be caught in the anti-Ahab purge (2 Kings 10; cf. R. D. Patterson and Hermann J. Austel, '1 and 2 Kings,' *Expositor's Bible Commentary*, 12 vols. [Grand Rapids: Zondervan, 1988], 4:165).

[12] Cf. Jeremiah 28:1-11. Hananiah proclaims a prophecy of restoration in opposition to Jeremiah's message of doom and gloom. Hananiah blabbers on and even uses Jeremiah's props for his visual aid (v. 10). Jeremiah's response? He turns and walks away (v. 11). Time will tell.

[13] This negative test may be the only sure test. If a prophet predicts something and it *does* come to pass, he could still be a false teacher (see Deut. 13:1-5).

Spirit' when their opponents fired their first salvo. The peasants broke and fled in panic while the enemy cavalry ran them down and slaughtered them by the hundreds.[14] God had spoken to Müntzer and promised him victory. How can you know that? Wait and, sadly, you will see.

It would be more convenient if we could dip messages into a prophetic fidelity solution and get immediate results: if it turns red, it's false; if blue, it's true. Such a procedure could have helped Micaiah, for the wait-and-see approach offers no instant vindication for the faithful prophet in the present. And so the humiliation of the word goes on, and the clergy with the most votes win the day. You can hardly expect to gain respectability if you are a stickler for speaking Yahweh's word (cf. v. 14). Suffering and isolation go with the prophetic turf (James 5:10). Don't despair if such is your lot. You are a member of a goodly fellowship. After all, don't you think Micaiah would've been heartened had he known that God's finest prophets would be smacked on the mouth (John 18:22; Acts 23:2-3)?

The Certainty of Yahweh's Word (vv. 29-38)

On to Ramoth-gilead (v. 29)![15] No details about how the decision was reached. On the basis of verse 18 we can surmise that Ahab pointed out to Jehoshaphat how blatantly mean-spirited Micaiah was, that he was hardly objective, and therefore they could not afford to take his word seriously.

But Ahab had not quite convinced himself. If Micaiah's word was so much rubbish, why was Ahab going into battle disguised as a buck private (v. 30)? Apparently Ahab had a secret foreboding that Micaiah was not all wet. Taking precautions might outsmart providence, if necessary. As partly stated already, Ahab is an interesting bundle of perversion: he hates the word (v. 8) yet wants the word (v. 16); he fears the word (v. 30ab) yet defies the word

---

[14] See Norman Cohn, *The Pursuit of the Millennium*, 2nd ed. (New York: Harper Torchbooks, 1961), 106, 268-70. Cohn's work provides multiple examples of defunct revelation-claims.

[15] For the general structure of this section, see the outline at the beginning of this chapter.

(vv. 29, 30c). A spitting image of the natural man in all his twistedness. Like a dupe – and almost a dead one (vv. 32-33) – Jehoshaphat complied with Ahab's battle plan.

The king of Aram had his own battle plan (v. 32). His charioteers were to ignore the small fry and go for the jugular, Israel's king. Ahab's death (if known), he thought rightly, would take the starch out of the Israelite assault. But Ahab's ruse (v. 30) nicely frustrated the careful plan of his opposite number (vv. 31-33). You won't ever kill what you can't identify.

Or won't you? 'But someone drew his bow at random and hit the king of Israel between the sections of his armor' (v. 34a, NIV). The writer has deliberately set verses 34-36 in direct contrast to verses 31-33. The king of Aram was specifically laying for the king of Israel and could not nail him; yet a no-name (the text literally reads, 'But a man ...') with no design except to hit another Joe Israelite released his shot and royal blood began dripping onto the chariot floorboard.[16] Yahweh's word comes to pass almost casually. It is not the order of the king of Aram that disposes of Ahab but the decree of Yahweh (v. 23b) – and that in the most 'accidental' way. 'Ahab was plated all over with iron and brass, but there is always a crevice through which God's arrow can find its way.'[17] That's what we call the *inerrancy* of the word.

The campaign is off (v. 36); the king is dead (v. 37a); the scene shifts back to Samaria (v. 37b). The writer appends a final picture with his theological comment:

> And someone rinsed off the chariot by the pool of Samaria, and the dogs licked his blood while the prostitutes bathed, in line with the word of Yahweh which he had spoken (v. 38).

Our writer stresses the fulfillment of Yahweh's word. What Ahab had tried to avoid, what the king of Aram could not achieve,

---

[16] When the text says the man drew his bow 'at random' (more literally, 'in his simplicity') it does not mean he did not aim his shot but only that he had no idea his target was special in any sense.

[17] Alexander Maclaren, *Expositions of Holy Scripture: Second Samuel and the Books of Kings* (reprint ed., Grand Rapids: Baker, n.d.), 313.

Yahweh has brought to pass in line with what he had spoken. Actually, verses 37-38 depict the fulfillment of three distinct prophecies: that of 20:42 (via the anonymous prophet), 21:19 (from Elijah), and 22:17, 23 (Micaiah). Hence a triple fulfillment concludes this triad of narratives (chaps. 20, 21, 22) about Ahab's failure under the word of Yahweh. Perhaps Micaiah will enjoy supper at home tonight while Zedekiah *et al.* eat crow.

Some puzzle, however, over whether verse 38 really 'fulfills' 21:19. There Elijah had threatened, 'In the place where the dogs have licked the blood of Naboth, the dogs will lick your blood, yes yours.' The writer seems to have 21:19 in mind in 22:38 when he writes, 'And the dogs licked his blood ... in line with the word of Yahweh which he had spoken.' The problem is that Naboth was stoned, most likely, outside of Jezreel (21:10, 13), whereas Ahab's chariot was washed down at the pool of Samaria. If, however, the pool of Samaria was outside that city (or at least outside the wall enclosing the fortified acropolis),[18] we could understand the 'place' of 21:19 as indicating not a precise but a generic location.[19] That is, dogs would also lick Ahab's blood outside of town (not necessarily Jezreel). At any rate, the biblical writer saw no major rubs between 21:19 and 22:38 or he would never have claimed the latter fulfilled the former. And what a moment: dogs feverish for every trace of blood, prostitutes calmly

---

[18] Excavators have discovered a pool (33 feet by some 16 feet) in the northwestern corner of the royal quarter or acropolis of Samaria. Some suggest this was the pool where Ahab's chariot was washed down. I doubt it. The pool of verse 38 seems very accessible to the public, to mangy, canine scavengers and to common prostitutes (the *zōnôt* here are not likely 'holy whores' who work the pagan chapels). I should think such visitors more likely to frequent a site outside the summit walls. On the excavations at Samaria, see N. Avigad, 'Samaria,' *Encyclopedia of Archaeological Excavations in the Holy Land*, 4 vols. (Englewood Cliffs, NJ: Prentice-Hall, 1978), 4:1032-46.

[19] See, for this view, K. C. W. F. Bähr, *The Books of the Kings*, Lange's Commentary on the Holy Scriptures, in vol. 3, *Samuel-Kings* (1868; reprint ed., Grand Rapids: Zondervan, 1960), 244, and J. R. Lumby, *The First and Second Books of the Kings*, Cambridge Bible for Schools and Colleges (Cambridge: CUP, 1909), 225, 238-39.

preparing for the night's work. Some things go on, even when kings die.

So the writer wants to tell you: that no-name prophet was right (chap. 20); Elijah was right (chap. 21); Micaiah was right (chap. 22). All this came upon Ahab 'in line with the word of Yahweh which he had spoken' (v. 38b). The King's word (cf. vv. 19-23) will come to pass. For the writer of Kings, history is no accident but is directed by the word Yahweh speaks. Both the unwilling and the unknowing only fulfill it. Precisely here a bit of gladness reaches out of this dark narrative and grabs the people of God, for if Yahweh's word is certain (the writer's point), we know that Yahweh's words of hope must be as solid as his words of judgment. His glory word must be as sure as his gory word. The coming of a kingdom (Dan. 2:44) is as sure as the departure of a king (Ahab); 2 Peter 3:13 must be as certain as 1 Kings 21:19. This point will not resolve all your personal problems – but it will pour some concrete into the bottom of your pit.

The Foolishness of Yahweh's Word (vv. 39-40)
Let the formulas begin! Here we are, after over six chapters, ready to wrap up the account of Ahab's reign. And the writer uses his stock language for such summaries, luring us into the usual cadence as we read ...

> And the rest of the deeds of Ahab, including all that he accomplished, and the ivory house he built, and all the cities he built – aren't they written in the record of the chronicles of the kings of Israel? (v. 39)

Now this verse is still speaking about the word of God, for the word of God is not only what Elijah and Micaiah and others actually declared but is also the written record which the writer of Kings has left us. And here, in verse 39, he tells us what he has omitted from his record. In case we hadn't noticed, the biblical writer confesses that he has given no attention to Ahab's achievements. You can find that kind of thing, he seems to say, in the royal chronicles in the Omride Memorial Library. By merely mentioning the king's accomplishments he tacitly admits Ahab's greatness but bluntly tells you he has included none of it. Why not? Because it doesn't matter.

Doesn't matter? Comparatively speaking, yes. In one of his *Peanuts* cartoon strips Charles Schulz depicts Charlie Brown – as he peruses the newspaper – complaining to Linus that the papers are full of horrible things every day. Charlie kicks the paper away in disgust and laments how he hates to 'see little Sally grow up in such a world.' Linus is no such pessimist. He urges Charlie Brown to forget the darker developments. 'Look on the bright side,' he counsels, 'think of the advancements – by the time she grows up, there'll be three major leagues!'[20] Now the writer of Kings would tell Linus that that doesn't matter. How can the progress of baseball hold any vital importance next to broad moral-social decay? Granted, any given phenomenon may be amazing or impressive, and yet be utterly trivial.

That is what the writer is saying about Ahab's attainments and why you can look elsewhere if you are interested in such matters. Are you enamored with his palace that boasts furniture and appointments inlaid with ivories? See the feature article in *Better Homes and Gardens.* If you're dying to know of Ahab's defense policies and of his extensive fortification programme, look in the recent copy of *Samaria News and World Report.*[21] That is the kind of thing our writer, by implication, is saying. What then does matter? Look back over the six-plus Ahab chapters and you cannot miss the focus of the biblical writer. For him there is only one question about Ahab that has any consequence: How did he stack up beside the word and commandments of God? It is the issue of Matthew 7:24-27. How then does verse 39 show us the 'foolishness' of the word? Because it shows us that *the word of God ignores what we regard as significant and prizes what we regard as mundane.* This is no dull, ho-hum verse; verse 39 is designed to leave your success in tatters and to lead you to repentance.

---

[20] One hesitates to call Linus a false prophet; American baseball still has only two major leagues, but – in the spirit of Linus, six total divisions.

[21] Or, better yet, read Ephraim Stern's fascinating article in *Biblical Archaeology Review*: 'How Bad Was Ahab?,' *BAR* 19/2 (1993): esp. 24-29.

Chapter 29

The Folly and the Folly

1 Kings 22:41-53

The end of 1 Kings might remind you of a home carpentry project. Imagine having finished. You are collecting your tools and replacing them in their assigned resting places. You stash left-over materials away for potential future use. Finally, you sweep up the sawdust and shavings and bent nails into the dustpan to flip into the trash. This last passage of 1 Kings may strike you as very much like those sweepings from a workshop floor. Here is no fascinating narrative, no connected story, but only bits and pieces about two kings, most of them in the form of familiar and unexciting formulas. A dull way to end a book. But that's just it. It's not the end of a book. The whole book or document consists of 1 and 2 Kings together and doesn't reach its proper end until 2 Kings 25. However, there's only so much text one can get on one scroll, and so the document has to be divided and that division comes after this somewhat bare-bones passage. And yet, though 22:41-53 is not an intended conclusion, it may be, for our purposes, an apt one. We might see it as an interim report on the fortunes of the kingdom of God. Our title suggests that 1 Kings can be summed up under the rubric of 'The Wisdom and the Folly'. Now 22:41-53 suggests we may want to revise that; perhaps try 'The Folly and the Folly'. It has come to that. The storm is coming over both kingdoms.

The Folly of the Righteous: Walking in Compromise (vv. 41-50)
Judah has nearly become a lost kingdom. Upon reading 'Now Jehoshaphat the son of Asa' (v. 41) we begin flipping back and find that we left Asa at 15:24. The writer has given no direct attention to Judah since that time. Nor will he give any more after

335

this slice on Jehoshaphat until 2 Kings 8:16-29; even so, it will be 2 Kings 11 before we settle in Jerusalem a while. One can assume that the writer of Kings does not want to focus just now on Judah in general or on Jehoshaphat in particular. The dynasty of Omri (1 Kings 16:23-2 Kings 10) consumes his attention.[1]

Jehoshaphat and his reign receive much more press in Chronicles. In 2 Chronicles 17-20 we find four leisurely chapters focusing on Jehoshaphat.[2] But not here. The writer of Kings indicates his interests when he tells you Jehoshaphat reigned for twenty-five years (v. 42) and gives him a mere ten verses (22:41-50), whereas Ahaziah, Ahab's son, reigns only two years (v. 51) but receives three verses in this chapter and all eighteen in 2 Kings 1. All this does not mean that Jehoshaphat holds no interest for our writer but that he holds a restricted interest.

Jehoshaphat does, however, receive ten verses. What then are we told? Fully half of the ten verses are couched in formulas familiar to us by now, which touch on chronology (vv. 41-42), theology (v. 43), bibliography (v. 45), and necrology (v. 50). Included with these formalized items are notes about statecraft (v. 44), sodomites (v. 46), and ships (vv. 47-49).

After spending so much literary time in apostate Israel one finds verse 43 refreshing. There is a kingdom that is not Baal-bent. 'And he walked in all the way of Asa his father (he did not turn away from it) by doing what is upright in Yahweh's eyes' (v. 43a). Even with the appended qualification (v. 43b) this is good news. Purging the land of remaining male cult prostitutes (or sodomites, v. 46; see 14:24 and 15:12) shows Jehoshaphat was no paper reformer.

But why three verses about ships? Verse 47 explains how it was that Jehoshaphat could aspire to shipping entrepreneur: Edom's power was in eclipse just then. Edomite politics boasted

---

[1] See discussion and structural layout in George Savran, '1 and 2 Kings,' *The Literary Guide to the Bible*, ed. Robert Alter and Frank Kermode (Cambridge, MA: Belknap, 1987), 148-49.

[2] Obviously, Jehoshaphat did figure in 1 Kings 22:1-40 (which 2 Chron. 18 parallels); still, Chronicles has much material on Jehoshaphat that Kings lacks.

no king, only a deputy acting as such. Edom was subservient, probably to Jehoshaphat and Judah (cf. 2 Kings 3 and 2 Chron. 20). Hence Jehoshaphat had unhindered access to ply his maritime pursuits from Ezion-geber on the Gulf of Aqaba. Shipbuilders found full employment, and the government, it was hoped, would enjoy lucrative commerce (v. 48a).[3] But the latter was not to be; the ships were smashed up while still in port (v. 48b). Perhaps the writer wants to portray Jehoshaphat as aspiring to Solomon-level ventures (9:26-28) while falling far short of Solomon-like success. In this way he could imply that the days of glory have given way to an era of decline.[4] But I doubt it. I think the writer mentions the naval fiasco because Ahaziah of Israel was mixed up in it (v. 49). It may be that when the fleet was bashed to bits Ahaziah had suggested they try again with a greater Israelite contribution. But Jehoshaphat had had enough (v. 49). This understanding would mesh with the parallel in 2 Chronicles 20:35-37.

The cooperative commercial venture was a product of Jehoshaphat's statecraft (v. 44). He had made peace with the king of Israel, certainly with Ahab (22:1-40) but also with Ahaziah his son. I think the writer of Kings views that alliance negatively, as a perilous precedent. Certainly Chronicles does; there prophets read the riot act to Jehoshaphat for teaming up with such apostate kings (2 Chron. 19:2-3; 20:37). But Kings is critical as well, if not so directly. The previous narrative had already rehearsed Jehoshaphat's insane naivete (22:29-33) when he had locked arms with Ahab. A few chapters later Kings will inform us that nuptials provided the cement for the alliance: Ahab's daughter became the wife of Jehoram, Jehoshaphat's son (2 Kings 8:18). Hence Jehoram aped Ahab rather than Jehoshaphat, as did Jehoram's son Ahaziah (8:18a, 25-27). In 2 Kings 11 our writer(s) will show that redemptive history almost ended in 841 BC. Why? Because Ahab's daughter remained very much alive after the deaths of

---

[3] On the ships of Tarshish or Tarshish-ships, see the array of opinion in ABD, 6:331-33, and ISBE, 4:734. On Ophir, see NBD, 3rd ed., 849-50, and my comments on 9:26-28.

[4] See Iain W. Provan, *1 and 2 Kings*, New International Biblical Commentary (Peabody, MA: Hendrickson, 1995), 168.

Jehoram and Ahaziah, and, as queen mother of Judah, nearly wiped out the whole divinely-chosen Davidic line of kings. How did such a tragedy ever get afoot? Because godly king Jehoshaphat imagined one could practice ecumenism with apostates (1 Kings 22:44). 'Now Jehoshaphat made peace with the house of Israel.' It was not astute but asinine. Look how it nearly decimated Yahweh's redemptive plan.

Several months ago I saw a report out of Corvallis, Oregon, in our newspaper. It stated that beneath the soil of the Malheur National Forest in eastern Oregon, a fungus that has been gradually wending its way through the roots of trees for centuries has become the largest living organism ever found. The Armillaria ostoyae, AKA honey mushroom, started from a single spore too minute to observe without a microscope and has been spreading its black shoestring filaments through the forest for an estimated 2,400 years, killing trees as it grows. The organism now covers 2,200 acres. Jehoshaphat's alliance was like that. Just a bit of matrimony. Perhaps he considered it a slick piece of diplomacy. But he wasn't around a dozen or so years later to see Athaliah turn Jerusalem into a butcher shop. And all because Jehoshaphat thought light could have a *little bit* of fellowship with darkness.

Please understand. I am not doubting the sincerity of Jehoshaphat's personal piety, but I am criticizing the stupidity of his public policy. The king's personal faith did not in this case affect his political – and covenantal – decisions. Such lapses are not his alone. One may possess personal faith in Yahweh without exercising discerning judgment in decisions. That should scare us to earnest prayer. How often do we see folks with undoubted faith, and yet that faith seems to have no carryover into their family life, their financial matters, or their understanding of social-moral questions? Have we not seen a disciple of Jesus convincing him/herself that marriage to a loving pagan could not prove such a giant disaster? The way of compromise is the folly of the righteous. And in 1-2 Kings it bodes ill for the kingdom Jehoshaphat ruled.

The Folly of the Wicked: Walking in Rebellion (vv. 51-53)

There is no compromise in Ahaziah's anatomy; he is given to sheer, undiluted wickedness. Again, this summary of his reign is almost wholly given through familiar formulas. The writer highlights (1) Ahaziah's tenure (v. 51); (2) his commitments (vv. 52-53a); and (3) his danger (v. 53b). According to verse 52, he is committed to a triple tradition: he walked in 'the way of his father and in the way of his mother and in the way of Jeroboam son of Nebat who caused Israel to sin.' In other words, Ahaziah embraced all the perversion and paganism that had accumulated in Israel to date, both the syncretism of Jeroboam and the Baalism of his parents. Lest we pass over the latter the writer specifically underscores it in verse 53a: 'So he served Baal and bowed down to him.' This is sheer rebellion; there can be no doubt about the destiny of such a kingdom.

The writer hints at Ahaziah's end in his very last line: 'so he provoked [traditional translation] Yahweh the God of Israel in line with all his father had done' (v. 53b). 'Provoked' is the verb *kāʿas* again. The writer means that Ahaziah's godlessness aggravated, galled, indeed goaded Yahweh to anger in order to destroy Ahaziah. It is almost as if Ahaziah has flaunted his wickedness, defying Yahweh to judge him. Had he any sense of his danger?

General John Sedgwick and his staff arrived near Spotsylvania Court House (Virginia) on May 8, 1864. Sedgwick, known affectionately as 'Uncle John' by his troops, commanded a Federal corps in the Wilderness Campaign about to begin. The next day, Sedgwick and his chief of staff, Martin McMahon, were standing by a battery and ordering some infantry near it to another position. At this point Confederate sharpshooters, located probably a mile away, opened up and Sedgwick's troops ducked, dodged, and cringed under the fire. The general amicably chastised his boys, claiming 'they couldn't hit an elephant at this distance.' At that very moment one man was walking in front of the general, heard a bullet whistling, and dove to the ground. Sedgwick nudged him with his boot. He was ashamed of the fellow, dodging bullets that way, again assuring that they 'couldn't hit an elephant at this distance'. The man stood, saluted, but, based on his experience, repeated his creed: 'I believe in dodging.' Sedgwick laughed and dismissed him. Another whistling sound. McMahon heard a dull thud. He was about to resume his conversation with Sedgwick when the general turned toward him, a hole under his left eye spurting a stream of blood. Sedgwick fell into McMahon's arms, knocking them both to the ground. The general was dead. Sedgwick had thought that the Confederates used only short-range rifles. He never knew that the sharpshooter who felled him with a hexagonal .45-caliber bullet was caressing a British-made Whitworth sniper rifle equipped with a telescopic sight.[5]

Sedgwick had no idea what he was facing. Do we? Did Ahaziah? If we goad Yahweh to anger by our defiance, by our insistence on our right to select from the cafeteria of deities our tolerant, pluralistic society offers us, by our clutching to that futile way of life handed down from our ancestors (1 Peter 1:18), do we realize what we are facing? Jesus does: we face the One who is 'able to destroy both soul and body in hell' (Matt. 10:28b). Now, really, that is no way to end a commentary. Can't we mix in a bit of sugary drivel to dilute the terror? No, for if you tremble, you may yet be saved.

---

[5] Clint Johnson, *Civil War Blunders* (Winston-Salem, NC: John F. Blair, 1997), 230-31.

Subject Index

Persons' Index

Scripture Persons Index

Focus on the Bible Commentaries

Deuteronomy	Alan Harman
Joshua	Ralph Davies
Judges	Ralph Davies
Judges/Ruth	Stephen Dray
1 Samuel	Ralph Davies
2 Samuel	Ralph Davies
Job	William Cotton
Proverbs	Eric Lane
Song of Solomon	Richard Brooks
Daniel	Robert Fyall
Hosea	Michael Eaton
Jonah–Zephaniah	John L Mackay
Haggai–Malachi	John L Mackay
Matthew	Charles Price
Mark	Geoffrey Grogan
Romans	Paul Barnett
1 Corinthians	Paul Barnett
2 Corinthians	Geoffrey Grogan
Thessalonians	Richard Mayhue
Pastoral Epistles	Douglas Milne
James	Derek Prime
1 Peter	Derek Cleave
2 Peter and Jude	Paul Gardner
Revelation	Paul Gardner

Mentor Commentaries

1 and 2 Chronicles – Richard Pratt (hardback, 512 pages)
The author is professor of Old Testament at Reformed Theo-logical Seminary, Orlando, USA. In this commentary he gives attention to the structure of Chronicles as well as the Chronicler's reasons for his different emphases from that of 1 and 2 Kings.

Psalms – Alan Harman (hardback, 456 pages)
The commentary includes a comprehensive introduction to the psalms as well as a commentary on each psalm.

Amos – Gary Smith (hardback, 456 pages)
Gary Smith, a professor of Old Testament in Midwestern Baptist Seminary, Kansas City, USA, exegetes the text of Amos by considering issues of textual criticism, structure, historical and literary background, and the theological significance of the book.

Exodus – John L Mackay (hardback, 624 pages)

Professor Mackay of the Free Church of Scotland theological college has produced a strong commentary on the Book of Exodus. It is filled with excellent material for the pastor and the serious-minded Bible student. I especially appreciate the work on application that is normally so difficult to draw out of historical literature. I recommend this work highly. It is a valuable tool for the study of this most important period in Israel's history.

John D. Currid,
Professor of Old Testament,
Reformed Theological Seminary, USA

A *tour de force* of conservative evangelical exposition. Massively researched, painstakingly explained, theologically nuanced, reliably expounded, simply expressed and sensitively applied; this volume will be of considerable value to all preachers and Bible students. For accessible and scholarly comment Mackay's work should quickly become the standard evangelical work on the Book of Exodus.

Stephen Dray
Moorlands College, Christchurch, England.